John Muir

Cruise of the Revenue Steamer Corwin in Alaska and the N. W. Arctic Ocean in 1881

John Muir

Cruise of the Revenue Steamer Corwin in Alaska and the N. W. Arctic Ocean in 1881

ISBN/EAN: 9783337318352

Printed in Europe, USA, Canada, Australia, Japan

Cover: Foto ©Andreas Hilbeck / pixelio.de

More available books at **www.hansebooks.com**

REVENUE-STEAMER CORWIN

IN

ALASKA AND THE N. W. ARCTIC OCEAN

IN

1881.

NOTES AND MEMORANDA: MEDICAL AND ANTHROPOLOGICAL;
BOTANICAL; ORNITHOLOGICAL.

WASHINGTON:
GOVERNMENT PRINTING OFFICE.
1883.

TREASURY DEPARTMENT,
Document No. 429.
Secretary—R. M.

LETTER

FROM

THE SECRETARY OF THE TREASURY,

IN RESPONSE TO

A resolution of the House of Representatives transmitting the observations and notes made during the cruise of the revenue-cutter Corwin in 1881.

MARCH 3, 1883.—Referred to the Committee on Commerce and ordered to be printed.

TREASURY DEPARTMENT, *March 3, 1883.*

SIR: I have the honor to acknowledge the receipt of resolution of the House, dated March 3, 1883, requesting that the Secretary of the Treasury furnish, as soon as convenient, to the Speaker of the House copies of documents in the possession of the Treasury Department containing observations on glaciation, birds, natural history, and the medical notes made upon cruises of revenue-cutters in the year 1881.

In reply, I transmit herewith the observations on glaciation in the Arctic Ocean and the Alaska region, made by Mr. John Muir; notes upon the birds and natural history of Bering Sea and the northwestern region, by Mr. E. W. Nelson; and medical notes and anthropological notes relating to the natives of Alaska and the northwestern Arctic region, made by Dr. Irving C. Rosse.

All these notes were made upon the cruise of the revenue-cutter Corwin in 1881.

Very respectfully,

H. F. FRENCH,
Acting Secretary.

Hon. J. W. KEIFER,
Speaker of the House of Representatives.

MEDICAL AND ANTHROPOLOGICAL NOTES ON ALASKA.

BY

IRVING C. ROSSE, M. D.

MEDICAL AND ANTHROPOLOGICAL NOTES.

LETTER OF TRANSMITTAL.

WASHINGTON, *April 29*, 1882.

SIR: I have the honor to transmit herewith a copy of medical and anthropological notes of the cruise of the revenue-cutter Corwin to Alaska and the Arctic Ocean.

Very respectfully, your obedient servant,

IRVING C. ROSSE, M. D.
(*Through Revenue Marine.*)

The Hon. SECRETARY OF THE TREASURY.

MEDICAL AND ANTHROPOLOGICAL NOTES.

GENERAL NOTES.

For the man of broad ideas and enthusiasm for humanity, more especially for the medical man, there exists but one people, namely, the human race, which he studies in all its varieties, physical and moral, in order not to hesitate, according to the expression of Hippocrates, in the treatment of disease. Experience and observation show, however, that no wide differences exist in the race when regarded from a biological or a medical aspect; and the infirmities of men, notwithstanding their physical inequalities and the extended range of the nosological table, are much the same the world over, no matter whether they be classified as belonging to the Caucasian, Mongolian, or Hyperborean races.

The object of this paper is to record, in a fragmentary way, some observations, as they have occurred to the writer during a late hyperborean experience, which afforded exceptional advantages for noting a few of the changes and variations that are brought about in the human economy by climatic influences and the environments of high latitudes—by the surroundings, in fact, of that part of the earth which Hippocrates places under the constellation of the Bear and beyond the Riphaean Mountains whence blows the north wind, and where the sun, says he, is near them only in the summer solstice, but warms these places only a short time; the winds which blow from warm countries reaching there but seldom and with little force.

These simple, true, and philosophical observations of the "divine old man," it may be remarked, are in striking contrast to those of Tacitus, who indulges in the usual mixture of true and false which fills the pages of the ancients when treating of geographical subjects.

Whether the early Greek conception of the people living beyond the north wind and giving rise to the Delian legends was based on any geographical relations at all, or was originally the mythical notion of the poets relative to an imaginary race, it is difficult to say—the question only raising a doubt that places us in a dilemma. Fabulous or not, we know that the subject was one of popular interest in high antiquity, giving rise to a work on the Hyperboreans in the time of Alexander the Great, and that when Virgil and Horace speak of the "Hyperboreæ oræ" and "Hyperborei campi" to indicate *most northerly*, they only made use of expressions which have served as connecting links in literature to extend the interest from the epoch of Hecateous of Abdera down to the days of Mr. James Gordon Bennett.

Among the numerous historic men who have sought adventure in this most weird, remote, and wonderful part of the globe from the early times of Naddod the Viking and Garder, down to Markham and De Long, we hear such tales of privation, disease, and suffering that the wonder is that men should still see about the mysterious regions of the north so much that is fascinating and romantic. But as the subject is not to be treated from a sentimental or an æsthetic point of view, these prefatory remarks must yield to considerations of a more practical and commonplace character.

THE VOYAGE.

In obedience to instructions I proceeded overland to San Francisco, Cal.; and after an unavoidable delay of several days from irregularities of railway travel, which had been interrupted by the floods of the Missouri-Mississippi River, I joined the Arctic Relief steamer Corwin on May 2. An inspection showed the Corwin to be in good sanitary condition with the exception of imperfect ventilation of the berth-deck and ward-room, the means for furnishing air to these overcrowded apartments being inadequate to supply every occupant with the twenty cubic feet of fresh air every minute which the best authorities agree that a healthy man requires. The insalubrity of the berth-deck was further increased by the humidity brought about by the habit of deluging the decks above and below every morning with water. At my suggestion this very reprehensible practice was happily abolished on the berth-deck, scraping and dry scrubbing being substituted, and the deck was not wetted oftener than once or twice a month, and only at times when the prevalence of fine weather would justify doing so.

After procuring such a medical outfit as the exigencies of the cruise might require, and after taking the necessary precautions as to the hygienic condition of the vessel and crew, we started on our humane mission, putting to sea on May 4 and meeting with seven or eight uneventful days of pleasant weather, exceptionally so for the season. The ocean, somewhat deserving of the adjective that designates it, displayed its prettiest combinations of lapis lazuli and ultramarine tints and sunset effects as we steamed through miles of medusidæ; and had it not been for the occasional sight of whales and little black divers, with the daily fall in the thermometer, we should not have known of our approach to the north. This happy state of affairs did not continue long on reaching a higher latitude, where we were beset by pelting hail and furious storms of snow and all the discomforts of sea life, causing a *pénible navigation* in every sense of the term. The increased cold, as we neared the north, had no perceptible effect for the worse on the health of the ship's company; and it is gratifying to state that but few serious cases, either surgical or medical, occurred during the entire voyage, a happy event, undoubtedly owing to the careful precautionary measures taken to secure full efficiency and to the excellent routine and discipline.

The Corwin is a good sea vessel, being tolerably dry in bad weather, and her oscillations are easy for a small craft. At the outset of the cruise, however, we were placed in the best possible conditions for studying both subjectively and objectively the strange phenomena of that doleful tribute of suffering that so many people are obliged to pay to the sea. Unfortunately so little is known of the nature and origin of this most distressing affection, and medical science has done so little to assuage its attacks, the wonder is that more extended experiments are not made by medical men in regard to seasickness. In spite of many theories and hypotheses that have been advanced to explain the phenomena of this so-called disease, we know that its causes are purely physical: the swinging of the diaphragm, the disturbance of the equilibrium in the fluid contents of the body—just as the mercury pumps up and down in a barometer—and the consequent reflex impressibility of the ganglionic, pneumogastric, and cerebro-spinal system of nerves producing a kind of trisplanchnic neurosis, which varies in different individuals according to peculiarity of structure and susceptibility.

Experience convinces that no drug known to the pharmacopœia will prevent or cure seasickness, notwithstanding the assertions of eminent medical authority to the contrary. Resolute effort of the will and the resort to such palliatives as drinks containing an excess of carbon dioxide, iced champagne and bottled Milwaukee beer for example, and oranges, were found to be the most efficacious modes of treatment adopted in the numerous cases of this almost unmitigated evil coming under my observation.

A portion of the crew suffered from violent phlegmon of the hand, arising doubtless from the combined influences of long confinement on shipboard, sea diet, and unusual climatic conditions. This affection was not confined to our vessel alone, for it prevailed extensively among the whalemen as well. The worst cases occurred among men whose history revealed the previous existence of syphilis. To remedy the condition it was recommended that the entire ship's company be allowed a run ashore as often as practicable, and that there be added to the usual dietary a ration of cranberries, a supply of which had been laid in among other antiscorbutics. Happily, these directions were complied with as far as possible, and I had the satisfaction to witness the good results.

Another affection prevailing extensively among the crew was a cutaneous eruption attended by excessive itching, which I at first suspected to be due to the presence of pediculi; but subsequent experience showed that temporary alleviation could be brought about by the administration of calcined magnesia and the topical application of vinegar and water. I may mention incidentally that my friend Dr. Charles Smart, U. S. A., who has cruised in the Arctic as far as latitude 82° on a Peterhead whaleman, says that he has often noticed the foregoing symptoms in connection with rheumatism among sailors, and also among soldiers in Arizona, who had been lying for some time on the army ration. He regards the symptoms to arise from inanition, and as the ones that usually precede an outbreak of scurvy.

A few cases of return of intermittent fever brought about by wet and fatigue, and of rheumatism—which seemed to be the prevailing ailment—the usual quota of headaches, constipation, and colic, with several cases of minor surgery, and a few cases of venereal contracted at Ounalaska, make up the sick-list so far as the crew proper is concerned.

It may not be foreign to the subject to remark that the sanitary condition of the Corwin, and indeed of other vessels in the revenue service, might be greatly improved by covering the berth-deck with a coating of shellac; and better ventilation might be secured by an arrangement similar to that found on the latest English naval vessels, where a flue passes up through the side of the ship until it opens just beneath the hammock-rail on the inside of the bulwarks, and is covered with a Venetian blind. Further advantage, especially in the way of lighting, would result from larger air-ports having a glass, convex externally and prismoidal on its inner surface, in order to facilitate the dispersion of light when the port is closed. The galley situated on the berth-deck of the Corwin was the source of excessive condensation and drip, which was always increased in the morning by shutting a small skylight when washing down decks; a proceeding seemingly inconsistent with enlightened common sense, especially when the decks have been wet the whole previous twenty-four hours from rain or the seas washing over them. The nuisance was in a measure abated by wiping the beams overhead and lighting a fire in a drying stove.

The facilities for warming were good throughout the ship, and the water supply was perhaps better than usual, owing to the fact that the water in the Arctic contains but a small percentage of organic or earthy impurities. At Ounalaska water was obtained from a small reservoir in an adjacent hill, but it had an unpleasant earthy taste. Better water was had at Saint Michael's. Here a spring wells up amid some rocks on the sea beach, and at low tide water may be obtained with great facility. Good water was procured nearly everywhere in the Arctic, notably at Chamisso Island and Choris Peninsula, and it was of unusual excellence at Cape Thompson, also at Herald and Wrangel Islands. Distilled water, supplied by the engineers, was occasionally used during the cruise, but as it was condensed from the main boiler without filtration it had that peculiar nauseating, oily flavor which rendered it unfit for potable purposes.

The articles of food, consisting of the regular rations, to which had been added pemmican and the usual antiscorbutics, such as potatoes, desiccated onions, sauerkraut, and cranberries, were of good quality and kept remarkably well, some butter in barrels being as good on our return as on the day we left. Frequent opportunities also occurred to get fish and game, the ration being varied from time to time with salmon and coregonus, auks, eider-ducks, geese, eggs (of which great quantities were found on the Diomede Islands), seal, bear, and reindeer. These supplementary articles proved not only an appetizing change from the regular ration, but their use was followed by a sense of well-being and by improved nutrition.

The ordinary clothing was supplemented with a hooded coat of reindeer skin, seal skin trousers, and a foot covering similar to that worn by the Eskimo. Over an ordinary pair of stockings were drawn a pair of reindeer socks, with the hair turned in, the foot being next thrust into an Eskimo boot of seal skin, into the bottom of which a small quantity of straw was placed as a non-conductor, and the whole secured by thongs after the manner of a sandal. This rig answered the purposes of warmth and comfort; but the effect was anything but picturesque, as the foot resembled a disabled extremity that some bungling hospital nurse had endeavored to inclose in a poultice.

Beyond the meteorological summary obtained from the signal station at Saint Michael's, there are no extended weather observations to report in regard to any fixed geographical point, for the reason that the ship seldom remained longer than a few days at a time in any one place, and it was impossible to get any definite information from the natives, whose knowledge in this respect does not extend beyond noticing whether the snowfall is great or little during the winter.

As regards the weather during the past season there is a marked contrast when compared to that experienced on the Corwin's former voyage. The sea was freer from ice, a fact doubtless owing to the preceding mild winter and other concurrent causes, but the number of fine days was comparatively few, and a series of gales and snow-storms continued throughout the summer. Even as late as July 18 the decks were covered with snow and hail, and a bitter cold wind penetrated our winter clothing. In striking opposition to this was the uncomfortably murky temperature of July 21, when the thermometer registered 45°. While the above is true of the weather in the more northern part of the Arctic, we found it in Kotzebue Sound, later in the season, much milder than it was at a corresponding date of the previous year. In the latter part of June at Saint Michael's we found the sun almost overpowering, although the thermometer registered but 60°. Why this incongruity should exist between the sensation of heat as experienced by the human body and the actual temperature as revealed by the thermometer, we are not prepared to say. All that we know from writers on the subject is that the sensations of heat and cold are relative and not absolute. In different latitudes, among the Andes in Peru, for instance, the opposite condition is often noticed, a disagreeable sensation of cold not indicated by the thermometer being one of the experiences of travelers in that part of the world; the cold is keen and penetrating with the thermometer standing at but 60°. An excellent distinction is that which mentions these phenomena as physical cold and physiological cold; the former indicating that revealed by the thermometer, the latter that not indicated by instruments.

Many Arctic travellers have noticed this relative sensation of cold as well as the impunity, and even a certain degree of comfort, with which they can expose themselves to a low temperature, which would be attended by serious results in a more southern clime. Dr. Hayes relates that in Greenland he went swimming in a pool of water on the top of an iceberg, and the captain of a New Bedford whaler has frequently gone swimming off the coast of Siberia. Taking advantage of one of these physiologically warm days, I took a plunge into the icy Arctic water, with no such motive, however, as that of Leander, nor did I, like Byron, have the ague after it; on the contrary, a swim of no great discomfort was followed by a pleasurable reaction.

The actual rise of temperature that follows upon stripping in a cold atmosphere or upon first entering into a cold bath, is not one of the least curious phenomena of the regulative function of the pyrogenetic mechanism. Nor is the busy activity of the metabolic tissues and the metabolism of the food within the alimentary canal, which accounts for the source of the heat of such homothermous animals as whales, seals, walrus, and the pygopodous birds, a subject to be passed by unmentioned. By what physical and chemical laws can we explain this morphological process—this physiological action of the protoplasm resulting in the evolution of kinetic energy sufficient to supply bodily heat to such animals as the seal and the whale, and enable them by remarkable adaptability to withstand the extreme cold of the Arctic? Does the *rete miribilia* of the whale and of the duck enable them to combine a greater quantity of oxygen with hæmoglobin and thereby act as a source of heat, or is the function of the liver the chief thermogenic source? By what means does the energy-yielding material become changed into actual energy? Does the nervous system, acting as a liberating force like the throttle-valve in a steam-engine, remove hinderances or impediments to the conversion of potential into kinetic energy, or do all the internal work of the animal organism, all the mechanical labor of the internal muscular mechanism, with their accompanying frictions, and the molecular labor of the nervous and other tissues produce a certain amount of heat, and thus account for the special function of calorification?

The foregoing physiological queries, with many others, suggested themselves on hearing the statements of whalemen and walrus hunters with reference to the scalding sensation produced by the spurting blood while handling the bodies of recently killed animals, and it occurred to me that a series of thermometric observations, something after the manner of the experiments of Dr. Kidder in connection with the Fish Commission, but having for their object the investigation of the manifestation of animal heat by the marine mammalia, would prove interesting and supply a scientific desideratum in addition to their novelty.

While ample opportunities occurred to make these experiments, yet it is to be regretted that the only available instrument, a clinical thermometer, was unfortunately broken early in the season. The experiments were, to say the least, so rough and inconclusive that any record of them would be of questionable value.

Another question in connection with the Arctic cold is, whether a sojourn in this region does not render one more susceptible to colds and disorders of the respiratory organs on returning to more temperate latitudes. The history of Eskimo who have spent any time in our comparatively moderate climate shows how they have suffered in this respect, and colds have been known to prevail endemically among the healthy crews of vessels lately arrived from the Arctic. It is related of a ship of the Franklin Search Expedition, the North Star, which was frozen up during one of the severest Arctic winters on record, in Wostenholm Sound, that the men maintained their health perfectly during all the trials to which they were exposed; but on their return to England in the early summer, every man within a week was on the sick list with some form of bronchial or pulmonary disorder. The reporter assigns the shaving off the beard as the cause of this illness. On board the Corwin on her return to San Francisco in October, and at a time, too, when "the glorious climate of California" appeared at its best, no such cause existed, yet colds of the most violent kind prevailed generally among a previously healthy crew.

Before dropping the question, it may be asked whether the psychical effects of climate were not apparent in some of the subjective sensations as experienced by myself and others. Something more than auditory spectra must account for some of them.

For instance, when climbing a steep cliff, with no sound to interrupt except the scream of wild sea-birds, or ascending a mountain side amid scenery the most desolate that can well be conceived, and in a stillness so great that the arterial pulsations are audible, how is it that certain trains of the most incongruous and absurd thoughts usurp a prominence in the mind? On such an occasion, why should the strains from wedding-marches be continually running through one's head? What gives birth to the floating succession of ideas regarding the delights of prospective dinners? And why does the presence of the midnight sun cause one to forget, like Horace Greeley, whether one has dined or not? While navigating through ice and fog, often within sight of a coast that is treeless and swardless, why should one dream of the laughing aspect of tropical vegetation, and of swinging in a hammock in a garden through which the summer wind bears the fragrance of flowers? And why should a diet of pork and beans cause a man during a series of nights to dream of sumptuous dinners, and at other times in his dreams to take part in a Barmicidal feast?

Among various meteorological phenomena witnessed during the cruise were parhelias and fog bows, which were of common occurrence off Wrangel Island; and toward the latter part of our stay in the Arctic, when the sun was no longer in the summer solstice, northern lights of varying intensity appeared, a peculiarity about one of them being a white arc extending across the heavens and accompanied by curtain-like fringes of light.

Not the least curious of the atmospheric phenomena are the modifications of nervous excitability in connection with the perception of light—the wonderful optical illusions witnessed from time to time during periods of extraordinary and unequal refraction. One day in July, at Saint Michael's, I saw on looking northward an island high up in the air and inverted; some distant peaks, invisible on ordinary occasions, loomed up at one time the very shape of a tower-topped building magnified, and suddenly changing assumed the shape of immense factory chimneys. Again, off Port Clarence, was witnessed the optical phenomenon of dancing mountains and the mirage of ice fifty miles away, which caused our experienced ice pilot to say, "No use to go in here; don't you see the ice!" Again, the mountains of Bering Straits have so betrayed the imagination that they have been seen to assume the most fantastical and grotesque shapes, at one moment that of a mountain not unlike Table Mountain, off the Cape of Good Hope; then the changing diorama shows the shape of an immense anvil, followed by the likeness of an enormous gun mounted *en barbette*, the whole standing out in silhouette against the background, while looking in an opposite direction at another time a whaling vessel turned bottom upward appeared in the sky. On another occasion, in latitude $70°$, when the state of the air was favorable to extraordinary refraction, a white gull swimming on the water in the distant horizon was taken for an iceberg, or more correctly a floeberg, other gulls in the distance, looming up, looked for all the world like white tents on a beach, while others resembled men with white shirts paddling a canoe. Again, two whaling ships that we knew to be sixty miles away, appeared on the distant sky as elongated afternoon shadows; minute stones and other small objects on a mountain side were so distinctly seen as to cause almost a glamour, a kind of witchery, to come over the eyesight, which, if there were no evidence to the contrary, might have been taken as one of the hallucinations that precede certain forms of insanity, where, for example, the sense of sight becomes so acute that a person reads a newspaper or tells the time of day from a small watch, on the opposite side of the street. Odd phenomena were occasionally witnessed while looking at the midnight sun, especially when he began to get low in the horizon. His disk would sometimes appear flattened like a door-knob, or to convey a more sensuous image, like a huge crimson pegtop with purple bands. It was easy, also, to distinguish by means of a marine glass the solar spots, the eye not being overwhelmed by the light but readily accommodating itself to the rays of the summer sun, which, owing to his low declination, are nowhere so delicate as they are in the far north.

Some of the strange acoustics experienced in this region are not unworthy of mention. A remarkable multiple echo was noticed between two mountains at Plover Bay, Siberia; another noticed by our sledge party in a cliff at Cape Onmann, Siberia, gives back more than a dozen echoes, and Baron Wrangel relates that a pistol fired near some cliffs on the River Lena is echoed a hundred times. The great distance to which small sounds are sometimes transmitted is also worthy of record. The first time this acoustic clearness of the atmosphere came under observation was at Saint Michael's, where a conversation carried on at an incredible distance could be distinctly heard. Amid the grim silence and desolation of heretofore untrodden Wrangel Island, at a time, too, when the air was acoustically opaque for that latitude, I distinctly heard our boatswain, a small man, with a voice of no great volume, giving orders two miles away, while laughter and sounds of the voice, when any one spoke above the ordinary tone, were heard with such amazing distinctness as to suggest telephonic communication. Where the conditions were so favorable to the reflection of sonorous waves, it was natural to expect the occurrence of a rarer phenomenon, an echo at sea, such as I once noticed in a fog off the Newfoundland Banks while crossing the Atlantic in a French steamer, whose fog-whistle was echoed in a surprising manner. But at no time was it observed that the nephelogical state of the atmosphere overhead or the prevalence of fog banks gave rise to anything like an aerial echo.

Although as a rule no very marked differences in the deep sea and surface temperatures were observed, yet a few of the anomalies noticed are deserving of mention. For instance, near Herald Island, on July 30, the temperature at the bottom was 48° and 49°. A few days later off the Siberian coast, 100 miles to the southward, it measured 37°; while later in Bering Sea, over 600 miles to the southward, it fell to 35°.

The density of the sea water, as observed by Mr. F. E. Owen, assistant engineer of the Corwin, is shown in the accompanying table. The instruments used in obtaining the results were a thermometer and a hydrometer. Water was drawn at about 6 feet below the surface and heated to a temperature of 200° F., and the saturation or specific gravity is shown by the depth to which the hydrometer sinks in the water. As sea water commonly contains one part of saline matter to thirty-two parts of water the instrument is marked in thirty-seconds, as $\frac{1}{32}$, $\frac{2}{32}$, &c., and the densities are fractional parts of one thirty-second:

Points of observation	Temperature	Density
At Saint Michael's, Bering Sea	30	1
Off Plover Bay, Asia	34	1
Arctic Ocean, near Bering Straits	32	1
Arctic Ocean, near ice on Siberian coast	32	1
Bering Sea, off Saint Lawrence Island	34	1
Golovnine Bay, Bering Sea, July 10	42	1
Bering Sea, between King's Island and Cape Prince of Wales, July 12	34	1
Entrance to Kotzebue Sound, July 13	47	1
Cape Thompson, Arctic Ocean, July 17	36	1
Icy Cape, July 21	36	1
Herald Island, in the ice, July 30	31	1
Cape Wankarem, Siberia, August 5	33	1
Wrangel Island (surface in ice) August 12	31	1
Wrangel Island (below surface 6 feet) August 12	31	1

The use of the dredge resulted in finding the usual bathybian forms that have been already described in works relating to Arctic voyages. In latitude 70°, longitude 170°—a spot known among the whalers as the "Post-Office"—the dredge brought up some mud of a temperature of 32°, while the water near the surface measured 34°. Microscopic examination of the mud revealed some shells of foraminifera.

In passing Bering Straits the brownish tint of the water was noticed. It resembled that often seen in the water of mill-ponds which has been discolored by decaying leaves. The phosphorescence of the sea was also observed in September in latitude 70°. And several patches of red snow were seen at Plover Bay and at Herald Island, but whether the tint was owing to the presence of some red protophyte or not I am unable to say.

The meteorological records kept on board the Corwin, being of use in connection with the navigation of the vessel only, are, therefore, untrustworthy so far as making any deductions from them in regard to climatology is concerned. In connection with this subject it may be inferred from the absence of glaciers above Bering Straits and the existence of huge ones in the more southern part of Alaska, compared with which the great Aletsch glacier of the Alps is a mere pygmy, that the amount of precipitation is much less in the higher latitudes of the Pacific Arctic. But the finding of terminal and lateral moraines, rock scratches, and other evidences of former glaciation, as well as of coal, which geology says is the sun's rays in potential form, and also the fossil remains of the mammoth along with luxuriant tropical or semi-tropical vegetation, would imply the existence at a remote period of a different climatological condition, a change in which has been brought about, according to the explanation of the meteorologists, in long lapses of time through the change in the eccentricity of the earth's orbit in combination with the precession of the equinoxes and the movement of the apsides. Whether a milder climate existed in former days, enabling the mammoth to subsist on vegetable food, as suggested by Professor Owen, or whether the mammoth, in his personal locomotions while endeavoring to overcome the influence of climate, was detained in his present position by the sudden freezing, it is impossible to say. Sir Charles Lyell seems to account satisfactorily not only for the presence of these animals in the northern parts of Siberia and America, but for the permanent masses of ice known as mammoth cliffs. His explanation is as follows:

This snow is commonly blown over the edges of steep cliffs, so as to form an inclined talus hundreds of feet high; and, when a thaw commences, torrents rush from the land and throw down from the top of the cliff alluvial soil and gravel. This new soil soon becomes covered with vegetation, and protects the foundation of snow from the rays of the sun. Water occasionally penetrates into the crevices and pores of the snow; but as soon as it freezes it serves the more effectively to consolidate the mass into compact ice. It may sometimes happen that cattle grazing in a valley at the base of such cliffs, on the borders of a river, may be overwhelmed by drift snow, and at length inclosed in solid ice, and then transported toward the polar region. Or a herd of mammoths, returning from their summer pastures in the north, may have been surprised, while crossing a stream, by the sudden congelation of the waters.

In the course of the summer we fell in with most of the vessels of the whaling fleet, to several of which medical services were rendered, the cases being such as are common to seafaring men. The most notable ones were of consumption and constitutional syphilis among men who should never have been shipped in the first place. There also came under notice a case of polydipsia, in which it would have been desirable to try large doses of valerian—a medicine not among the stores—consequently the patient was unbenefited by treatment; and there occurred two deaths, one each from consumption and ascites.

One man of the escaped crew of the bark Daniel Webster, which was crushed in the ice, on being rescued, after two weeks of exposure, terror, and starvation, was completely insane, but subsequently regained his reason. It seems that the act of deserting ship in the Arctic not only taxes all the resources of manliness but the situation conduces to bringing about mental derangement. One of the oldest and most experienced Arctic whalers tells me that he has seen men from an abandoned ship so lose their wits as to cry like children, sit helpless on the ice, and refuse to move until the most rigorous measures were taken to force them. Another whaleman told me that some years ago, having to retreat from his crushed ship across the ice, two of his crew, becoming raving maniacs, finally drowned themselves; and the insane seamen of the Jeannette party is fresh in the minds of every one. The rescued crew of the Webster were on the verge of starvation when picked up, and among the nine taken on board the Corwin there prevailed for some weeks a peculiar disturbance of the digestive organs, characterized by a furred tongue, indigestion, and a sense of heaviness and pain in the epigastric region.

But the demands for medical services were more urgent among the inhabitants of several remote places where the Corwin touched, notably at Ounalaska and at Saint Michael's, the most northern station of the Alaska Commercial Company, and one of the few unprovided with a physician.

Arrived at Oonalaska and securely moored in a land-locked harbor surrounded by Alp-like hills, which presented a dreary picture of snowy desolation, we found the air uncommonly chilly and apparently disagreeable enough to give a seal bronchitis, although the inhabitants called it mild weather. An epidemic, from which a large portion of the native population of the island had died, prevailed in the little village off which we anchored, and the only physician of the place being also dangerously ill, the sick were without medical advice or attendance. During the few days of our stay every assistance in our power was rendered the sufferers, and we hope that our advent among them was the means of averting several funerals that otherwise would have taken place.

DISEASES PECULIAR TO THE ABORIGINAL POPULATION.

Clinical observation of the disease in question showed marked dyspnœa, broncophony, imperfect arterialization of the blood, cough, with expectoration, pain, insomnia, and great depression both physical and psychical: in fact the latter symptom was the most characteristic; and it seemed impossible to impart the least ray of hope to a patient who had made up his mind to die from the offset of his attack. The disease was very rapid in its course and, considering the gravity of these assembled phenomena, there was but little of the fever that usually attends pneumonitis. The main symptom calling for relief seemed to be the marked asthenia, to combat which the administration of quinia, stimulants, and milk were resorted to with beneficial effects. It may be mentioned that the administration of quinia to these natives is attended with the happiest results. The attending physician at Oonalaska informs me that most of the ailments he has to treat among them being of an adynamic character he invariably gives quinia, the effect of which, he says, is almost magical. It is very much to be regretted that time and opportunity forbade a necropsy in one of these cases, for among the different and varied forms under which pneumonitis presents itself, and this type differing from any I have heretofore seen, it is not at all incredible that there may have been something distinctive about its morbid anatomy.

What connection there may have been between the outbreak of the epidemic and the prevailing climatic and telluric influences it is impossible to say; but the well-known relations of meteorological conditions to certain diseases would lead one to infer that the previous occurrence of several earthquake shocks, or, what is more probable, a relatively mild winter, with an unusual amount of precipitation, may have been the predisposing cause: not to mention the interminable diet of fish and whale of the Aleutian, his fondness for "quass," and his inability to resist slight causes of psychical depression.

So far as it is possible to ascertain the disease seems to have been confined almost exclusively to the native population. At Oonalaska the only sufferer not a native was from the Island of Mauritius. The epidemic also prevailed extensively at Saint Paul's, Unga, Kodiak, Cook's Inlet, and Prince William Sound, a singular coincidence connected with the outbreak being its appearance at these places immediately or soon after the arrival of the first vessel in port. This circumstance so impressed itself on the native mind as to give rise to a general and strong belief in the importation of the disease.

It is not at all unlikely that sickness of the foregoing character has occurred from time to time among the Aleutians. We have a mention of at least one outbreak, where it is stated that during a few days of unusually warm weather an epidemic of bilious pneumonia made its appearance at Kodiak, one of the adjacent islands, attacking about fifty of the natives.*

The same authority reports the prevalence of intermittent fever at Cook's Inlet among a white population who lived on a bluff several hundred feet high in houses exposed to a strong breeze directly from the inlet. The reporter states that the disease might have been contracted elsewhere; but happening after a sea voyage of forty days, and in persons previously in good health, he attributes it to locality. In a conversation with Mr. Petroff, whose topographical knowledge of this part of Alaska qualifies him to give an intelligent opinion, he informed me that for many miles around the bluff in question the land is low and marshy, but he thinks it is not malarious, and quotes the opinion of Dr. Govorlivo, a Russian surgeon, who says that in summer the weather of Cook's Inlet is warm and clear; in winter the thermometer falls to 40° below freezing; rain and fog are rare, and the atmosphere is clear, bracing, and healthy. These observations, the Doctor adds, are supported by Admiral Tebenkoff.

* Pacific Medical and Surgical Journal, 1870, vol. iv, p. 337.

Another observer, Assistant Surgeon John Brooke, U. S. A., in a report to the War Office, 1870-'74, speaking of the execrable climate of a part of Alaska in the same latitude, as Kodiak, remarks:

It might naturally be supposed that, in such a climate, acute rheumatism and acute pulmonary inflammations would be very common; but such is not the case. During a tour of nearly fifteen months I have seen but one case of typical acute rheumatism, and not a single case of uncomplicated pneumonia or pleuritis. Cases of sub-acute rheumatism, however, and pains and aches of a few days' duration, are very frequent. Pulmonary phthisis is not uncommon, and forms a large percentage of the cases of disease even among the native Indians.

Cases of sickness not infrequently occur in which there is a general adynamic condition of the system, without definable disease, a condition which is doubtless due to the depressing influences of almost continuous wet, and cool, and cloudy weather; a monotonous diet, in which fresh fruits and vegetables play an insignificant part; the almost entire absence of out-door amusements, and the want of opportunities for sufficient exercise in the open air.

The subject cannot be dismissed without some further historical mention, for which, by the way, I am largely indebted to Mr. Petroff, who has obtained his information from original Russian sources not generally accessible to the ordinary reader. From 1800 to 1820 no special diseases existed in the Russian colonies exclusive of scurvy and syphilis. At the end of 1819 a fever accompanied by a reddish eruption broke out, from which forty-two deaths occurred at Kodiak and twenty-five at Sitka. No physicians were in the colonies at that time, except those accompanying the ships of the company from St. Petersburg. It seems that subsequently two hospitals were established in 1844, one at Sitka of forty beds, and one at Kodiak of ten beds; and in 1862 the company had in its service three physicians, eleven stewards, five surgeons and apothecaries' assistants, two midwives and two assistants. From 1840 to 1860 a most fatal epidemic in the form of an exanthematous fever prevailed at Onnalaska. The same disease in 1848 prevailed at Uniga, Sitka, and the Alaska Peninsula, three hundred natives having died therefrom. The reporter further says that the great mortality was owing to loss of courage and refusal to take medicine. Tikhmenief, in his historical review of the Russian colonies, says that the prevailing diseases among the native population of Alaska are consumption, ulcers, scurvy, and syphilis, they being indebted to the Russians for the importation of the latter. He also mentions the occurrence of epidemic pneumonia in 1852 at Sitka, Kodiak, and the missionary establishment at Bristol Bay. At the first-mentioned place the disease occurred principally among children. In 1853 there were sixty-four cases of scurvy at Sitka, of which nine died; and in 1855 an epidemic typhoid fever like yellow fever occurred. It was believed to have been imported by a ship which had come around the globe from Russia. The mortality, however, does not appear to have been excessive, for out of three hundred and forty-one cases there were but thirteen deaths. The same year there was also an epidemic of pneumonia, three hundred and ninety-eight cases having occurred at Sitka and Kodiak with sixty deaths. In 1860 epidemic measles attacked both adults and children, causing eighty-one deaths in the whole colonies.

From a report of the Russian American Company on the sanitary condition of New Archangel and other posts from May 1, 1861, to May 1, 1862, it is learned that for 1861 and the first third of 1862 and those of previous years there existed both in the number and character of the cases a marked difference that was very gratifying. The mean daily number of patients in the New Archangel Hospital was ten persons, besides the fact is worthy of attention that scorbutic and syphilitic diseases had almost entirely disappeared. In April, 1862, there was not a single case of the latter disease. Dr. Markoffski ascribes this circumstance to many judicious measures taken for the extirpation of these diseases by the chief director of the colony, as well as to the greatly improved treatment of such patients. The number of patients admitted to the New Archangel Hospital was 663, of whom 626 recovered and 8 died. In the Kodiak Hospital there were 360 admissions, with 330 recoveries and 7 deaths. At Afognak typhus fever appeared but was promptly suppressed. Inoculation (?) is reported to have been carried out generally and successfully in the colonies. A medical and sanitary inspection of the northern districts in 1861 showed the accommodations of the unmarried workmen of the coal expedition to be in excellent condition; the hearty and healthy appearance of the men showing that they had been well cared for, notwithstanding the difficult under-ground character of their work; and the surgery is reported to have been in good condition. Dr. Markoffski also makes a favorable report for Michalowski (Saint Michael's) and speaks of the new *Kaskarn* as light, spacious, and very comfortable; and of the lazarette and surgery as well provided and in good order.

H. Ex. 105——3

No epidemics are mentioned, except one of gastric fever, the result of immoderate eating, which prevailed on Saint George's Island. It yielded to treatment. The houses of this island are reported to be in a satisfactory condition, sanitary conditions being observed as far as possible, also order and cleanliness; and the Kashim (or club-house) comes in for favorable mention.

On the Island of Saint Paul the regulations established for cleanliness are reported to have been generally obeyed. Inoculation (?) was generally carried out, and almost all the children were vaccinated except at Ikogmut Mission, where the natives refused to adopt this method of protection; but it is stated that this obstinacy may be overcome by time or accidental circumstances such as the prevalence of an epidemic.

A disease called the "black measles" appeared at Kodiak and the adjoining islands in 1875, from which the Alaska Herald of August 3, 1875, reports the following deaths to July of that year:

Kodiak		40
Wood Island		50
Afognak		20
Yeloma		10
Eagle Harbor		10
Total		130

The natives of the Pribylof Islands, being better housed than those on the Aleutian Islands, appear of late to have fared better as regards health than their more southern neighbors. The wonder is, though, after visiting these islands, that so little sickness exists among a population most of whom live but a few hundred yards away from the carcasses of thousands of seals in all stages of decomposition. On the island of Saint Paul, for instance, where the climate is as humid and disagreeable as possible, the carcasses of the 80,000 seals that are slaughtered yearly are left to decay in the open air in the immediate vicinity of the village, and the stench therefrom is anything but pleasant. One night the Corwin anchored under the lee of the island, about a mile off shore, and the stench was so great as to preclude sleep during the night.

A stroll ashore on Saint Paul afforded a fine opportunity to study comparative anatomy, especially of the marine mammalia; for in addition to the millions of live seals to be seen hauled up on the rookeries, we walked through the green, slimy ooze, the remains of thousands of seals slain years ago, occasionally sinking over our ankles in a substance resembling adipocere; picked our way through the scattered anatomy of last year's seal and walrus; witnessed the remains of the 1,500 seals killed but yesterday and of the 1,200 killed the day before.

From information furnished by Special Agent Otis, it is learned that the prevailing diseases are of a pulmonary and cutaneous character, but the mortality returns of a late year show three deaths each from scrofula and cerebro-spinal meningitis. Since 1869, out of a population of about 300, the increase has been but slight, the births and deaths having about balanced each other. The mortality per thousand being nearly three times greater than that among more civilized communities under more favorable conditions, and the Aleutian women, as a rule, being unprolific, it is hardly reasonable to look for any decided increase in the population except under changed and more favorable conditions.

Mr. George Kennan, the genial author of "Tent Life in Siberia," has kindly furnished a translation of the chapter from Veniaminoff's History of the Aleutian Islands, relative to "Diseases and their Treatment," from which the following notes are taken:

"It appears that in the early days of the Russian occupation the Aleutians had some crude notions of human anatomy, which they acquired from the dissection of the dead bodies of their slaves, and they also had considerable knowledge of medicine and surgery the practice of which, being prohibited and suppressed by the Russians, is now entirely lost. Among the diseases most common to them were a skin disease known as 'seep;' itch, boils, diarrhœa, and fever—the latter called 'common' because no one escaped it—and consumption of two kinds generally considered incurable. The first variety was simply a decay of the lungs attended by such symptoms as cough, spitting of blood, and shortness of breath; the second, proceeding from decay of the liver, was accompanied by griping of the intestines and rapid emaciation.

"They were also acquainted with another disease which they called the 'inward disease.' Scurvy and venereal disease were formerly unknown to them.

"Their principal therapeutic measures consisted in patience and strict diet, the patient being allowed only a gargle and two spoonfuls of water in the twenty-four hours. Dangerous wounds were treated by prolonged fasting, as they considered food and drink extraordinarily dangerous for the patient, and creating a liquid in the wound which caused inflammation and even death. The writer states that this method of treatment is still pursued, and thinks that even now it saves many from death. Accidental wounds from fox-traps were quite common, the barbed iron teeth usually taking effect in or near the knee-joint. At Oonalaska out of forty or fifty cases but two are known to have died. In gunshot wounds, aside from diet, they used for cleansing and keeping unds alive the fat of fishes and various land animals, especially fat from the head of the fox. Over deep wounds they sifted burnt teeth reduced to powder and applied a fresh mouse-skin every day. Swellings and rheumatisms they treated with various fomentations and ointments, or by poultices made of roots. Other external diseases they hardly treated at all, except by employing the universal medicines, diet and patience.

"In fevers they employed decoctions of bitter herbs and guarded the patient carefully from the external air. Herbs were also used in consumption of the first kind, but if the expectoration proved troublesome, the patient was submitted further to the operation of 'pricking.' In both kinds of consumption the Aleut doctors supposed the bad symptoms to proceed from bad blood, or a ferment, or spirit. The operation just mentioned was performed by thrusting stone lancets on both sides immediately under the ribs, and was done by the most skillful surgeons only, because it required accurate knowledge of the internal parts and of just how much of the spirit to let out, as there was danger of letting it all out and thus sending the patient to the other world. The operation, also used as a remedy for 'internal disease,' was considered the most approved treatment for colic, and patients expressed themselves as having received decided benefit therefrom. 'Puncture' in critical conditions was resorted to as the last and sole remedy. It was also used in many other diseases, for example in diseases of the eyes, where the skin was pricked between the eyes or on the nape of the neck. In fact, this operation was done on all parts of the body, and an instance was known of an Aleut having submitted to it forty times, various parts of his body having been punctured. The operators were men famous for their skill, and imparted their knowledge to the best-beloved of their children or nephews; for this reason the art is of late become almost lost. Common bleeding from the arm and leg was employed to reduce large swellings and correct morbid conditions of the blood; also to combat sluggishness or weakness, headache, and loss of appetite.

"For diarrhœa astringent roots and diet were employed or the root of the 'makarsha.' Another treatment in 'internal diseases,' generally resorted to by old women, consisted in a sort of manipulation of the belly while the patient was lying on his back. It was used principally against griping pains, and elicited high praise from the men who have experienced the treatment."

EFFECTS OF ALCOHOL.

The principal vices among these people, who are generally mild and inoffensive, seem to be a fondness for games of chance and an uncontrollable craving for alcoholic drinks—an appetite which, by the way, two seasons of personal observation and experience in the Arctic convince me is something of a physiological necessity. The taste, however, seems to be an acquired one by the aborigines, for I saw a man at Nounivak Island to whom the taste was foreign, and on tasting both brandy and whiskey he made a wry face and spat them out with evident disgust.

Late authorities testify strongly in favor of the benefit to be derived from moderate indulgence in drink during an Arctic sojourn. In looking over a *précis* of the evidence taken by the Parliamentary Committee appointed to inquire into the adequacy of the provision in the way of food, medicines, and medical comforts furnished to the Nares Arctic Search Expedition, we learn that Sir Edward Parry attributed the greatest antiscorbutic effect to beer; and Dr. Colan, R. N., fleet surgeon (Alert), says it is the opinion of all the men he has read about who spoke about beer in the Arctic regions. Dr. Barnes believes beer decidedly antiscorbutic and recommends it should be given. Sir George Nares says abstainers are no better off than others as regards scurvy. Captain Markham says he would as soon take a man of temperate habits on an expedition as an abstainer; the two total abstainers of his sledge suffered severely, and he himself felt better after he took to drinking his rum. Sir L. McClintock says there is no advantage in teetotalers; Mr. Alexander

Gray, that there is no advantage in health in abstainers on board whalers, while Dr. A. Envall, who accompanied Nordenskiöld, condemns excess, but says he believes spirituous liquors to be of great use in small and moderate quantities. Further mention may be made to Professor Nordenskiöld and Lieutenant Palander, who in 1873 undertook a sledging journey from their winter quarters in Spitzbergen, in latitude 79° 53' north, and were away sixty-six days. During the whole journey, there was no scurvy, though the party had no lime juice. The diet consisted of pemmican, biscuit, salt pork, butter, coffee in abundance, and a little spirits daily. All returned in excellent health. Comparison may be made between the Alert, of the Nares Expedition, aboard which scurvy prevailed notwithstanding the careful daily administration of lime juice, and H. M. S. Assistance, in 1850–'51. In the Assistance there was beer brewed on board, while the Alert had no such advantage. No scurvy prevailed on board the former ship. Captain Markham, speaking of the prevention of scurvy in any future expedition wintering in high latitudes, says that the dietetic causes may be reduced to a minimum by varying the diet with condensed milk, butter, eggs, beer, and wine. He also observes in regard to the adequacy and completeness of outfit that former expeditions had the means of brewing beer on board, while the Nares Expedition had no such advantage.

Markham moreover says that Captain Hall, of the Polaris, who died of apoplexy, was a teetotaler and was much annoyed at seeing others drink.

Whatever conclusions may be deduced from the foregoing, it is evident that there is an absolute consensus of opinion both among executive and medical officers of late Arctic Expeditions in regard to the judicious use of alcoholic beverages. It only remains to add that personal experience and observation convince that there is an indescribable something in the Arctic atmosphere that produces what is called the northern craving for drink, even among persons who care nothing for it in temperate latitudes. Being of abstemious habits, I would not for the world say anything to favor intemperance, but facts warrant in testifying to the undeniable good effects of whiskey when served out to the crew after unusual fatigue and exposure; and I know of no place, circumstance, or condition under which such beverages as beer and claret are more palatable or more valuable from a hygienic point of view than when taken at meals during an Arctic voyage.

Illicit traders, taking advantage of this northern craving for drink, have of late years been in the habit of supplying the most villainous compounds, in exchange for small quantities of which the improvident Eskimo gives his choicest furs. Some captured specimens of these prohibited articles, bearing the respective labels of *Bay Rum*, *Jamaica Ginger*, *Pain Killer*, and *Florida Water*, with a view to defrauding the revenue, proved on examination to be nothing but cheap alcohol of a highly inflammable nature to which a little coloring matter had been added. Loath as I am to give the least encouragement to intemperance, being rather an advocate of temperance, I cannot help thinking that it would be a step in the right direction, and one productive of good, if instead of the present prohibitory measures the fur companies were allowed to sell small quantities of beer and claret. In addition to their value as antiscorbutics, their use would be eminently better for the natives from a moral point of view than the present use of "quass," a vile native decoction made from sugar and flour, both of which articles the traders have a right to dispose of in unlimited quantities.

To the alleged introduction of spirituous liquors is said to be due the famine and excessive mortality among the natives of Saint Lawrence Island, one thousand of whom it is estimated have died in the last three years. Several visits to this island revealed the fact that it is fast becoming depopulated. The first village at which we landed was entirely deserted; at a second not a living being was to be seen, but in and around the houses were counted fifty-four dead bodies, all adults. Many laid unburied on the adjacent hills, while others had died in bed, where they still remained. A third village, which must have been a very old settlement, judging from the thousands of walrus skulls strewn in every direction and from the character of the kitchen-middens, was also depopulated. It was a Golgotha in every sense of the word. A great many dead were found here, laid promiscuously out of doors, and in one house we found sixteen bodies. Among these remains were those of several children, a fact which tended to remove previous suspicions of cannibalism on the part of the sufferers. At these villages was made a fine collection of Innuit crania and other ethnological curiosities for the Smithsonian Institution. Finally we visited at the northwest extremity of the island a settlement where lived several hundred Eskimo. They informed us that two hundred people of the village had died of famine, as near as we could make out from a very imperfect interpretation, and that food became so scarce they were obliged to eat dried walrus skins and their dogs, having but one dog left, when happily the capture of a whale afforded timely relief. A number of these fur and feather-clad aborigines, having their heads shaved after the manner of Zurbaran's pictures of monks in the middle ages, were clamorous in importuning for whiskey, and the chief of the village refused to sell us a few reindeer skins unless we gave him liquor in exchange, this too while the poor remaining dog, looking wistfully up into his face, seemed to be a living warning not to try as a remedy the hair of the dog that had bitten the village.

To attribute the late cause of death among these people entirely to intemperance admits of some doubt. It seems impossible for them, owing to lack of means, to have procured enough drink to last more than a few days, or at least during the short stay of any trading vessel that may have arrived. Then again it is probable that some epidemic influence was the main factor, if we may rely upon the statement of a whaling captain who visited the island during the time so many were dying. He tells me that the disease was what he calls "measles or black tongue." Admitting the prevalence of sickness of this kind among an improvident and shiftless people, starvation must follow as an inevitable and necessary result. Similar conditions having prevailed among the Asiatic Eskimo of Plover Bay and East Cape, many of whom have died in the last few years, it would, perhaps, be nearer the truth to say that the mortality in question was due to the combined influences of intemperance, sickness, and starvation.

EFFECTS OF CLIMATE.

At Saint Michael's, almost under the Arctic Circle, I found that pulmonary troubles and the constitutional effects of syphilis prevailed among the small population to an alarming extent. Here also, as in most every northern place we touched at, the wicked thirst for rum exercised a dominating influence. The winters are long and cold, with high winds and gales and a great deal of snow; the thermometer falls to $-45°$, and the winter previously to our coming was so severe that owing to the great and long continued cold Eskimo dogs and wild geese are reported to have frozen to death. The accompanying meteorological summaries from the records of the Signal Office give a more detailed account of the weather:

METEOROLOGICAL SUMMARY.

July, 1879, to end of June, 1880.	BAROMETER.				THERMOMETER.				Mean relative humidity	WIND.			AMOUNT OF RAIN AND MELTED SNOW.		
	Mean	Highest	Lowest	Difference	Mean	Maximum	Minimum	Difference		Prevailing direction	Maximum velocity during month	Total	Amount in inches	Number of days on which rain or snow fell	Number of auroras
1879.											Miles.				
July	29.850	30.211	29.121	1.120	53.1	68	36	32	82.6	North	37	7,473	.65	16	0
August	29.731	30.186	29.237	.800	50.2	62	35	27	88.8	North	53	8,870	.85	18	0
September	29.622	30.097	29.723	.764	45.1	58	19	39	88.3	North	49	7,878	.64	21	0
October	29.716	30.514	29.290	1.254	26.1	42	13	30	91.7	South	76	12,580	.25	16	1
November	29.747	30.198	29.011	1.187	17.1	36	12	18	98.5	North	74	10,742	.03	11	1
December	30.175	30.797	29.583	1.414	6.0	36	-32	68	99.7	North	68	7,987	.07	10	3
1880.															
January	30.037	31.012	28.951	2.068	-19.	15	-45	60	100	North	64	1,671	0	9	5
February	29.881	30.652	29.083	1.560	-1	11	-26	?	99.4	South	75	11,436	?	17	0
March	29.992	30.662	30.125	1.537	8.53	?	-37	?	98.0	South	69	12,598	?	20	0
April	29.874	30.665	29.229	1.436	19.3	?	-27	?	97.8	N. E.	19	7,042	.10 (?)	14	0
May	29.963	30.190	29.517	.982	28.0	?	-1	?	97.9	North	82	6,808	.21	11	0
June															

GENERAL REMARKS.

1879. July.—Cold and damp, rain or fog nearly every day.
August.—Cold and rainy.
September.—Winter commenced the last of the month; remarkably early.
October.—Almost a continuous series of gales all the month.
November.—Series of gales the last of the month.
December.—Mild temperatures and gales the first half of month, ending abruptly in severely cold weather.
  Station, Saint Michael's, Alaska.
1880. January.—Remarkably high barometer the first of month; long continued cold weather with high winds the last.
February.—A continuous series of gales accompanied by snow all the month.
March.—Extraordinarily large snow fall during the month; but the accompanying gales, as in February, prevented measurement.
April.—Very cold; unusually fine weather toward the last of month, but low temperatures still prevailed.
May.—Winter continued unbroken until the 18th inst., when it became suddenly warm, and the water-fowl began arriving

METEOROLOGICAL SUMMARY.

FORT SAINT MICHAEL'S, ALASKA.

Date	Barometer — Local observations	Barometer — Mean of Telegraphic observations (Corrected for temperature, instrumental error, and elevation) A. M.	P. M.	Midnight	Corrected for temperature and instrumental error only. A. M.	P. M.	Midnight	Range — Highest	Range — Lowest	Difference	Thermometer — Local observations	Thermometer — Mean of Telegraphic observations A. M.	P. M.	Midnight	Range — Maximum*	Range — Minimum	Difference	Mean relative humidity—local observations (per cent.)	Prevailing direction	Wind — Number of miles † Noon to 6 p.m.	6 p.m. to midnight †	Midnight to 6 a.m. †	6 a.m. to noon †	Total	Maximum velocity during month	Amount of rain or melted snow (inches and hundredths)	Number of days on which rain or snow fell	Number of auroras
July	29.879	29.846	29.864	29.947	29.954	29.746	30.353	29.292	0.961	52.6	56.9	54.2	54.5			17	Blank	N. x N.					6,516	39	.65	11	8
August	29.770	29.772	29.734	29.756	29.730	29.723	30.551	29.366	0.905	52.3	54.6	54.5	53.2			15	do	x. 6 E.					7,663	67	4.46	23	0
September	29.644	29.648	29.614	29.581	29.567	29.584	29.927	29.176	0.851	41.2	39.0	41.7	42.0			29	do	79.6 N.					9,064	64	5.60	21	5
October	29.850	29.854	29.833	29.856	29.810	29.825	30.400	29.193	1.207	24.3	27.2	39.2	24.8			3	do	93.7 N.					10,802	67	22.50	26	2
November	29.861	29.873	29.857	29.872	29.828	29.863	30.043	29.227	1.416	21.4	21.6	25.0	21.0			−7	do	96.1 N.					9,954	64	1.63	14	4
December	29.946	29.941	29.937	29.891	29.875	29.942	30.798	29.073	1.725	11.3	10.3	11.7	11.2			−43	do	96.8 E.					8,771	59	1.91	12	11

*Maximum thermometer broken. † This data is incomplete.

Copied from records on file at the office of the Chief Signal Officer, United States Army, Washington, D.C., on February 1, 1882.

HAIDA SAINT-LAWRENCE CENTRE
2 (front)

HAIDA BONE AGGLUTINATION, SAINT-LAWRENCE CENTRE
22 (front view)

In addition to the frequent disorders of the respiratory organs, rheumatism and affections of the alimentary canal are quite common. The latter are principally due to overloading the stomach after a long fast, and indigestion from this cause is so frequent that it is no uncommon thing to find an Eskimo suffering for several days from all the remorse of a guilty stomach. The women, too, are at times violently hysterical, and in this respect do not differ much from their more civilized sisters.

AFFECTIONS OF THE EYE.

Diseases of the eye and its appendages are quite numerous, and among them I noticed several cases of opacity of the crystalline lens and of the cornea, and of fatty and pigmental degeneration. Ophthalmia tarsi in its chronic form and granular inflammation of the conjunctiva are common along with amblyopia and asthenopia, and it is not at all unlikely that a specialist might exhaust the ophthalmological vocabulary in describing the diseases he might observe.

Among these numerous eye diseases, however, I observed but two cases of total blindness; one in a man at Saint Lawrence Island and another at Saint Michael's in a native from the interior. Mr. Petroff, whose duties as census agent have afforded him great facilities for observing the interior population, informs me that blindness is almost universal among the older people, most of whom get blind on reaching the age of fifty. This blindness, common also to the lower animals, was once observed by him in a bear at Prince William Sound. The bear with several others was seen approaching his party on the beach, and the singular actions of this particular bear attracting attention, from the uncertain way in which he walked and was pushed about by the noses of the other bears, it was singled out and shot, when an examination showed the previous existence of total blindness, which of course accounted for the odd movements of the animal.

These eye affections are not caused by smoke as has been erroneously supposed; they are mostly the result of snow blindness, in which the sensibility of the end-organs, the rods and cones, is diminished or exhausted by the prolonged illumination from the constant sunlight and the glare from broad expanses of brightly glistening snow. The rarefaction of the arctic atmosphere, the insufficient and impoverished condition of the blood brought about by bad feeding and the strumous diathesis, may likewise be mentioned as predisposing causes.

It may not be digressing from the subject to cite an observation of Mr. Edwards, surgeon to Sir Edward Parry's second expedition, who has noticed in the Eskimo what he believed to be a rudimentary nictitating membrane resembling that which protects the eyes of some animals. The peculiarity he points out as common to many individuals of Melville Peninsula, and consists in the inner corner of the eye being covered by a duplication of the adjacent loose skin. This fold is lightly stretched over the edges of the eyelids, covering the caranculus lachrymalis, which in Europeans is exposed, and forms, as it were, a third lid of crescentric shape. This singularity was ascertained to be very remarkable in childhood, less so toward the adult age, and then frequently disappearing altogether, the proportion in which it existed in grown up persons being small compared with that observed among the young.*

An interesting question in this connection is the form of the fibres of the cones and rods in the retina of the Eskimo. It is known that in animals, the habits of which are nocturnal, such as owls and bats, the cones are wholly wanting, and rods alone are present; so a variation may have occurred in the eye of the Eskimo in this particular as one of the results of his conflict with his circumstances. But this is mere speculation, and the incorrect observation of Mr. Edwards, when viewed in the light of more recent ophthalmological knowledge, would seem to be nothing more nor less than a congenital defect, owing to the laxity of the skin at the root of the nose and of the folds on a level with the inner canthus of the eye known as epicanthus, which often disappears with the development of the bones of the nose, and is remediable by an operation or the application of electricity to the muscles of the face.

Although applications from the Eskimo for "eye-medicine" were quite frequent, yet I was unable to find out much regarding the means taken by them to treat or prevent eye diseases. In the quaint old book of Hans Egede, a missionary who spent twenty-five years among the Greenlanders, is an account of an operation that he has seen Eskimo perform for removing a film from

---
* Edinburgh Philosophical Journal, vol. 36, 1844.

the eye with a hooked needle and a knife, which from the description appears to be the same as the modern operation for pterygium. No operative procedure of the kind came under observation; but it was noticed that the use of a shade for protection was quite common, also eye-blinkers made of wood in which was cut a slit after the manner of the stenopaic slit of oculists used to correct astigmatism.

From imperfect observation and the difficulty experienced in communicating intelligently with the Eskimo I was unable to determine whether acritochromacy existed among them to any great extent. That this functional trouble does exist we know from Nordenskiöld, who ascertained the fact after actual experiment. Many of them, however, possess eye-sight that is perfectly wonderful, being endowed with the acuity of vision peculiar to nomads and hunters who spend a great deal of time in the open air, which enables them to descry distant objects only discernible to ordinary eyes by means of a spy glass.

At several places I saw Eskimo using spy-glasses and opera-glasses, with the use of which they were perfectly familiar. As far north as Point Barrow, the northwestern extremity of America, I saw an old fellow with a pair of opera-glasses of French manufacture, which he carried carefully protected in a skin bag hung around his neck. Another pair was in possession of a man at Cape Krusenstern, who showed how they were useful to him in stalking reindeer.

ARCTIC MOSQUITOES.

Mosquitoes were found to be quite troublesome at Saint Michael's. How strange that the busy drone of these little dipterous insects, recalling the solicitations for a *pour boire* in a French café, should importune one's ears at a spot so far north beyond the domain of the ordinary "globe trotter" and unknown to tourists! The little pests are more widely distributed than the Innuit race or the reindeer, to both of whom they cause great annoyance during the short Arctic summer. Frail as they are in body they have reached as far north as man has penetrated, having been found by the Nares Expedition, and unlike other insects they seem to have no relations to the external conditions by which they are surrounded, being in fact cosmopolitan and having no zoological province. Not only are they unconfined to any limited or definite area, their distribution in time is contemporaneous with if not antecedent to man, as their fossil remains have been found in the Tertiary beds of the Lower White River, Colorado; and an instance is even recorded of their affording material for Eskimo wit at Lieutenant Schwatka's expense, who was facetiously styled by these people "the big mosquito."

Mr. Seebohm, a naturalist who visited Northern Siberia to study the birds, writes:

But there is one great drawback to visiting this charming country, and that is the reason why it is so frequented by birds—the myriads of mosquitoes. Life without a veil I believe would be perfectly unendurable. I was obliged to wear thick leather gloves, and on many occasions, when shooting, if I was too long in taking aim, I had to shake the barrel to get the mosquitoes off, and then take another aim quickly before they lighted again, otherwise I could not see the bird at all.

Arctic mosquitoes as encountered by us surpassed anything I have ever seen in New Jersey, for instance, where it is said they collect at times in such clouds around village church steeples as to be mistaken for smoke and cause an alarm of fire. Although they were worse than anything that I ever experienced at such places as Tybee Island, Georgia, the New Orleans quarantine station, or on the Rio Grande River, they differ from the southern insect in several respects. In the first place they are more pilose and more plumose, and have not so much nimbleness and activity, in consequence of which they are unable to get out of the way quickly and can easily be killed almost by the handful; but they seem to be just as venomous and persistent as their southern congeners.

Owing to their excessive annoyance, at times it was found to be almost impossible to use the instruments in taking observations when the position of a spot on shore was to be determined. On one occasion at a desolate spot on the top of Chamisso Island, about 200 feet above the sea level, we found an astronomical station, which had been established by parties from English ships in search of Sir John Franklin, and near it was a notice telling something about a bottle buried so many feet to the magnetic north. Curiosity, of course, prompted to get it by all means, but the mosquitoes coming in such myriads actually caused the search to be abandoned. Many of the men of the Corwin's crew were seriously incommoded by their bites and stings on exposed parts of the body, one man's neck and face being so swollen from this cause that he was temporarily deprived of eyesight.

MEDICAL AND SURGICAL REMARKS.

No serious epidemics have occurred at Saint Michael's since 1840, when small-pox was introduced by the Russians. This is probably the northern limit of that disease on the Pacific American coast. Of 550 cases occuring at Saint Michael's and Kolmakovsky 200 died, and a famine ensued because of the death of so many of the hunters and providers.*

This post having been for a long time in possession of the Russians before the Alaskan purchase, numerous half-breeds are found in the vicinity, for whom the so-called strumous diathesis seems to have the preference. That diseases of the latter character have prevailed for some time may be assumed from examination of an aboriginal skull exhumed from the neighboring graveyard at Saint Michael's. There is shown extensive necrosis of the bones composing the apex of the skull, also of the temporal and occipital bones and the left half of the inferior maxilla.

It appears that variola prevailed among the Alaskans previously to the Russian occupation, for several early Spanish navigators mention having noticed the marks of small-pox among the natives of Sitka Bay and Port Bucareli on Prince William Sound. The first mention is made by Don Francisco Antonio Maurelle, who explored the coast in 1775. "Journal of a Voyage in 1775 to explore the coast of America northward of California," published in English, Edinburgh, 1802. The other reference is "Relacion del Viaga Heche por los Goletas dutil y Mexicana en el año de 1792, Madrid, 1801."

Hagemeister (Report on Russian Colonies, 1820) says that the first vaccine matter was brought to Alaska in 1808 by the ship Neva, and the surgeon, Mardhorst, who introduced vaccination, instructed the agents of the company in performing the operation. From Tikhmenieff we learn that 400 natives and 1 Russian died of small-pox at Sitka in 1836, and the disease being carried to Kodiak the following year, in March, it caused the death of 737 people.

On the Alaskan Peninsula vaccination seems to have afforded protection from the disease, for but 27 deaths occurred out of 243 cases. At Ounalaska there were 180 cases, of which 130 died. At Cook's Inlet, the natives refusing to be vaccinated, the mortality is reported to have been greater, but no figures are given. The last cases occurred there in 1840. The reappearance of small-pox was noticed at Sitka in 1862, and it traveled northward, but vaccination is alleged to have lessened the mortality of previous epidemics.

On reaching Saint Lawrence Bay, Siberia, a native was taken aboard at his own request with a view to utilize his services, as he spoke a little English. This fellow had a fatuous expression of countenance and a choreic affection which kept up an intermittent twitching of his head. After several days he suffered from constipation and insomnia, for which the usual remedies were administered, with the effect best described in the patient's own phraseology when questioned at morning sick call: "Lass night big sick; to-day small sick; all same bime by good." However, the bustle and stir on board a steam-vessel, with the unusual surroundings, caused a return of the insomnia, and the fellow's state of mind was not improved by seeing our collection of aboriginal crania nor by the chaff and gibes of the men in the forecastle, who made him believe that he was to be taken to San Francisco in a box as an anatomical curiosity, all of which causes tended to produce an illusion of the imagination that exercised a despotism over his weak and uncultivated intellect. High authority asserts that all suicides originate either from insanity or moral cowardice. Here undoubtedly is an instance in which the disorder of the relations between mental and physical functions was of such a nature as to destroy the current presumptions founded on these relations as existing in health—the man stabbed himself and jumped into the sea. Happily he was fished aboard with great promptness, a boat being alongside at the time. An inspection showed a penetrating wound of the chest just under the left nipple, the knife having entered several inches; blood and air escaped from the wound every time the patient coughed, and the hand placed over the surface of the chest showed extensive effusion of blood into the thoracic cavity with the peculiar mucous bubbling or gurgling of traumatopnœa. With such a formidable array of symptoms the patient ought to have perished promptly from asphyxia, notwithstanding the application of an occlusive dressing to the wound, a tight roller bandage around the chest, and the administration of the usual stimulant and opiate. After considerable delirium, followed by orthopnœa, it was

---

* Tikhmenieff: Historical Review of the Russian Colonies. Vol. I. p. 311-13.

surprising to notice the presence of favorable symptoms and ultimate improvement. In a few days the patient was landed at Plover Bay, Siberia, where he recovered sufficiently to start on foot for his home over a rugged mountain way 150 miles distant.

Some weeks thereafter the Corwin happening to stop in at Plover Bay, I inquired of a native, remarkable for his whaleman's English and apothegmatical way of putting things, whether my patient had got well, to which he replied, "Yes; small well." I learned subsequently from a whaling vessel, on board which this man had made a visit at Saint Lawrence Bay, that he had entirely recovered from his wound, but still labored under the delusion that his life had been attempted by the captain of the Corwin.

One case of hermetical sealing of a wound of the foregoing description does not prove much, to be sure, and it is hardly necessary to advocate a subject that has been the occasion of much discussion; but it does seem that the occlusive treatment, which has been sanctioned and practiced by such masters as Guy de Chauliac, John de Vigo, Paré, Graefe, of Berlin, and others, has its virtues, notwithstanding a different and unwarrantable assumption put before the public in a late official publication.

Wounds seem to heal uncommonly well in the Arctic, a fact doubtless owing to the highly ozonized condition of the atmosphere and the absence of disease germs and organic dust. It is noticeable both in man and animals. At King's Island I saw a whale's rib in which reunion had taken place after a fracture probably caused by a bomb lance, and I have also seen a bear with several reunited ribs which had been fractured by a musket ball that had previously passed through the skull. A fossil rib of a reindeer, taken from the mammoth cliff in Kotzebue Sound, likewise showed reunion after a fracture.

Several extraordinary recoveries from scalp wounds, more extensive in character than anything of the kind I have ever seen in hospital or described in surgical works, came under my observation. One occurred off the Siberian coast in an old Eskimo who denuded a large portion of the *os frontis* from a fall on the ice. Careful approximation of the edges of the wound and the application of a retentive bandage were followed by rapid healing unaccompanied by complications. But the two most notable ones were in Eskimo, who in encounters with bears had been pawed and terribly lacerated about the head and face—a favorite amusement of this animal when he gets a man in his clutches. The first fellow's scalp, neck, and face, in the region of the parotid gland, were extensively mutilated; the second was similarly torn, with the additional loss of his left eye, and fracture of his inferior maxilla. Both men, though much deformed, had recovered without surgical assistance, and the wounds were well cicatrized.

Occasional gunshot wounds, usually the result of accident, are also met with among the Eskimo. At Saint Lawrence Bay I saw an old man who had been struck by a ball which entered the left side of his face just under the zygomatic process, and, passing downwards, had emerged from the neck, in the vicinity of the right carotid artery.

Among other things observed surgically were three cases of angular ankylosis of the knee joint, two occurring in adults and one in a boy; a case of paraplegia, due to traumatic causes; a case of periostitis of the bones of the forearm, another of necrosis of the superior maxilla; several of tumors occurring on the neck, and one case of hemorrhoids. The latter affection and boils are quite common, according to Mr. Nelson, who has spent some time at Saint Michael's. Mr. Petroff tells me that he has seen among the Innuit population of the interior extensive serpiginous ulcers, which yielded readily to treatment; and has also noticed a great many instances of disabled extremities from the effects of frost-bite. Among the more northern Eskimo, however, it appears that frost-bites are extremely rare. I have never seen an instance, and this observation seems to accord with the experience of others. More rare still is the occurrence of malformation, deformity, or idiocy. Whether the Spartan rule obtains relative to the destruction of weak or deformed infants, I am unable to say. However that may be, I can recall but a single instance in which there was observed anything approaching to deformity, and that was a girl with a supernumerary digit.

Skin diseases, principally of the vesicular and squamous varieties, were found to prevail extensively, a fact not to be wondered at, since they are just the diseases the medical man would expect to see developed in subjects among whom are recognized the conditions most favorable to their origin. The existence of the dartrous, scrofulous, rheumatic, and even syphilitic diseases, along with personal uncleanliness, must necessarily result in such lesions of the skin as eczema, psoriasis, ichthyosis, pityriasis, and tinea favosa, all of which I saw among the Eskimo. Although affections of the scalp were quite common, especially in children, I noticed but one case of baldness, which leads me to doubt the statement of several medical men to the effect that wearing fur caps is one of the causes of loss of the hair. If this were true every Eskimo pate ought to be as bald as the palm of the hand.

It is also doubtless true that the numerous catarrhs and bronchial and pulmonary troubles are only internal manifestations of the diatheses previously mentioned. When the Corwin was along the Siberian coast in June and July not a man on board had a cold, yet nearly all the natives we met with were suffering from coughs and colds. The same thing was observed by our sledge party who went up the coast, and Lieutenant Schwatka informs me that rheumatic and pulmonary complaints were the principal ones noticed by him. Notwithstanding Mr. Kennan's mention of a reindeer picket in an atmosphere of —60°, it is indeed questionable whether Eskimo can endure cold as well as well-fed white men. Though clad in furs, I have often seen them shivering from cold, when our crew, with only the ordinary winter clothes of sailors, experienced no discomfort.

Among their more common ailments are boils and epistaxis, the latter having been noticed by former travelers, and Mr. Nelson informs me that it is quite common among the fur traders of the Upper Yukon, who attribute it to a plethoric condition brought about by an almost exclusive diet of animal food.

Our hyperborean nosology would be incomplete without some mention of nervous diseases, which late authorities assume to be one of the sequelæ of civilization. They would, perhaps, come nearer the truth to ascribe them, as Dr. Draper has done, to the introduction and extension of that senseless and filthy habit, the use of tobacco. Mr. Petroff informs me that hysteria, epilepsy, and paralysis are common diseases among the interior tribes, who also believe in and practice Shamanism. Instances of excessive nervousness have come under my notice, one of a man so shaky that his infirmity was a source of merriment to his companions. I treated one patient for insomnia and another for epilepsy. I saw also two cases of chorea, one each of paraplegia and of cerebral hemorrhage with hemiplegic symptoms (both at Point Barrow), one of suicidal mania, and I know of at least three deaths from cerebro-spinal meningitis.

To what cause a late authority would assign the existence of these diseases I am unable to say, but enough has been seen to convince that nervous diseases are not confined to civilized communities, as many persons believe; and, indeed, a distinguished medical author, who sees in spiritualism a form of nervous derangement, might, after observing Shamanism and its results, be in possession of enough neurological material for a new chapter in his work on that subject.

GENERAL REMARKS ON THE NORTHERN INHABITANTS.

But it is from an anthropological point of view that the Eskimo coming under observation proved most interesting. The term Eskimo may be held to include all the Innuit population living on the Aleutian Islands, the islands of Bering Sea, and the shores both of Asia and America north of about latitude 64°. In this latitude on the American coast the ethnical points that difference the North American Indian from the Eskimo are distinctly marked. It cannot, however, be said that the marks of distinction are so plain between the American Eskimo and the so-called Tsuchtschi of the Asiatic coast. I have been unable to see anything more in the way of distinction than exists between Englishmen and Danes, for instance, or between Norwegians and Swedes. Indeed, it may be said that much of the confusion and absurdity of classification found in ethnographic literature may be traced to a tendency to see diversities where few or none exist. To the observant man of travel who has given the matter any attention, it seems that the most sensible classification is that of the ancient writers who divide humanity into three races, namely, white, yellow, and black. Cuvier adopted this division, and the best contemporary British authority, Dr. Latham, also makes three groups, although he varies somewhat in details from Cuvier. In accordance with the nomenclature of Latham, the Eskimo may be spoken of as Hyperborean Mongolidæ of essentially carnivorous and ichthyophagous habits, who have not yet emerged from the hunting and fishing stage.

PHYSICAL APPEARANCES.

Their physical appearance and structure having been already described by others, it is unnecessary to mention them here, except incidentally and by way of noting a few peculiarities that seem to have been heretofore overlooked or slightly touched upon by other writers. Although as a rule they are of short build, averaging about five feet seven inches, yet occasional exceptions were met with among the natives of Kotzebue Sound, many of whom were tall and of commanding appearance. At Cape Krusenstern a man was seen who measured six feet six inches in height. This divergence from the conventional Eskimo type, as usually described in the books, may have been caused by intermarriage with an inland tribe of larger men from the interior of Alaska, who come to the coast every summer for purposes of trade.

The complexion, rarely a true white, but rather that of a Chinaman, with a healthy blush suffusing each cheek, is often of a brownish-yellow and sometimes quite black, as I have seen in several instances at Tapkan, Siberia. Nor was the broad and flat face and the small nose without exception. In the vicinity of East Cape, the easternmost extremity of Asia, a few Eskimo were seen having distinctive Hebrew noses and a physiognomy of such a Jewish type as to excite the attention and comment of the sailors composing our crew; others were noticed having a Milesian cast of features and looked like Irishmen, while others resembled several old mulatto men I know in Washington. However, the Mongoloid type in these people was so pronounced that our Japanese boys on meeting Eskimo for the first time took them for Chinamen; on the other hand the Japs were objects of great and constant curiosity to the Eskimo, who doubtless took them for compatriots, a fact not to be wondered at, since there is such a similarity in the shape of the eyes, the complexion, and hair. In regard to the latter it may be remarked that scarcely anything on board the Corwin excited greater wonder and merriment among the Eskimo than the presence of several persons whom Professor Huxley would classify in his Xanthocroic group because of their fiery red hair.

The structure and arrangement of the hair having lately been proposed as a race characteristic upon which to base an ethnical classification, I took pains to collect various specimens of Innuit hair, which in conjunction with Dr. Kidder, U. S. N., I examined microscopically and compared with the hair of fair and blue-eyed persons, the hair of negroes, and as a matter of curiosity with the reindeer hair and the hair-like appendage found on the fringy extremity of the baleen plates in the mouth of a "bowhead" whale. Some photomicrographs of these objects are shown in the accompanying illustrations.

To the man willing and anxious to make more extended research into the matter of race characteristics, I venture to say that a northern experience will afford him ample opportunity for supplementing Mr. Murray's paper on the Ethnological Classification of Vermin; and he may further observe that the Eskimo, whatever may be his religious belief or predilection, apparently observes the prohibitions of the Talmud in regard both to filth and getting rid of noxious entomological specimens that infest his body and habitation.

Whatever modification the bodily structure of the Eskimo may have undergone under the influence of physical and moral causes, when viewed in the light of transcendental anatomy, we find that the mode, plan, or model upon which his animal frame or organs are founded is substantially that of other varieties of men.

Some writers go so far, in speaking of the Eskimo's correspondence, mental and physical, to his surroundings as to mention the seal as his correlative, which, in my opinion, is about as sensible as speaking of the reciprocal relations of a Cincinnati man and a hog. Unlike the seal, which is pre-eminently an amphibian and a swimmer, the Eskimo has no physical capability of the latter kind, being unable to swim and having the greatest aversion to water except for purposes of navigation. He wins our admiration from the expert management at sea of his little shuttle-shaped canoe, which is a kind of marine bicycle, but I doubt very much the somersaults he is reported to be able to turn in them. In fact, after offering rewards of that all-powerful incentive, tobacco, on numerous occasions, I have been unsuccessful in getting any one of them to attempt the feat, and when told that we had heard of their doing it they smiled rather incredulously. The Eskimo is clearly not a success in a cubistic or saltatorial line, as I have had ample opportunities to observe. They seem to be unable to do the simplest gymnastics, and were filled with the greatest delight

HAIR—ALEUTIAN ESKIMO
(polarized)

and astonishment at some exhibitions we gave them on several occasions. Receiving a challenge to run a foot-race with an Eskimo, I came off easy winner, although I was handicapped by being out of condition at the time; a challenge to throw stones also resulted in the same kind of victory; I shouldered and carried some logs of drift-wood that none of them could lift, and on another occasion the captain and I demonstrated the physical superiority of the Anglo-Saxon by throwing a walrus lance several lengths farther than any of the Eskimo who had provoked the competition. As a rule they are deficient in biceps, and have not the well developed muscles of athletic white men. The best muscular development I saw was among the natives of Saint Lawrence Island, who, by the way, showed me a spot in a village where they practiced athletic sports, one of these diversions being lifting and "putting" heavy stones, and I have gracefully to acknowledge that a young Eskimo got the better of me in a competition of this kind. It is fair to assume that one reason for this physical superiority was the inexorable law of the survival of the fittest, the natives in question being the survivors of a recent prevailing epidemic and famine.

ESKIMO APPETITES.

As far as my experience goes the Eskimo have not the enormous appetites with which they are usually accredited. The Eskimo who accompanied Lieutenant May, of the Nares Expedition, on his sledge journey, is reported to have been a small eater, and the only case of scurvy, by the way; the Eskimo employed on board the Corwin as dog drivers and interpreters were as a rule smaller eaters than our own men, and I have observed, on numerous occasions, among the Eskimo I have visited, that instead of being great gluttons they are on the contrary moderate eaters. It is, perhaps, the revolting character of their food—rancid oil, a tray of hot seal entrails, a bowl of coagulated blood, for example—that causes overestimation of the quantity eaten. Persons in whom nausea and disgust are awakened at tripe, putrid game, and moldy and maggoty cheese affected by so-called epicures, not to mention the bad oysters which George I preferred to fresh ones, would doubtless be prejudiced and incorrect observers as to the quantity of food an Eskimo might consume. From some acquaintance with the subject I, therefore, venture to say that the popular notion regarding the great appetite of the Eskimo is one of the current fallacies. The reported cases were probably exceptional ones happening in subjects who had been exercising and living on little else than frozen air for perhaps a week. Any vigorous man in the prime of life who has been shooting all day in the sharp, crisp air of the Arctic will be surprised at his gastronomic capabilities; and personal knowledge of some almost incredible instances among civilized men might be related, were it not for fear of being accused of transcending the bounds of veracity.

ORIGIN AND DEVELOPMENT.

There is so much about certain parts of Alaska to remind one of Scotland, that we wonder why some of the more southern Eskimo have not the intrepidity and vigor of Scotchmen, since they live under almost the same topographical conditions amid fogs and misty hills. Perhaps if they were fed on oatmeal, and could be made to adopt a few of the Scotch manners and customs, religious and otherwise, they might, after infinite ages of evolution, develop some of the qualities of that excellent race. It is probably not so very many generations ago that our British progenitors were like these original and primitive men as we find them in the vicinity of Bering Straits. Here the mind is taken back over centuries, and one is enabled to study the link of transition between the primitive men of the two continents at the spot where their geographical relations lead us to suspect it. Indeed the primitive man may be seen just as he was thousands of years ago, by visiting the village perched, like the eyry of some wild bird, about 200 feet up the side of the cliff at East Cape on the Asiatic side of the Straits. This bold, rocky cliff, rising sheer from the sea to the height of 2,100 feet, consists of granite with lava here and there, and the indications point to the overflow of a vast ice sheet from the north, evidences of which are seen in the trend of the ridges on the top and the form of the narrow peninsula joining the cliff to the mainland. From the summit of the cape the Diomedes, Fairway Rock, and the American coast are so easily seen that the view once taken would dispel any doubts as to the possibility of the aboriginal denizens of America having crossed over from Asia, and it would require no such statement to corroborate the opinion as that of an officer of the Hudson Bay Company, then resident in Ungava Bay, who relates that in 1839 an Eskimo family crossed to Labrador from the northern shore of Hudson's Straits on a raft of drift-wood. Natives cross and recross Bering Straits to-day on the ice and in primitive skin canoes, not unlike Cape Cod dories, which have not been improved in construction since the days of prehistoric man. Indeed the primitive man may be seen at East Cape almost as he was thousands of years ago. Evolution and development, with the exception of fire-arms, seem to have halted at East Cape. The place with its cave-like dwellings and skin-clad inhabitants, among whom the presence of white men creates the same excitement as the advent of a circus among the colored population of Washington, makes one fancy that he is in some grand prehistoric museum and that he has gone backward in time several thousand years in order to get there.

While we may do something towards tracing the effects of physical agents on the Eskimo back into the darkness that antedates history, yet his geographical origin and his antiquity are things concerning which we know but little. Being subjects of first-class interest deserving of grave study and so vast in themselves, they cannot be touched upon here except incidentally. Attempting to study them is like following the labyrinthal ice mazes of the Arctic in quest of the North Pole, and only ends in a wild-goose chase.

We may, however, venture the assertion that the Eskimo is of autochthonic origin in Asia, but is not autochthonous in America. His arrival there and subsequent migrations are beyond the reach of history or tradition. Others, though, contend from the analogy of some of the western tribes of Brazil, who are identical in feature to the Chinese, that the Eskimo may have come from South America; and the fashion of wearing labrets, which is common to the indigenous population both of Chili and Alaska, has been cited as a further proof.

Touching the subject of early migrations Mr. Charles Wolcott Brooks, whose sources of information have been exceptionally good, reports in a paper to the California Academy of Sciences a record of sixty Japanese junks, which were blown off the coast and by the influence of the Kuro-Shiwo were drifted or stranded on the coast of North America, or on the Hawaiian or adjacent islands. As merchant ships and ships of war are known to have been built in Japan prior to the Christian era, a great number of disabled junks containing small parties of Japanese must have been stranded on the Aleutian Islands and on the Alaskan coast in past centuries, thereby furnishing evidence of a constant infusion of Japanese blood among the coast tribes.

Leaving aside any attempt to show the ethnical relations of these facts, the question naturally occurs whether any of these waifs ever found their way back from the American coast. On observing the course of the great circle of the Kuro-Shiwo and the course of the trade winds, one inclines to the belief that such a thing is not beyond the range of possibility. Indeed, several well-authenticated instances are mentioned by Mr. Brooks; and in connection with the subject he advances a further hypothesis, namely, the American origin of the Chinese race, and shows in a plausible way that—

"The ancestry of China may have embarked in large vessels as emigrants, perhaps from the vicinity of the Chincha Islands, or proceeded with a large fleet, like the early Chinese expedition against Japan, or that of Julius Cæsar against Britain, or the Welsh Prince Madog and his party, who sailed from Ireland and landed in America A. D. 1170; and, in like manner, in the dateless antecedure of history, crossed from the neighborhood of Peru to the country now known to us as China."

If America be the oldest continent, paleontologically speaking, as Agassiz tells us, there appears to be some reason for looking to it as the spot where early traces of the human race are to be found, and the fact would seem to warrant further study and investigation in connection with the indigenous people of our continent, thereby awakening new sources of inquiry among ethnologists.

LINGUISTIC PECULIARITIES.

The sienite plummet from San Joaquin Valley, California, goes back to the distant age of the Drift; and the Calaveras skull, admitting its authenticity, goes back to the Pliocene epoch, and is older than the relics or stone implements from the drift gravel and the European caves.

It is doubtful, though, whether these sources enable us to make generalizations equal in value to those afforded by the study of vocabularies. It is alleged that linguistic affinities exist between some of the tribes of the American coast and our Oriental neighbors across the Pacific. Mr. Brooks,

whom I have already quoted, reports that in March, 1860, he took an Indian boy on board the Japanese steam-corvette Kanrin-maru, where a comparison of Coast-Indian and pure Japanese was made at his request by Funkuzawa Ukitchy, then admiral's secretary; the result of which he prepared for the press and published with a view to suggest further linguistic investigation. He says that quite an infusion of Japanese words is found among some of the Coast tribes of Oregon and California, either pure or clipped, along with some very peculiar Japanese "idioms, constructions, honorific, separative, and agglutinative particles;" that shipwrecked Japanese are invariably enabled to communicate understandingly with the Coast Indians, although speaking quite a different language, and that many shipwrecked Japanese have informed him that they were enabled to communicate with and understand the natives of Atka and Adakh Islands of the Aleutian group.

With a view to finding out whether any linguistic affinity existed between Japanese and the Eskimo dialects in the vicinity of Bering Straits, I caused several Japanese boys, employed as servants on board the Corwin, to talk on numerous occasions to the natives, both of the American and Asiatic coasts; but in every instance they were unable to understand the Eskimo, and assured me that they could not detect a single word that bore any resemblance to words in their own language.

The study of the linguistic peculiarities which distinguish the population around Bering Straits offers an untrodden path in a new field; but it is doubtful whether the results, except to linguists like Cardinal Mezzofanti, or philologists of the Max Müller type, would be at all commensurate with the efforts expended in this direction; since it is asserted that the human voice is incapable of articulating more than twenty distinct sounds, therefore whatever resemblnaces there may be in the particular words of different languages are of no ethnic value. Although these may be the views of many persons not only in regard to the Eskimo tongue but in regard to philology in general, the matter has a wonderful fascination for more speculative minds.

Much has been said about the affinity of language among the Eskimo—some asserting that it is such as to allow mutual intercourse everywhere—but instances warrant us in concluding that considerable deviations exist in their vocabularies if not in the grammatical construction. For instance, take two words that one hears oftener than any others: On the Alaskan coast they say "na-koo-ruk," a word meaning "good," "all right," &c.; on the Siberian coast "ma-zink-ah," while a vocabulary collected during Lieutenant Schwatka's expedition gives the word "mah-muk'-poo" for "good." The first two of these words are so characteristic of the tribes on the respective shores above the straits that a better designation than any yet given to them by writers on the subject would be *Nakoorooks* for the people on the American side and *Mazinkahs* for those on the Siberian coast. These names, by which they know each other, are in general use among the whalemen and were adopted by every one on board the Corwin.

Again, on the American coast " Am-a-luk-tuk" signifies plenty, while on the Siberian coast it is "Num-kuck-ee." "Tee-tee-tah" means needles in Siberia, in Alaska it is "mitkin." In the latter place when asking for tobacco they say "te-ba-muk," while the Asiatics say "salopa." That a number of dialects exists around Bering Straits is apparent to the most superficial observer. The difference in the language becomes apparent after leaving Norton Sound. The interpreter we took from Saint Michael's could only with difficulty understand the natives at Point Barrow, while at Saint Lawrence Island and on the Asiatic side he could understand nothing at all. At East Cape we saw natives who, though apparently alike, did not understand one another's language. I saw the same thing at Cape Prince of Wales, the western extremity of the New World, whither a number of Eskimo from the Wankarem River, Siberia, had come to trade. Doubtless there is a community of origin in the Eskimo tongue, and these verbal divergencies may be owing to the want of written records to give fixity to the language, since languages resemble living organisms by being in a state of continual change. Be that as it may, we know that this people has imported a number of words from coming in contact with another language, just as the French have incorporated into their speech "le steppeur," "l'outsider," "le high life," "le steeple chase," " le jockey club," &c.—words that have no correlatives in French—so the Eskimo has appropriated from the whalers words which, as verbal expressions of his ideation, are undoubtedly better than anything in his own tongue. One of these is "by and by," which he uses with the same frequency that a Spaniard does his favorite *mañana por le mañano*. In this instance the words express the state of development and habits of thought—one the lazy improvidence of the Eskimo, and the other the "to-morrow" of the Spaniard, who has indulged that propensity so far that his nation has become one of yesterday.

The change of the Eskimo language, brought about by its coming in contact with another, forms an important element in its history, and has been mentioned by the older writers, also by Gilder, who reports a change in the language of the Iwillik Eskimo to have taken place since the advent among them of the white men. Among other peculiarities of their phraseology occurs the word "tanuk" signifying whiskey, and it is said to have originated with an old Eskimo employed by Moore as a guide and dog driver when he wintered in Plover Bay. Every day about noon that personage was in the habit of taking his appetizer and usually said to the Eskimo, "Come, Joe, let's take our tonic." Like most of his countrymen, Joe was not slow to learn the meaning of the word, and to this day the firm hold "tanuk" has on the language is only equalled by the thirst for the fluid which the name implies. Among the Asiatic Eskimo the word "um-muck" is common for "rum," while "em-nik" means water. Even words brought by whalers from the South Sea Islands have obtained a footing, such as "kow-kow" for food, a word in general use, and "pow" for "no," or "not any." They also call their babies "pick-a-nee-nee," which to many persons will suggest the Spanish word or the southern negro idiom for "baby." The phrase "pick-a-nee-nee kowkow" is the usual formula in begging food for their children. An Eskimo, having sold us a reindeer, said it would be "mazinkah kowkow" (good eating), and one windy day we were hauling the seine, and an Eskimo seeing its empty condition when pulled on to the beach, said "'Pow' fish; bimeby 'pow' wind, plenty fish."

The fluency with which some of these fellows speak a mixture of pigeon English and whaleman's jargon is quite astonishing, and suggests the query whether their fluency results from the aggressiveness of the English or whether it is an evidence of their aptitude? It seems wonderful how a people we are accustomed to look upon as ignorant, benighted, and undeveloped, can learn to talk English with a certain degree of fluency and intelligibility from the short intercourse held once a year with a few passing ships. How many "hoodlums" in San Francisco, for instance, learn anything of Norwegian or German from frequenting the wharves? How many "wharf rats" or stevedores in New York learn anything of these languages from similar intercourse? Or, for that matter, we may ask, How many New York pilots have acquired even the smallest modicum of French from boarding the steamers of the Compagnie Générale Transatlantique?

From a few examples it will be seen that the usage followed by the Eskimo in its grammatical variations rests on the fixity of the radical syllable and upon the agglomeration of the different particles intended to modify the primitive sense of this root, that is to say upon the principle of agglutinative languages. One or two instances may suffice to show the agglutinate character of the language. Canoe is "o-me-uk;" ship, "o-me-uk-puk;" steamer, "o-me-uk-puk-ignelik;" and this composite mechanical structure reaches its climax in steam-launch, which they call "o-me-uk-puk-ignelik-pick-a-nee-nee."

For snow and ice in their various forms there are also many words, which show further the polysynthetic structure of the language—a fact contrary to that primitive condition of speech where there are no inflections to indicate the relations of the words to each other. It will not do to omit "O-kee-chuck" from this enumeration—a word signifying trade, barter, or sale, and one most commonly heard among these people. When they wish to say a thing is bad they use "A-shu-ruk," and when disapproval is meant they say "pe-chuk." The latter word also expresses general negation. For instance, on looking into several unoccupied houses a native informs us "Innuit peehuk," meaning that the people are away or not at home; "Allopar" is cold, and "allopar peehuk" is hot. Persons fond of tracing resemblances may find in "Ignik" (fire) a similarity to the Latin *ignis* or the English "ignite," and from "Un-gi-doo-ruk" (big, huge) the transition down to "hunky-dory" is easy. Those who see a sort of complemental relation to each other of linguistic affinity and the conformity in physical characters may infer from "Mikey-doo rook" (a term of endearment equivalent to "Mavourneen" and used in addressing little children) that the inhabitants within the Polar Circle have something of the Emerald Isle about them. But no, they are not Irish, for when they are about to leave the ship or any other place for their houses they say "to-hum;" consequently they are Yankees.

I do not wish to be thought frivolous in my notions regarding the noble science of philology; but when one considers the changes that language is constantly undergoing, the inability of the human voice to articulate more than twenty distinct sounds, and the wonderful amount of ingenious learning that has been wasted by philologists on trifling subjects, one is disposed to associate many of their deductions with the savage picture writing on Dighton Rock, the Cardiff Giant, and the old wind-mill at Newport.

ESKIMO DIETETICS.

Attempts to trace or discover the origin of races through supposed philological analogies do not possess the advantage of certainty afforded by the study of the means by which individuals of the race supply the continuous demands of the body with the nutriment necessary to maintain life and health.

Everybody has heard of the seal, bear, walrus, and whale in connection with Eskimo dietetics, and doubtless the stomachs of most persons would revolt at the idea of eating these animals, the taste for which, by the way, is merely a matter of early education or individual preference, for there is no good reason why they should not be just as palatable to the northern appetite as pig, sheep, and beef are to the inhabitants of temperate latitudes. As food they renew the nitrogenous tissues, reconstruct the parts, and restore the functions of the Eskimo frame, prolong his existence, and produce the same animal contentment and joy as the more civilized viands of the white man's table. There are more palatable things than bear or eider-duck, yet I know many persons to whom snails, olive oil, and *paté de fois gras* are more repugnant. A tray full of hot seal entrails, a bowl of coagulated blood, and putrid fish are not very inviting or lickerish to ordinary mortals, yet they have their analogue in the dish of some farmers who eat a preparation of pig's bowels known as "chitterlings," and in the blood-puddings and Limburger cheese of the Germans. Blubber-oil and whale are not very dainty dishes, yet consider how many families subsist on half-baked saleratus biscuits, salted pork, and oleomargarine.

On the mess table of the fur company's establishment at Saint Paul Island, seal meat is a daily article of consumption, and from personal experience I can testify as to its palatability, although it reminded one of indifferent beef rather overdone. Hair seal and bear steaks were on different occasions tried at the mess on board the Corwin, but everybody voted eider-duck and reindeer the preference. It is not so very long since that whale was a favorite article of diet in England and Holland, and Arctic whalemen still, to my personal knowledge, use the freshly tried oil in cooking; for instance, in frying cakes, for which they say it answers the purpose as well as the finest lard, while others breakfast on whale and potatoes prepared after the manner of codfish balls. The whale I have tasted is rather insipid eating, yet it appears to be highly nutritious, judging from the well-nourished look of natives who have lived on it, and the air of greasy abundance and happy contentment that pervades an Eskimo village just after the capture of a whale. Being ashore one day with our pilot, we met a native woman whom he recognized as a former acquaintance, and on remarking to her that she had picked up in flesh since he last saw her, she replied that she had been living on whale all the winter, which explained her plumpness.

It must not be supposed, however, that the whale, seal, and walrus constitute the entire food supply of the Arctic. There is scarcely any more toothsome delicacy than reindeer, the tongue of which is very dainty and succulent. There is one peculiarity about its flesh—in order to have it in perfection it must be eaten very soon after being killed; the sooner the better, for it deteriorates in flavor the longer it is kept. Indeed, the Eskimo do not wait for the animal heat to leave the carcass, as they eat the brains and paunch hot and smoking.

While our gastronomic enthusiasm did not extend this far, we dined occasionally on fresh trout from a Siberian mountain lake, young wild ducks as fat as squabs, and reindeer, any of which delicacies could not be had in the same perfection at Delmonico's or any similar establishment in New York for love or money. There is scarcely any better eating in the way of fish than *coregonus*—a new species discovered at Point Barrow by the Corwin—and certainly no more dainty game exists than the young wild geese and ptarmigan to be found in countless numbers in Hotham Inlet. At the latter place, doubtless the warmest inside the Straits, are found quantities of cranberries about the size of a pea, which not only make a delicious accessory to roasted goose, but act as a valuable antiscorbutic. These berries, and a kind of kelp, which I have seen Eskimo eating at Tapkan, Siberia, seem to be the only vegetable food they have. The large quantities of eggs easily procurable, but in most cases doubtful, also constitute a standard article of diet among these people, who have no scruples about eating them partly hatched. They seemed never to comprehend our fastidiousness in the matter and why our tastes differed so much from theirs in this respect. They will break an egg containing an embryonic duck or goose, extract the bird by one leg and devour it with all the relish of an epicure. Gull's eggs, however, are in disrepute among them, for the women—who, by the way, have the same frailties and weakness as their more civilized sisters—believe that eating gulls' eggs causes loss of beauty and brings on early decrepitude. The men, on the other hand, are fond of seal eyes, a tid-bit which the women believe increases their amorousness, and feed to their lords after the manner of "Open your mouth and shut your eyes."

Game is as a rule very tame, and during the moulting season, when the geese are unable to fly, it is quite possible to kill them with a stick. At one place, Cape Thompson, Eskimo were seen catching birds from a high cliff with a kind of scoop net, and I saw birds at Herald Island refuse to move when pelted with stones, so unaccustomed were they to the presence of man. In addition to being very tame, game is plentiful, and not an uncommon sight, off the Siberian coast, were flocks of eider ducks darkening the air and occupying several hours in passing overhead. It was novel sport to see the natives throw a projectile known as an "apluketat" into one of these flocks with astonishing range and accuracy, bringing down the game with the effectiveness of a shotgun.

Game keeps so well in the Arctic that an instance is known of its being perfectly sweet and sound on an English ship after two years' keeping, and whalemen kill a number of pigs, which they hang in the rigging and keep for use during the cruise. It is also noticeable that leather articles do not mildew as they generally do at sea, some shoes kept in a locker on board the Corwin having retained their polish during the entire cruise.

The food of the Eskimo satisfies their instinctive craving for a hydrocarbon, but they do not allow themselves to be much disturbed or distracted in its preparation, as most of it is eaten raw. They occasionally boil their food, however, and some of them have learned the use of flour and molasses, of which they are very fond.

Their aversion to salt is a very marked peculiarity, and they will not eat either corned beef or pork on this account. It may be that physiological reasons exist for this dislike.

SOCIAL AND DOMESTIC RELATIONS.

Omitting other ethnographic facts relative to the Eskimo, which might be treated in a systematic way except for their triteness, we pass from the means of the renewal of the animal economy to its reproduction. Courtship and marriage, which, it is said, are conducted in the most unsentimental manner possible, are for that reason not to be discussed; and for obvious reasons many of the prenatal conditions cannot here be dwelt upon. Having never witnessed the act of parturition in an Eskimo my knowledge of the subject is merely second-hand, and consequently not worth detailing. It appears, though, that parturition is a function easily performed among them, and that it is unattended by the post-partem accidents common to civilization. As a rule the women are unprolific, it being uncommon to find a family numbering over three children, and the mortality among the new-born is excessive, owing to the ignorance and neglect of the ordinary rules of hygiene. They seem, however, to be kind to their children, who in respect to crying do not show the same peevishness as seen in our nurseries; indeed, the social and demonstrative good nature of the race seems to crop out even in babyhood, as I have often witnessed under such circumstances as a baby enveloped in furs in a skin canoe which lay along side the ship during a snow storm; its tiny hands protruding held a piece of blubber, which it sucked with apparent relish, the unique picture of happy contentment. It was quick to feel itself an object of attraction, and its chubby face returned any number of smiles of recognition.

The manner of carrying the infant is contrary to that of civilized custom. It is borne on the back under the clothes of the mother, which form a pouch, and from which its tiny head is generally visible over one or the other shoulder, but on being observed by strangers it shrinks like a

snail or a marsupian into its snug retreat. When the mother wants to remove it she bends forward, at the same time passing her left hand up the back under her garments, and seizing the child by the feet, pulls it downward to the left; then, passing the right hand under the front of the dress, she again seizes the feet and extracts it by a kind of pedalic delivery. Another common way of carrying children is astride the neck. The subject is one that the Chuckchii artist often carves in ivory.

The play-impulse manifests itself among these people in various ways. They have such mimetic objects as dolls, miniature boats, &c. I have seen a group of boys, sailing toy boats in a pond, behave under the circumstances just as a similar group has been observed to do at Provincetown, Cape Cod, and the same act, as performed in the Frog Pond of the Boston Common, may be called only a differentiated form of the same tendency. Their dolls, of ivory and clothed with fur, seem to answer the same purpose that they do in civilized communities—namely, the amusement of little girls—for at one place where we landed a number of Eskimo girls, stopping play on our approach, sat their dolls up in a row, evidently with a view to give the dolls a better look at the strange visitors. Spinning tops, essentially Eskimo and unique in their character, are held in the hand while spinning; on the Siberian Coast foot ball is played, and among other questionable things acquired from contact with the whalemen, a knowledge of card playing exists. We were very often asked for cards, and at one place where we stopped and bartered a number of small articles with the natives they gave evidence of their aptitude at gaming. The game being started, with the bartered articles as stakes, one fellow soon scooped in everything, leaving the others to go off dead broke amid the ridicule of some of our crew, and doubtless feeling worse than dead, for among no people that I have seen, not even the French, does ridicule so effectually kill.

PERSONAL ORNAMENTATION.

Among the means taken by these people to produce personal ornamentation that of tattooing the face and wearing a labret is the most noticeable. The custom of tattooing having existed from the earliest historical epochs is important not only from an ethnological but from a medical and pathological point of view, and even in its relation to medical jurisprudence in cases of contested personal identity.

Without going into the history of the subject, it may not be irrelevant to mention that tattooing was condemned by the Fathers of the Church, Tertullian among others, who gives the following rather singular reason for interdicting its use among women: "Certi sumus Spiritum Sanctum magis masculis tale aliquid subscribere potuisse si feminis subscripsisset."*

In addition to much that has been written by French and German writers, the matter of tattoomarks has of late claimed the attention of the law courts of England, the chief-justice, Cockburn, in the Tichbourne case, having described this species of evidence as of "vital importance," and in itself final and conclusive. The absence of the tattoo-marks in this case justified the jury in their finding that the defendant was not and could not be Roger Tichbourne, whereupon the alleged claimant was proved to be an impostor, found guilty of perjury, and sentenced to penal servitude.†

The accompanying representations, showing extensive markings on different parts of the body, are from photographs obtained in Japan.

Why the ancient habit of tattooing should prevail so extensively among some of the primitive tribes as it does, for instance, in the Polynesian Islands and some parts of Japan, and we may say as a survival of a superstitious practice of paganism among sailors and others, is a psychological problem difficult to solve. Whether it be owing to perversion of the sexual instinct, which is not unlikely, or to other cause, it is not proposed to discuss. Be that as it may, the prevalence of the habit among the Eskimo is confined to the female sex, who are tatooed on arriving at the age of puberty. The women of Saint Lawrence Island, in addition to lines on the nose, forehead, and chin, have uniformly a figure of strange design on the cheeks, which is suggestive of cabalistic import. It could not be ascertained, however, whether such was the case. The lines drawn on the chin were exactly like the ones I have seen on Moorish women in Morocco. Another

---

* De Virginibus velandis. Lutetiæ Parisiorum, 1675fº., p. 178.
† See Guy's Hospital Report, XIX, 1874; also "Histoire Médicale du Tatouage," in Archives de Médecine Navale, Tom. 11 et 12, Paris, 1869.

outlandish attempt at adornment was witnessed at Cape Blossom in a woman who wore a bunch of colored beads suspended from the septum of her nose. These habits, however, hardly seem so revolting as the use of the labret by the "Mazinka" men on the American coast, of

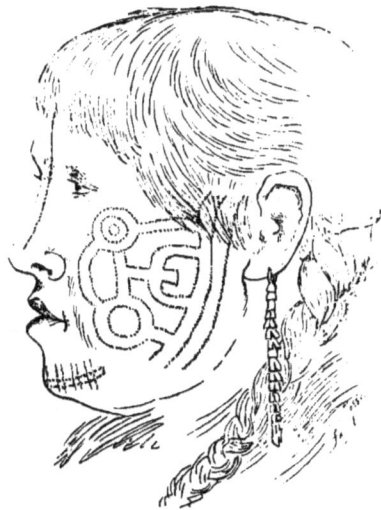

Style of personal ornamentation adopted by the women of Saint Lawrence Island.

whom it is related that a sailor seeing one of them for the first time, and observing the slit in the lower lip through which the native thrust his tongue, thought he had discovered a man with two mouths. The use of the labret, like many of the attempts at primitive ornamentation, is very old, it having been traced by Dall along the American Coast from the lower part of Chili to Alaska. Persons fond of tracing vestiges of savage ornamentation amid intellectual advancement and æsthetic sensibility far in advance of the primitive man, may observe in the wearers of bangles and ear-rings the same tendency existing in a differentiated form.

DIVERSIONS.

I doubt whether Shakespeare's dictum in regard to music holds good when applied to the Eskimo, for they have but little music in their souls, and among no people is there such a noticeable absence of "treason, stratagem, and spoil." A rude drum and a monotonous chant consisting only of the fundamental note and minor third, are the only things in the way of music among the more remote settlements of which I have any knowledge. Mrs. Micawber's singing has been described as the table-beer of acoustics. Eskimo singing is something more. The beer has become flat by the addition of ice. One of our engineers, who is quite a fiddler, experimented on his instrument with a view to see what effect music would have on the "savage breast," but his best efforts at rendering Madame Angot and the Grande Duchesse were wasted before an unsympathetic audience, who showed as little appreciation of his performance as some people do when listening to Wagner's "Music of the Future."

Where they have come in contact with civilization, their musical taste is more developed. At Saint Michael's I was told that some of their songs are so characteristic that it is much to be regretted that some of them cannot be bottled up in a phonograph and sent to a musical composer.

On the coast of Siberia I heard an Eskimo boy sing correctly a song he had learned while on board a whaling vessel, and on several of the Aleutian Islands the natives play the accordion quite well, have music-boxes, and even whistle strains from Pinafore.

From music to dancing the transition is obvious, no matter whether the latter be regarded in a Darwinian sense as a device to attract the opposite sex or as the expression of joyous excitement. This manifestation of feeling in its bodily discharge, which Moses and Miriam and David indulged in, which is ranked with poetry by Aristotle, and which old Homer says is the sweetest and most perfect of human enjoyments, is a pastime much in vogue among the Eskimo, and it required but little provocation to start a dance at any time on the Corwin's decks when a party happened to be on board. Their dancing, however, had not the cadence of "a wave of the sea," nor was there the harmony of double rotation circling in a series of graceful curves to strains like those of Strauss or Gungl. On the contrary, there was something saltatorial and jerky about all the dancing I saw both among the men and women. It is the custom at some of their gatherings, after the hunting season is over, for the men to indulge in a kind of terpsichorean performance, at the same time relating in Homeric style the heroic deeds they have done. At other times the women, more décolleté than our beauties at the German, for they strip to the waist, do all the dancing, and the men take the part of spectators only in this choregraphical performance.

ART INSTINCT.

The aptitude shown by Eskimo in carving and drawing has been noticed by all travellers among them. Some I have met with show a degree of intelligence and appreciation in regard to charts and pictures scarcely to be expected from such a source. From walrus ivory they sculpture figures of birds, quadrupeds, marine animals, and even the human form, which display considerable individuality notwithstanding their crude delineation and imperfect detail. I have also seen a fair carving of a whale in plumbago. Evidences of decoration are sometimes seen on their canoes, on which are found rude pictures of walruses, &c., and they have a kind of picture-writing by means of which they commemorate certain events in their lives, just as Sitting Bull has done in an autobiography that may be seen at the Army Medical Museum.

When we were searching for the missing whalers off the Siberian Coast some natives were come across with whom we were unable to communicate except by signs, and wishing to let them know the object of our visit, a ship was drawn in a note-book and shown to them with accompanying gesticulations, which they quickly comprehended, and one fellow, taking the pencil and note-book, drew correctly a pair of reindeer horns on the ship's jib-boom—a fact which identified beyond doubt the derelict vessel they had seen. At Point Hope an Eskimo, who had allowed us to take sketches of him, desired to sketch one of the party, and taking one of our note-books and a pencil, neither of which he ever had in his hand before, produced the accompanying likeness of Professor Muir:

At Saint Michael's there is an Eskimo boy who draws remarkably well, having taught himself by copying from the Illustrated London News. He made a correct pen-and-ink drawing of the Corwin, and another of the group of buildings at Saint Michael's, which, though creditable in many respects, had the defect of many Chinese pictures, being faulty in perspective. As these drawings equal those in Dr. Rink's book, done by Greenland artists, I regret my inability to reproduce them here. As evidences of culture they show more advancement than the carvings of English rustics that a clergyman has caused to be placed on exhibition at the Kensington Museum.

Sir John Ross speaks highly of his interpreter as an artist; Beechy says that the knowledge of the coast obtained by him from Innuit maps was of the greatest value, while Hall and others show their geographical knowledge to be as perfect as that possible of attainment by civilized men unaided by instruments. I had frequent opportunities to observe these Eskimo ideas of chartography. They not only understood reading a chart of the coast when showed to them, but would make tracings of the unexplored part, as I knew a native to do in the case of an Alaskan river, the mouth only of which was laid down on our chart.

Manifestation of the plastic art, which is found among tribes less intelligent, is rare among the

Eskimo. In fact, the only thing of the kind seen was some rude pottery at Saint Lawrence Island, the design of which showed but crude development of ornamental ideas. The same state of advancement was shown in some drinking cups carved from mammoth ivory and a dipper made from the horn of a mountain sheep.

COMBATIVENESS.

In one of the acts of Shakespeare's Seven Ages the Eskimo plays a very unimportant rôle. Perhaps in no other race is the combative instinct less predominant; in none is quarreling, fierceness of disposition, and jealousy more conspicuously absent, and in none does the desire for the factitious renown of war exist in a more rudimentary and undeveloped state. Perhaps the constant fight with cold and hunger is a compensation which must account for the absence of such unmitigated evils as war, taxes, complex social organization, and hierarchy among the curious people of the icy north. The pursuits of peace and of simple patriarchal lives, notwithstanding the fact that much in connection therewith is wretched and forbidding to a civilized man, seem to beget in these people a degree of domestic tranquillity and contentment which, united to their light-hearted and cheery disposition, is an additional reason for believing the sum of human happiness to be constant throughout the world.

MENTAL CHARACTER AND CAPACITY.

The intellectual character of the Eskimo, judging from the information which various travellers have furnished, as well as my personal knowledge, produces more than a feeble belief in the possibility of their being equal to anything they choose to take an interest in learning. The Eskimo is not "muffled imbecility," as some one has called him, nor is he dull and slow of understanding, as Vitruvius describes the northern nation to be "from breathing a thick air"—which, by the way, is thin, elastic, and highly ozonized—nor is he, according to Dr. Beke, "degenerated almost to the lowest state compatible with the retention of rational endowments." On the contrary, the old Greenland missionary, Hans Egede, writes: "I have found some of them witty enough and of good capacity;" Sir Martin Frobisher says they are "in nature very subtle and sharp-witted;" Sir Edward Parry, while extolling their honesty and good nature, adds, "Indeed, it required no long acquaintance to convince us that art and education might easily have made them equal or superior to ourselves;" Sauer tells of a woman who learned to speak Russian fluently in rather less than twelve months, and Beechy and others have acknowledged the intelligent help they have received from Eskimo in making their explorations.

Before going further, it may not be amiss to speak in a general way of the bony covering which protects the organ whose function it is to generate the vibrations known as thought. Of one hundred crania, collected principally at Saint Lawrence Island, a number were examined by me at the Army Medical Museum, through the courtesy of Dr. Huntington, with the result of changing and greatly modifying some of the previous notions of the conventional Eskimo skull as acquired from books on craniology. Perhaps after the inspection and examination of a large collection of crania it may be safe to pronounce upon their differential character; but whether the differences in configuration are constant or only occasional manifestations admits of as much doubt as the exceptions in Professor Sophocles's Greek grammar, which are often coextensive with the rule.*

The typical Eskimo skull, according to popular notion, is one exhibiting a low order of intelligence, and characterized by small brain capacity, with great prominence of the superciliary ridges, occipital protuberance, and zygomatic arches, the latter projecting beyond the general contour of the skull like the handles of a jar or a peach basket; and lines drawn from the most projecting part of the arches and touching the sides of the frontal bone are supposed to meet over the forehead, forming a triangle, for which reason the skull is known as pyramidal.

The first specimen, examined from a vertical view, shows something of the typical character as figured in A, and when viewed posteriorly there is noticed a flattening of the parietal walls with an elongated vertex as shown in D; while a second specimen, represented by B, shows none of the foregoing characteristics, the form being elongated and the parietal walls so far overhanging as to conceal the zygomatic arches in the vertical view, so that if lines be drawn as previously men-

---
*See Retzius, Finska Kranier, Stockholm: 1878.

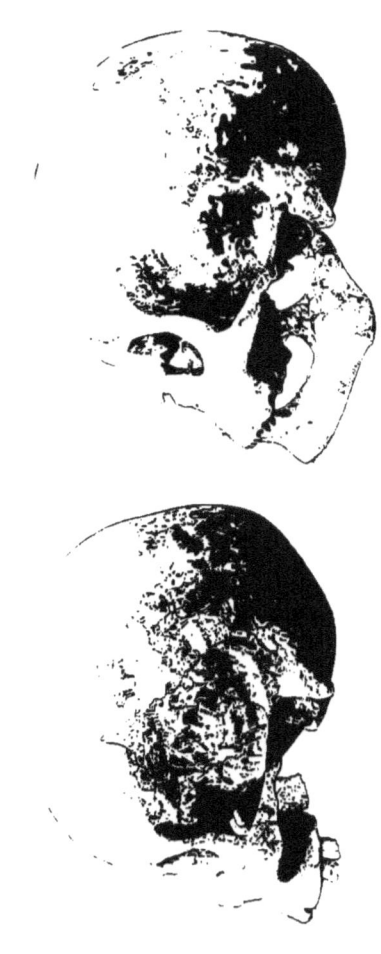

tioned, instead of forming a triangle they may, like the asymptotes of a parabola, be extended to infinity and never meet:

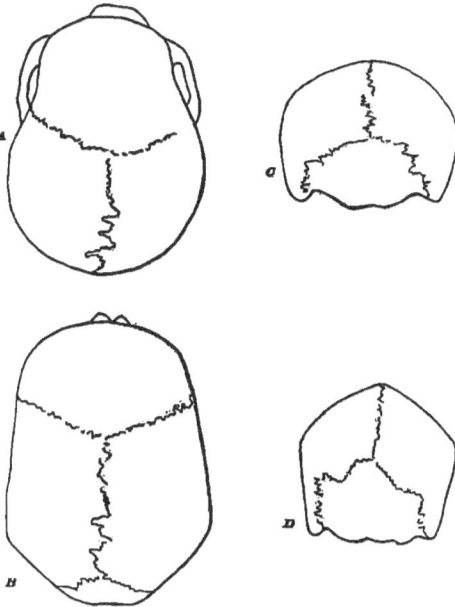

For purposes of comparison a number of orthographic outlines, showing the contour of civilized crania from a vertical point of observation, are herewith annexed. No. 1 is that of an eminent mathematician who committed suicide; No. 2, a prominent politician during the civil war; No. 3, a banker; and No. 4, a notorious assassin. Nos. 5 and 6 are negro skulls. Further comparison may be made with the Jewish skull, as represented in No. 7, in which the nasal bones project so far beyond the general contour as to form a bird-like appendage:

A collection of Aleutian heads, as seen from a vertical point of observation, when I looked down from the gallery of the little Greek church at Onnalaska, presented at first sight certain collective characters by which they approach one another. But anatomists know that a careful comparison of any collection will show extremely salient differences. In fact, individual differences, so numerous and so irregular as to prevent methodical enumeration, constitute the stumbling-block of ethnic craniology. Take, for instance, a number of the skulls under consideration: In proportions they will be found to present very considerable variations among themselves. The skulls figured by A and B are respectively brachycephalic and dolichocephalic. The former has an internal capacity of 1,400, the latter 1,214 cubic centimeters; but the facial angle of each is 80°, and in one Eskimo cranium it runs up to 84°. If the facial angle be trustworthy, as a measure of the degree of intelligence, we have shown here a development far in excess of the negro, which is placed at 70°, or of the Mongolian at 75°, and exceeding that observed by me in many German skulls, which do not as a rule come up to the 90° of Jupiter Tonans or of Cuvier, in spite of the boasted intelligence of that nationality.

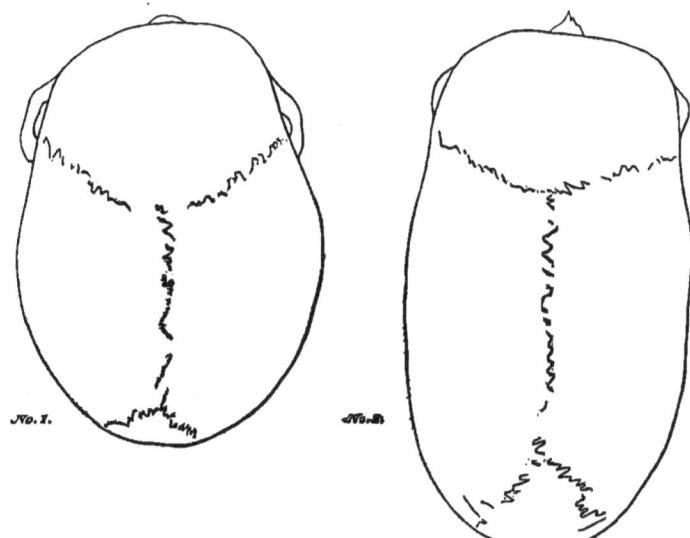

In none of the skulls of the collection is there observable the heavy superciliary ridges alleged to be common in lower races, but which exist in many of the best-formed European crania—shall we say as anomalies or as individual variations? Nor is the convexity of the squamo-parietal suture such as characterizes the low-typed cranium of the chimpanzee or of the Mound Builder. On the contrary, the orbits are cleanly made and the suture is well curved. Besides, a low degree of intelligence is not shown by observing the index of the foramen magnum, which is about the same as that found in European crania; and the same may be said of the internal capacity of the cranium. To illustrate the latter remark is appended a tabular statement made up from Welcker, Broca, Aitken, and Meigs:

	Cubic centimeters.
Australian	1,228
Polynesian	1,230
Hottentot	1,230
Mexican	1,296
Malay	1,328
Ancient Peruvian	1,361
French	1,403 to 1,461
German	1,448
English	1,572

An average of the Eskimo skulls, some of which measure as much as 1,650 and 1,715 c. c., will show the brain capacity to be the same as that of the French or of the Germans. None of them, however, approaches the anomalous capacities of two Indian skulls on exhibition at the Army Medical Museum, one of which shows 1,785 c. c., and the other the unprecedented measurement of 1,920 c. c.

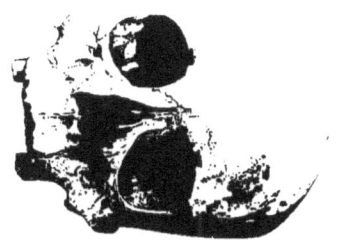

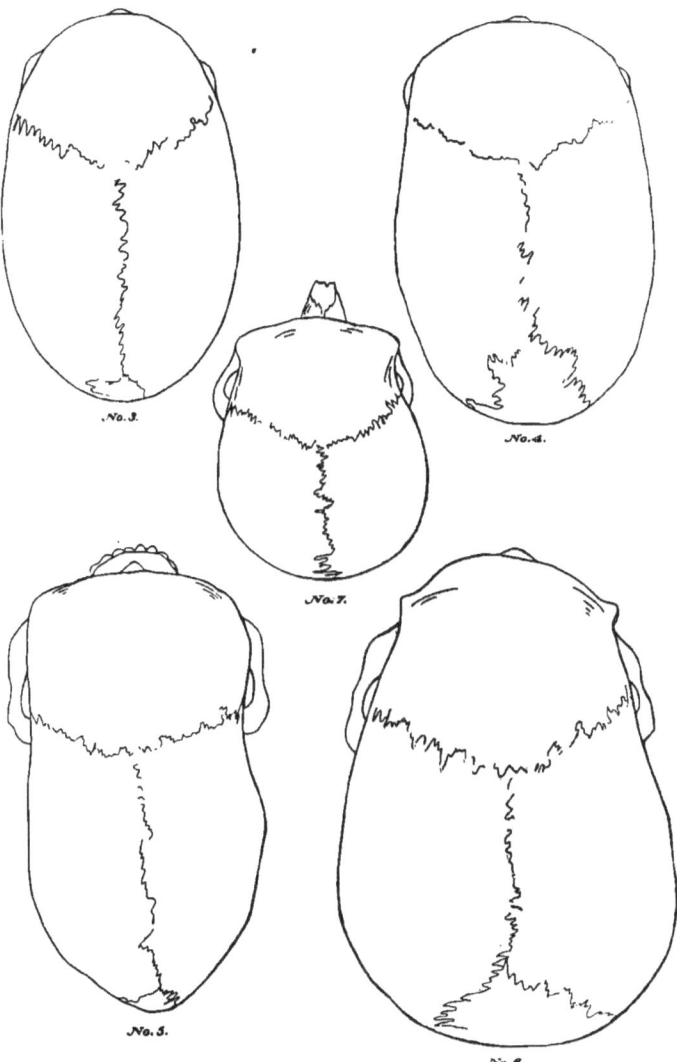

If the foregoing means for estimating the mental grasp and capacity for improvement be correct, then we must accord to the most northern nation of the globe a fair degree of brain energy—potential though it be. Aside from the mere physical methods of determining the degree of intelligence it is urged by some writers, among them the historian Robertson, that tact in commerce and correct ideas of property are evidence of a considerable progress toward civilization. The natural inference from this is that they are tests of intellectual power, since mind is a combination of all the actual and possible states of consciousness of the organism, and an examination of the Eskimo system of trade draws its own conclusion. Their fondness for trade has been known for a long time, as well as the extended range of their commercial intercourse. They trade with the Indians, with the fur companies, the whalers, and among themselves across Bering Straits. Many of them are veritable Shylocks, having a thorough comprehension of the axiom in political economy regarding the regulation of the price of a thing by the demand.

THE MORAL SENSE AND THE RELIGIOUS INSTINCT.

With the aptitudes and instincts of our common humanity Eskimo morals, as manifested in truth, right, and virtue, also admit of remark. Except where these people have had the bad example of the white man, whose vices they have imitated not on account of defective moral nature but because they saw few or no virtues, they are models of truthfulness and honesty. In fact their virtues in this respect are something phenomenal. The same cannot be said, however, for their sexual morals, which as a rule are the contrary of good. Even a short stay among the hyperboreans causes one to smile at Lord Kames's "frigidity of the North Americans" and at the fallacy of Herder who says, " the blood of man near the pole circulates but slowly, the heart beats but languidly; consequently the married live chastely, the women almost require compulsion to take upon them the troubles of a married life," &c. Nearly the same idea, expressed by Montesquieu, and repeated by Byron in "happy the nations of the moral north," are statements so at variance with our experience that this fact must alone excuse a reference to the subject. So far are they from applying to the people in question, that it is only necessary to mention, without going into detail, that the women are freely offered to strangers by way of hospitality, showing a decided preference for white men, whom they believe to beget better offspring than their own men. In this connection one is soon convinced that salacious and prurient tastes are not the exclusive privilege of people living outside of the Arctic Circle; and observation favors the belief in the existence of pederasty among Eskimo, if one may be allowed to judge from circumstances, which it is not necessary to particularize, and from a word in their language signifying the act.

Since morality is the last virtue acquired by man and the first one he is likely to lose, it is not so surprising to find outrages on morals among the undeveloped inhabitants of the north as it is to find them in intelligent Christian communities among people whose moral sense ought to be far above that of the average primitive man in view of their associations and the variations that have been so frequently repeated and accumulated by heredity; and where there is no hierarchy nor established missionaries it is still more surprising to find any moral sense at all among a people whose vague religious belief does not extend beyond Shamanism or Animism, which to them explains the more strange and striking natural phenomena by the hypothesis of direct spiritual agency.

It must not be understood by this, however, that these people have no religion, as many travellers have erroneously believed; that would be almost equivalent to stating that races of men exist without speech, memory, or knowledge of fire. A purely ethnological view of religion which regards it as "the feeling which falls upon man in the presence of the unknown," favors the idea that the children of the icy north have many of the same feelings in this respect as those experienced by ourselves under similar conditions, although there is doubtless a change in us produced by more advanced thought and nicer feeling. On the other hand, how many habits and ideas that are senseless and perfectly unexplainable by the light of our present modes of life and thought can be explained by similar customs and prejudices existing among these distant tribes. Is there no fragment of primitive superstition or residue of bygone ages in the supposed influence of the "Evil Eye" in Ireland, or in the habit of "telling the bees" in Germany? Is there not something of intellectual fossildom in the popular notion about Friday and thirteen at table, and in the ancient rite of exorcising oppressed persons, houses, and other places supposed to be haunted by unwelcome spirits, the form for which is still retained in the Roman ritual? And is not our enlightened America "the land of spiritualists, mesmerism, soothsaying, and mystical congregations"?

When the native of Saint Michael's invokes the moon, or the native of Point Barrow his crude images previously to hunting the seal, in order to bring good luck, is not the mental and emotional impulse the same as that which actuates more civilized men to look upon "outward signs of an inward and spiritual grace," or not to start upon any important undertaking without first invoking the blessing of Deity? And are not the rites observed by the natives on the Siberian coast, when the first walrus is caught, the counterpart of our Puritan Thanksgiving Day?

Perhaps the untutored Eskimo has the same fear of the dangerous and terrible, the unknown, the infinite, as ourselves, and parts with life just as reluctantly; but it cannot be said that our observation favors the fact of his longevity, although long life seems to prevail among some of the circumpolar tribes, the Laps, for instance, who, according to Scheffer, in spite of hard lives enjoy good health, are long lived, and still alert at eighty and ninety years.—(De Medecina Laponum.)

Owing to his hard life, the conflict with his circumstances, and his want of foresight, the Eskimo soon becomes a physiological bankrupt, and his stock of vitality being exhausted, his bodily remains are covered with stones, around which are placed wooden masks and articles that have been useful to him during life, as I have seen at Nounivak Island, or they are covered with drift wood as observed in Kotzebue Sound, or as at Tapkan, Siberia, where the corpse is lashed to a long pole and is taken some distance from the village, when the clothes are stripped off, placed on the ground and covered with stones. The cadaver is then exposed in the open air to the tender mercies of crows, foxes, and wolves. The weapons and other personal effects of the decedent are placed near by, probably with something of the same sentiment that causes us to use chaplets of flowers and immortelles as funeral offerings—a custom that Schiller has commemorated in "Bringet hier die letzten Gaben."

The future destiny of these people is a question in which the theologian and politician are not less interested than the man of science. Some observers seem to think that their numbers are diminishing under the evil influence of so-called civilization. But as every race participates in the same moral nature, and the entire history of humanity, according to Herder, is a series of events pointing to a higher destiny than has yet been revealed, there is no reason why the sum of human happiness, under proper auspices, should not be increased among the Innuit race. Archdeacon Kirkby, a Church-of-England clergyman who has lately visited them in a missionary capacity as far as Boothia, speaks in the highest terms of their intelligence and capacity for improvement. Here then is a brilliant opportunity for some one full of propagandism and charity to imitate the acts of the modern Apostles, and extend the influence of civilization to the gay, lively, curious, and talkative hyperboreans whose home is under the midnight sun and on the borders of the Icy Sea.

BOTANICAL NOTES ON ALASKA.

BY

JOHN MUIR.

BOTANICAL NOTES.

By John Muir.

INTRODUCTORY.

The plants named in the following notes were collected at many localities on the coasts of Alaska and Siberia, and on Saint Lawrence, Wrangel, and Herald Islands, between about latitude 54° and 71°, longitude 161° and 178°, in the course of short excursions, some of them less than an hour in length.

Inasmuch as the flora of the arctic and subarctic regions is nearly the same everywhere, the discovery of many species new to science was not to be expected. The collection, however, will no doubt be valuable for comparison with the plants of other regions.

In general the physiognomy of the vegetation of the polar regions resembles that of the alpine valleys of the temperate zones; so much so that the botanist on the coast of Artic Siberia or America might readily fancy himself on the Sierra Nevada at a height of 10,000 to 12,000 feet above the sea.

There is no line of perpetual snow on any portion of the arctic regions known to explorers. The snow disappears every summer not only from the low sandy shores and boggy tundras but also from the tops of the mountains and all the upper slopes and valleys with the exception of small patches of drifts and avalanche-heaps hardly noticeable in general views. But though nowhere excessively deep or permanent, the snow-mantle is universal during winter, and the plants are solidly frozen and buried for nearly three-fourths of the year. In this condition they enjoy a sleep and rest about as profound as death, from which they awake in the months of June and July in vigorous health, and speedily reach a far higher development of leaf and flower and fruit than is generally supposed. On the drier banks and hills about Kotzebue Sound, Cape Thompson, and Cape Lisbourne many species show but little climatic repression, and during the long summer days grow tall enough to wave in the wind, and unfold flowers in as rich profusion and as highly colored as may be found in regions lying a thousand miles farther south.

OUNALASKA.

To the botanist approaching any portion of the Aleutian chain of islands from the southward during the winter or spring months, the view is severely desolate and forbidding. The snow comes down to the water's edge in solid white, interrupted only by dark outstanding bluffs with faces too steep for snow to lie on, and by the backs of rounded rocks and long rugged reefs beaten and overswept by heavy breakers rolling in from the Pacific, while throughout nearly every month of the year the higher mountains are wrapped in gloomy dripping storm-clouds.

Nevertheless vegetation here is remarkably close and luxuriant, and crowded with showy bloom, covering almost every foot of the ground up to a height of about a thousand feet above the sea—the harsh trachytic rocks, and even the cindery bases of the craters, as well as the moraines and rough soil beds outspread on the low portions of the short narrow valleys.

On the 20th of May we found the showy *Geum glaciale* already in flower, also an arctostaphylos and draba, on a slope facing the south, near the harbor of Ounalaska. The willows, too, were then beginning to put forth their catkins, while a multitude of green points were springing up in sheltered spots wherever the snow had vanished. At a height of 400 and 500 feet, however, winter was still unbroken, with scarce a memory of the rich bloom of summer.

During a few short excursions along the shores of Ounalaska Harbor and on two of the adjacent mountains, towards the end of May and beginning of October we saw about fifty species of flowering plants—empetrum, vaccinium, bryanthus, pyrola, arctostaphylos, ledum, cassiope, lupinus, zeranium, epilobium, silene, draba, and saxifraga being the most telling and characteristic of the genera represented. *Empetrum nigrum*, a bryanthus, and three species of vaccinium make a grand display when in flower and show their massed colors at a considerable distance.

Almost the entire surface of the valleys and hills and lower slopes of the mountains is covered with a dense spongy plush of lichens and mosses similar to that which cover the tundras of the Arctic regions, making a rich green mantle on which the showy flowering plants are strikingly relieved, though these grow far more luxuriantly on the banks of the streams where the drainage is less interrupted. Here also the ferns, of which I saw three species, are taller and more abundant, some of them arching their broad delicate fronds over one's shoulders, while in similar situations the tallest of the five grasses that were seen reaches a height of nearly six feet, and forms a growth close enough for the farmer's scythe.

Not a single tree has yet been seen on any of the islands of the chain west of Kodiak, excepting a few spruces brought from Sitka and planted at Ounalaska by the Russians about fifty years ago. They are still alive in a dwarfed condition, having made scarce any appreciable growth since they were planted. These facts are the more remarkable, since in Southeastern Alaska lying both to the north and south of here, and on the many islands of the Aexander Archipelago, as well as on the mainland, forests of beautiful conifers flourish exuberantly and attain noble dimensions, while the climatic conditions generally do not appear to differ greatly from those that obtain on these treeless islands.

Wherever cattle have been introduced they have prospered and grown fat on the abundance of rich nutritious pasturage to be found almost everywhere in the deep withdrawing valleys and on the green slopes of the hills and mountains, but the wetness of the summer months will always prevent the making of hay in any considerable quantities.

The agricultural possibilities of these islands seem also to be very limited. The hardier of the cereals—rye, barley, and oats—make a good vigorous growth, and head out, but seldom or never mature, on account of insufficient sunshine and overabundance of moisture in the form of long-continued drizzling fogs and rains. Green crops, however, as potatoes, turnips, cabbages, beets, and most other common garden vegetables, thrive wherever the ground is thoroughly drained and has a southerly exposure.

SAINT LAWRENCE ISLAND.

Saint Lawrence Island, as far as our observations extended, is mostly a dreary mass of granite and lava of various forms and colors, roughened with volcanic cones, covered with snow, and rigidly bound in ocean ice for half the year.

Inasmuch as it lies broadsidewise to the direction pursued by the great ice-sheet that recently filled Bering Sea, and its rocks offered unequal resistance to the denuding action of the ice, the island is traversed by numerous ridges and low gap-like valleys all trending in the same general direction, some of the lowest of these transverse valleys having been degraded nearly to the level of the sea, showing that had the glaciation to which the island has been subjected been slightly greater we should have found several islands here instead of one.

At the time of our first visit, May 28, winter still had full possession, but eleven days later we found the dwarf willows, drabas, erigerons, saxifrages pushing up their buds and leaves, on spots bare of snow, with wonderful rapidity. This was the beginning of spring at the northwest end of the island. On July 4 the flora seemed to have reached its highest development. The bottoms of the glacial valleys were in many places covered with tall grasses and carices evenly planted and forming meadows of considerable size, while the drier portions and the sloping grounds about them were enlivened with gay highly-colored flowers from an inch to nearly two feet in height—*Aconitum Napellus*, L. var. *delphinifolium* ser. *Polemonium cœruleum*, L. *Papaver nudicaule*, *Draba alpina*, and *Silene acaulis* in large closely flowered tufts, Andromeda, Ledum Linnæa, Cassiope, and several species of Vaccinium and Saxifraga.

SAINT MICHAEL'S.

The region about Saint Michael's is a magnificent tundra, crowded with Arctic lichens and mosses, which here develop under most favorable conditions. In the spongy plush formed by the lower plants, in which one sinks almost knee-deep at every step, there is a sparse growth of grasses, carices, and rushes, tall enough to wave in the wind, while empetrum, the dwarf birch, and the various heathworts flourish here in all their beauty of bright leaves and flowers. The moss mantle for the most part rests on a stratum of ice that never melts to any great extent, and the ice on a bed rock of black vesicular lava. Ridges of the lava rise here and there above the general level in rough masses, affording ground for plants that like a drier soil. Numerous hollows and watercourses also occur on the general tundra, whose well drained banks are decked with gay flowers in lavish abundance, and meadow patches of grasses shoulder high, suggestive of regions much farther south.

The following plants and a few doubtful species not yet determined were collected here:

Linnæa borealis, Gronov.
Cassiope tetragona, Desv.
Andromeda polifolia, L.
Loiseleuria procumbens, Desv.
Vaccinium Vitis Idæa, L.
Arctostaphylos alpina, Spring.
Ledum palustre, L.
Nardosmia frigida, Hook.
Saussurea alpina, DC.
Senecio frigidus, Less.
    palustris, Hook.
Arnica angustifolia, Vahl.
Artemisia arctica, Bess.
Matricaria inodora, L.
Rubus chamæ morus, L.
    arcticus, L.
Potentilla nivea, L.
Dryas octopetala, L.
Draba alpina, L.
    incana, L.
Eutrema arenicola, Hook?
Pedicularis sudetica, Willd.
    euphrasioides, Steph.
    Langsdorffii, Fisch, var. *lanata*, Gray.
Diapensia Lapponica, L.
Polemonium cœruleum, L.
Primula borealis, Daly.

Oxytropis podocarpa, Gray.
Astragalus alpinus, L.
    frigidus, Gray, var. *littoralis*.
Lathyrus maritimus, Bigelow.
Arenaria lateriflora, L.
Stellaria longipes, Goldie.
Silene acaulis, L.
Saxifraga nivalis, L.
    hieracifolia, W. and K.
Anemone narcissiflora, L.
    parviflora, Michx.
Caltha palustris, L., var. *asarifolia*, Rothr.
Valeriana capitata, Willd.
Lloydia serotina, Reichnb.
Tofieldia coccinea, Richards.
Armeria vulgaris, Willd.
Corydalis pauciflora.
Pinguicula Villosa, L.
Mertensia paniculata, Desv.
Polygonum alpinum, All.
Epilobium latifolium, L.
Betula nana, L.
Alnus viridis, DC.
Eriophorum capitatum.
Carex vulgaris, Willd, var. *alpina*.
Aspidium fragrans, Swartz.
Woodsia Ilvensis, Rv.

GOLOVIN BAY.

The tundra flora on the west side of Golovin Bay is remarkably close and luxuriant, covering almost every foot of the ground, the hills as well as the valleys, while the sandy beach and a bank of coarsely stratified moraine material a few yards back from the beach were blooming like a garden with *Lathyrus maritimus*, *Iris sibirica*, *Polemonium cœruleum*, &c., diversified with clumps and patches of *Elymus arenarius*, *Alnus viridis*, and *Abies alba*.

This is one of the few points on the east side of Bering Sea where trees closely approach the shore. The white spruce occurs here in small groves or thickets of well developed erect trees 15 or 20 feet high, near the level of the sea, at a distance of about 6 or 8 miles from the mouth of the bay, and gradually become irregular and dwarfed as they approach the shore. Here a number of dead and dying specimens were observed, indicating that conditions of soil, climate, and relations to other plants were becoming more unfavorable, and causing the tree-line to recede from the coast.

The following collection was made here July 10:

Pinguicula villosa, L.
Vaccinium vitis Idaea, L.
Spiraea betulifolia, Pallas.
Rubus arcticus, L.
Epilobium latifolium, L.
Polemonium coeruleum, L.
Tofieldia coccinea, L. var. arctica, Ledeb.
Eutrema arenicola, Hook.
Iris sibirica, L.
Hoydea serotina, Reichenb.
Chrysanthemum arcticum, L.
Artemisia Tilesii, Ledeb.
Arenaria peploides, L.
Gentiana glauca, Pallas.
Elymus arenarius, L.
Poa trivialis, L.
Carex vesicaria, L. var. alpigena, Fries.
Aspidium spinulosum, Sw.

KOTZEBUE SOUND.

The flora of the region about the head of Kotzebue Sound is hardly less luxuriant and rich in species than that of other points visited by the Corwin lying several degrees farther south. Fine nutritious grasses suitable for the fattening of cattle and from 2 to 6 feet high are not of rare occurrence on meadows of considerable extent and along streambanks wherever the stagnant waters of the tundra have been drained off, while in similar localities the most showy of the Arctic plants bloom in all their freshness and beauty, manifesting no sign of frost, or unfavorable conditions of any kind whatever.

A striking result of the airing and draining of the boggy tundra soil is shown on the ice-bluffs around Escholtze Bay, where it has been undermined by the melting of the ice on which it rests. In falling down the face of the ice-wall it is well shaken and rolled before it again comes to rest on terraced or gently sloping portions of the wall. The original vegetation of the tundra is thus destroyed, and tall grasses spring up on the fresh mellow ground as it accumulates from time to time, growing lush and rank, though in many places that we noted these new soil beds are not more than a foot in depth, and lie on the solid ice.

At the time of our last visit to this interesting region, about the middle of September, the weather was still fine, suggesting the Indian Summer of the Western States. The tundra glowed in the mellow sunshine with the colors of the ripe foliage of vaccinium, empetrum, arctostaphylos, and dwarf birch; red, purple, and yellow, in pure bright tones, while the berries, hardly less beautiful, were scattered everywhere as if they had been sown broadcast with a lavish hand, the whole blending harmoniously with the neutral tints of the furred bed of lichens and mosses on which the bright leaves and berries were painted.

On several points about the sound the white spruce occurs in small compact groves within a few miles of the shore; and pyrola, which belongs to wooded regions, is abundant where no trees are now in sight, tending to show that areas of considerable extent, now treeless, were once forested.

The plants collected are:

Pyrola rotundifolia, L. var. pumila, Hook.
Arctostaphylos alpina, Spring.
Cassiope tetragona, Desr.
Ledum palustre.
Vaccinium Vitis Idaea, L.
Uliginosum, L. var. mucronata, Hender.
Empetrum nigrum.
Potentilla, anserina, L. var.
  biflora, Willd.
  fruticosa.
Stellaria longipes, Goldie.
Cerastium alpinum, L. var. Behringianum, Regel.
Mertensia maritima, Dcrr.
Papaver nudicale, L.
Saxifraga tricuspidata, Retg.
Tofieldia coccinea, L. var. artica, Ledeb.
Lupinus arcticus, Watson.
Hedysarum boreale, Nutt.
Galium boreale, L.
Armeria vulgaris, Willd, var. Arctica, Cham.
Allium schaenoprasum, L.
Polygonum Viviparum, L.
Castilleia pallida, Kunth.
Pedicularis sublitica, Willd.
  verticillata, L.
Senecio palustris, Hook.
Salix polaris, Wahl.
Luzula hyperborea, R. Br.

CAPE THOMPSON.

The Cape Thompson flora is richer in species and individuals than that of any other point on the Arctic shores we have seen, owing no doubt mainly to the better drainage of the ground through the fissured frost cracked limestone, which hereabouts is the principal rock.

Where the hill-slopes are steepest the rock frequently occurs in loose angular masses and is entirely bare of soil. But between these barren slopes there are valleys where the showiest of the Arctic plants bloom in rich profusion and variety, forming brilliant masses of color—purple, yellow, and blue—where certain species form beds of considerable size, almost to the exclusion of others.

The following list was obtained here July 19:

Phlox Sibirica, L.
Polemonium humile, Willd.
    coeruleum, L.
Myosotis sylvatica, var. alpestris.
Eritrichium nanum, var. arctioides, Hedu.
Dodecatheon media, var. frigidum, Gray.
Andromce chamæjasme, Willd.
Anemone narcissiflora, L.
    multifida, Poir.
    parviflora, Michx.
    parviflora, Michx. var.
Ranunculus affinis, R. Br.
Caltha asarifolia, Dl.
Geum glaciale, Fisch.
Dryas octopetala, L.
Polygonum Bistorta, L.
Rumex Crispus, L.
Boykinia Richardsonii, Gray.
Saxifraga tricuspidata, Retg.
    cernua, L.
    flagellaris, Willd.
    Davurica, Willd.
    punctata, L.
    nivalis, L.
Nardosmia corymbosa, Hook?
Erigeron Muirii, Gray, n. sp.
Taraxacum palustre, Dl.
Senecio frigidus, Less.
Artemisia glomerata, Ledt.

Potentilla biflora, Willd.
    nivea, L.
Draba stellata, Jacq. var. nivalis, Regel.
    incana, L.
Cardamine pratensis, L. ?
Cheiranthus pygmæus, Adans.
Parrya nudicaulis, Regel. var. aspera, Regel.
Hedysarum borealis, Nutt.
Oxytropis podocarpa, Gray.
Cerastium alpinum, L. var. Behringianum, Regel.
Silene acaulis, L.
Arenaria verna, L. var. rubella, Hook, f.
    Arctica, Stev.
Stellaria longipes, Goldie.
Artemisia tomentosa.
Pedicularis capitata, Adans.
Papaver nudicaule, L.
Epilobium latifolium, L.
Cassiope tetragona, Desr.
Vaccinium uliginosum, L. var. Macrocarpa, Hender.
    Vitis Idæa, L.
Salix polaris, Wahl, and two other species undetermined.
Festuca Sativa?
Glyceria, ———
Trisetum subspicatum, Beauv. var. Molle, Gray.
Carex rariflora, Wahl.
    vulgaris, Fries, var. Alpina, (?, rigida, Good).
Cystopteris fragilis, Bernt.

CAPE PRINCE OF WALES.

At Cape Prince of Wales we obtained:

Loiseleuria procumbens, Desr.
Andromeda polifolia, L. fa na arctica.
Vaccinium Vitis Idæa, L.
Andromeda chamæjasme, Willd.

Tofieldia coccinea, Richards.
Armeria arctica, Ster.
Taraxacum palustre, Dl.

TWENTY MILES EAST OF CAPE LISBOURNE.

Lychnis apetala, L.
Andromce chamæjasme, Willd.
Geum glaciale, Fisch.
Potentilla nivea, L.
    biflora, Willd.
Phlox Sibirica, L.
Primula borealis, Daly.
Anemone narcissiflora, L. var.

Oxytropis campestris, Dl.
Erigeron uniflorus, L.
Artemisia glomerata, Ledb.
Saxifraga escholtzii, Sterub.
    flagellaris, Willd.
Chrysosplenium alternifolium, L.
Draba hirta, L.

CAPE WANKEREM, SIBERIA.

Near Cape Wankerem, August 7 and 8, we collected:

Claytonia Virginica, L.?
Ranunculus pygmæus, Wahl.
Pedicularis Langsdorffii, Fisch.
Chrysosplenium alternifolium, L.
Saxifraga cernua, L.
    stellaris, L. var. cornusa.
    rivularis, L. var. hyperborea, Hook.
Polemonium coeruleum, L.
Lychnis apetala, L.
Nardosmia frigida, Hook.

Chrysanthemum arcticum, L.
Senecio frigidus, Less.
Artemisia vulgaris, var. Telesii, Ledeb.
Elymus arenarius, L.
Alopecurus alpinus, Smith.
Poa arctica, R. Br.
Calamagrostis deschampsioides, Trin. ?
Luzula hyperborea, R. Br.
    spicata Desv.

PLOVER BAY, SIBERIA.

The mountains bounding the glacial fiord called Plover Bay, though beautiful in their combinations of curves and peaks as they are seen touching each other delicately and rising in bold, picturesque groups, are nevertheless severely desolate looking from the absence of trees and large shrubs, and indeed of vegetation of any kind dense enough to give color in telling quantities, or to soften the harsh rockiness of the steepest portions of the walls. Even the valleys opening back from the water here and there on either side are mostly bare as seen at a distance of a mile or two, and show only a faint tinge of green, derived from dwarf willows, heathworts, and sedges chiefly.

The most interesting of the plants found here are *Rhododendron Kamtschaticum*, Pall., and the handsome blue-flowered *Saxifraga oppositifolia*, L., both of which are abundant.

The following were collected July 12 and August 26:

Gentiana glauca, Pall.
Geum glaciale, Fisch.
Dryas octopetala, L.
Aconitum Napellus, L. var. delphinifolium, Ser.
Saxifraga oppositifolia, L.
    punctata, L.
    cespitosa, L.
Diapensia Lapponica, L.

Rhododendron Kamtschaticum, Pall.
Cassiope tetragona, Desv.
Anemone narcissiflora, L.
Arenaria macrocarpa, Pursh.
Draba alpina, L.
Parrya Ermanni, Ledb.
Oxytropis podocarpa, Gray.

HERALD ISLAND.

On Herald Island the common polar cryptogamous vegetation is well represented and developed. So also are the flowering plants, almost the entire surface of the island, with the exception of the sheer crumbling bluffs along the shores, being quite tellingly dotted and tufted with characteristic species. The following list was obtained:

Saxifraga punctata, L.?
    serpyllifolia, Pursh.
    silenifolia, Sternb.
    branchialis, L.
    stellaris, L. var. comosa, Poir.
    cirralaris, L. var. hyperborea, Hook.
    hieracifolia, Waldst & Kit.
Papaver nudicaule, L.

Draba alpina, L.
Gymnandra Stelleri, Cham. & Schlecht.
Stellaria longipes, Goldie, var. Edwardsii T. & G.
Senecio frigidus, Less.
Potentilla frigida, Vill.?
Salix polaris, Wahl.
Alopecurus alpinus, Smith.
Luzula hyperborea, R. Br.

WRANGEL ISLAND.

Our stay on the one point of Wrangel Island that we touched was far too short to admit of making anything like as full a collection of the plants of so interesting a region as was desirable. We found the rock formation where we landed and for some distance along the coast to the eastward and westward to be a close grained clay slate, cleaving freely into thin flakes, with here and there a few compact metamorphic masses that rise above the general surface. Where it is exposed along the shore bluffs and kept bare of vegetation and soil by the action of the ocean, ice, and heavy snow-drifts the rock presents a surface about as black as coal, without even a moss or lichen to enliven its sombre gloom. But when this dreary barrier is passed the surface features of the country in general are found to be finely molded and collocated, smooth valleys, wide as compared with their depth, trending back from the shore to a range of mountains that appear blue in the distance, and round topped hills, with their side curves finely drawn, touching and blending in beautiful groups, while scarce a single rock-pile is seen or sheer-walled bluff to break the general smoothness.

The soil has evidently been derived mostly from the underlying slates, though a few fragmentary wasting moraines were observed containing traveled boulders of quartz and granite which doubtless were brought from the mountains of the interior by glaciers that have recently vanished—so recently that the outlines and sculptured hollows and grooves of the mountains have not as yet suffered sufficient post glacial denudation to mar appreciably their glacial characters.

The banks of the river at the mouth of which we landed presented a striking contrast as to vegetation to that of any other stream we had seen in the Arctic regions. The tundra vegetation was not wholly absent, but the mosses and lichens of which it is elsewhere composed are about as feebly developed as possible, and instead of forming a continuous covering they occur in small separate tufts, leaving the ground between them raw and bare as that of a newly ploughed field. The phanerogamous plants, both on the lowest grounds and the slopes and hilltops as far as seen, were in the same severely repressed condition and as sparsely planted in tufts an inch or two in diameter, with about from one to three feet of naked soil between them. Some portions of the coast, however, farther south presented a greenish hue as seen from the ship at a distance of eight or ten miles, owing no doubt to vegetation growing under less unfavorable conditions.

From an area of about half a square mile the following plants were collected:

Saxifraga flagellaris, Willd.
    stellaris, L. var. *comosa*, Poir.
    silenefora, Sternb.
    hieracifolia, Waldst. & Kit.
    rivularis, L. var. *hyperborea*, Hook.
    bronchialis, L.
    serpyllifolia, Pursh
Anemone parviflora, Michx.
Papaver nudicaule, L.
Draba alpina, L.
Cochlearia officinalis, L.
Artemisia borealis, Willd.
Nardosmia frigida, Hook.
Saussurea monticola, Richards.

Senecio frigidus, Less.
Potentilla nivea, L.
    frigida, Vill.?
Armeria maccrocarpa, Pursh.
    vulgaris, Willd.
Stellaria longipes, Goldie, var. *Edwardsii* T. & G.
Cerastium alpinum, L.
Gymnandra Stelleri, Cham & Schlecht.
Salix polaris, Wahl.
Luzula hyperborea, R. Br.
Poa arctica, R. Br.
Aira caespitosa, L. var. *Arctica*.
Alopecurus alpinus, Smith.

BIRDS OF BERING SEA AND THE ARCTIC OCEAN.

BY

E. W. NELSON.

The last of June, 1881, the United States revenue steamer Corwin reached Saint Michaels, Alaska, on her cruise to Bering Sea and the Arctic Ocean. The object of this cruise was to search the various accessible portions of the Arctic for traces of the Jeannette and two missing whaling vessels which were lost the same season that the Jeannette entered the ice. Through the courtesy of the Secretary of the Treasury, I was taken on board and accompanied the Corwin throughout the remainder of the season.

On June 21, we left Saint Michaels and crossed Bering Sea to Saint Lawrence Island and Plover Bay on the Siberian coast; thence along this coast through the Straits and northwest in the Arctic to the vicinity of Nordenskiöld's winter quarters, where we took on board a sledge party which had been left there earlier in the season to search the coast in that district. Thence we returned again to Saint Lawrence Island and to Saint Michaels. After remaining here a short time, we returned to the Arctic, touching at all the islands in Bering Straits; and during the remainder of the summer visited in succession the entire Alaskan coast line from Bering Straits to Point Barrow, including Kotzebue Sound and on the Siberian shore from the Straits to North Cape. We also cruised along the edge of the ice-pack, landing upon Herald and Wrangel Islands. On September 14, we passed through Bering Straits bound south; and after remaining some time at Onnalaska in the Aleutian islands, fitting the vessel for a voyage to San Francisco, we left, October 4, homeward bound.

The observations on which the present paper is based were made both during the cruise just detailed, and in addition are the results of observations made by myself during over four years' residence at Saint Michaels, and explorations carried on in various directions from that point. In addition, I have used information obtained from various reports which have been issued regarding the region in question, so far as the limited time at my disposal would allow.

The species given for the Alaskan coast and the islands of Bering Sea are almost, or quite, a complete list of the birds found there; but the species mentioned upon the Siberian coast form only a small quota of those occurring in that region. This is mainly due to the little that is known concerning that region and the inaccessibility of its literature.

The Arctic waters lying between Greenland and Europe on the southeast, and America on the southwest, have been visited by so many naturalists accompanying the various exploring and other expeditions, that the vertebrate fauna, at least, has become pretty well known. This is certainly true as regards the distinction of most of the species, though the life histories of many undoubtedly yet require the patient research of some enthusiastic student ready to face the discomfort, and often misery, entailed by such work in boreal regions.

Leaving this comparatively well-trodden field, however, where is the naturalist who is prepared to state authoritatively just what is found at other portions, or on other coasts of this great frozen ocean? The reply is simple, for as yet no one has been able to do more than to touch at some remote corners of the coast; or a vessel's prow may have pressed into the shifting ice-pack a short distance only to be rebuffed or else caught and held in an unyielding grasp.

Exceptionally favorable opportunities of the writer in the unknown region of Bering Sea and the adjoining portion of the Arctic Ocean to the north have been detailed in the present paper, with such other information as could be obtained from other sources; as we visited all parts of the basin lying to the south of the solid ice-pack, and between Alaska on the east and south, Bering straits and part of Siberia completing the southern limit, and the same portion of Siberia and Wrangel Island forming, with the ice-pack, the western border. Within this area, visiting all the shores named, among which as specially noteworthy may be mentioned Herald and Wrangel Islands, respecting which the only knowledge existing was that two bodies of land were known to lie there, one of which, in fact, was previously considered almost mythical till the work of the

Rogers and the Corwin has defined it. Further work will undoubtedly add other species to the list and widen the range of others.

But it is thought the present paper will give a very good idea of the bird life of the regions visited. Having the continent of America on the one side and Asia on the other, it might be anticipated that we should secure specially rich results from the combinations of two faunas; yet, although this is true to a certain extent, there are predominating reasons to prevent the very marked exhibition of this. The first is the location of the region within the limits inhabited by a circumpolar fauna, and in consequence frequented by many species of wide distribution. The next is the similarity of the two barren coast lines and outlying islands, offering but small inducements to land birds, while the sea birds, as usual, are species common to extended areas.

The usually low but rolling coast country, a monotonous grass-grown plain, varied by lichen or moss-covered slopes, or wind-swept hills reaching back far into the interior, are the only variations to the general level. Here and there a few weathered pieces of driftwood break the cold gray of the shingly beach, while clusters of native huts or tents lend a passing interest to the cheerless coast, thus offering but slight inducements for birds.

As might well be expected, the former region north of Bering Straits is entirely Arctic; and south of Bering Straits in Bering Sea the water birds may be divided into two groups—those frequenting the deep water surrounding the Aleutian, Fur Seal, and Bering Strait Islands, and the adjoining Siberian coast for the first group; and the shallow-water species occurring along the Alaskan shore from the mouth of the Kuskoquin River to the vicinity of Bering Straits. The former group includes the auks and allied species; also the Rogers Fulmar and Steller's eider; and the second group such species as the emperor goose, the spectacled eider, and many of the fresh and brackish water ducks.

This distinction of the two shores holds also, to a certain extent, north of Bering Straits, these two shores having there somewhat the same relationship I have just mentioned. There is also a difference still more striking to be noted between the species frequenting the sea north of Bering Straits and those to the south. North of the straits the auks are very rare, while south throughout the Aleutian Islands, over all the other islands of Bering Sea, except along its eastern border, including even the islands in Bering Straits, they swarm in the greatest abundance; while the presence in Bering Sea of several other species, including gulls and petrels not found north of the straits, makes the difference still more striking. Beyond these differences, however, it is difficult to divide the region into any well-marked faunal districts.

Though along some parts of the coast the breeding water fowl fill the marshes with life, yet the rocky islands of Bering Sea are the places about which birds exist in the greatest numbers; and as Baron Nordenskiöld well remarks in his account of the Vega's voyage, "It is not the larger inhabitants of the Polar regions, such as the whale, walrus, bear, and seal, which first attract the explorer's attention, but the innumerable flocks of birds that swarm around the polar traveller during the long summer day of the North. And this is especially striking about any of the islands which birds—the gulls, guillemots, and auks—seek as breeding-places. The islands of Bering Straits resemble enormous bee-hives, about which the birds swarm in countless numbers, filling the air with their swiftly moving forms in every direction, and the waters are covered with them all about the islands, while every jutting point and place where foothold can be obtained is taken possession of by them for breeding-places.

Although Herald Island is almost perpetually surrounded by the ice-pack, yet we found it swarming with murres, guillemots, and gulls; as were also some of the cliffs on Wrangel Island. Still to the westward, on some of the islands visited by the Jeannette crew on their retreat towards the Siberian coast, this was also found to be the case, as Mr. Newcomb informs me and they found there guillemots in extreme abundance, although the islands were surrounded by an almost unbroken ice-pack.

For the benefit of naturalists visiting this region in future, I will mention a few localities where certain species of considerable interest may be obtained. The Emperor Goose is quite abundant on the southwestern portion of Saint Lawrence Island, frequenting the low, flat portion of the island intersected by lagoons. The islands of Bering Strait are all of them resorted to by the Crested Parrot-billed and Least Auks, and the Diomede Islands in particular are frequented by myriads of them throughout the summer season. Along the coast of Siberia from just north of Bering Straits to wherever the shore is low and bordered by lagoons or shallow river mouths, occur the Steller's and the King Eider in great numbers. According to Nordenskiöld the Emperor Goose also visits this coast. At Tapkan we found Steller's Eider in excessive abundance during our stay there, as detailed in the following pages. The Alaskan coast, from Icy Cape to Point Barrow, is also frequented by the King Eider in great abundance.

The Kotzebue Kittiwake nest in large numbers upon a small rocky islet just off Chamisso Island at the head of the Kotzebue Sound, and also upon the cliffs bordering the northern shore of Norton Sound in Bering Sea, especially those at Cape Darby and Cape Denbigh. Adams's Loon is found rather commonly upon the rivers flowing into the head of Kotzebue Sound, especially along the Kunguk.

Some small rocky islets in the middle of Akutan Pass near Unalaska, in the Aleutian Islands, are the breeding places of the beautiful little Forked-tailed petrel; and the coast line of Alaska from Cape Vancouver to the middle of the Yukon delta is the great breeding-ground of the Emperor geese. From the northern border of the Yukon delta north to Norton Bay the Spectacled Eider breeds among the brackish water lagoons and ponds where the shore is flat and marshy. North of Saint Michaels, however, this species is rare, occurring in its greatest abundance between Saint Michaels and the Yukon mouth.

The principal sources from which information has been derived, in addition to my own observations, have been Dall and Bannister's list of birds in the "Transactions of the Chicago Academy of Sciences" for 1869, and Dr. Coues' Ornithology of the Pribylov Islands in Elliott's "Condition of Affairs in Alaska," Treasury Department, 1874.

The seasons of navigation upon the two shores of Bering Sea are usually somewhat uneven, the ice remaining longer in spring upon the Alaskan coast than it does on the Siberian shore; and the reverse in autumn, when the ice from the Arctic forces its way through Bering Strait and fills the western portion of this sea for some distance before ice commences to form on the east coast. On shore we have the reverse, and in the spring of 1881, when we left Saint Michaels, the last of June, the hills were covered with green grasses, and willows and alders were commencing to show their summer foliage, while numerous northern flowers were already in blossom. Only a rare patch of snow was to be seen here and there on the distant hillsides, and summer was apparently at hand. When we reached the Siberian coast, however, winter still appeared in force, and the snow reached from the tops of the highest hills to the water's edge in immense banks and drifts, although many places where the snow or wind had opportunity to exert its influence showed the bare lichen-covered rocks; but the vegetation was extremely backward, only just commencing to start, in fact. This, however, is accounted for from the fact that the waters of western Bering Sea are deeper and far colder than those of the eastern shore in summer, where the shallow water and great amount of warm fresh water brought down by the numerous rivers flowing into the sea change the temperature very rapidly and at the same time rapidly affect the surrounding atmosphere. On the Siberian coast, on the contrary, the ice is swept away by the strong currents which flow north and in spring carrying with it ice, leaving the coast free from the latter, but at the same time surrounding the shores with water at an icy temperature which falls but little throughout the summer. The basin-like character of Norton Sound, as also of Kotzebue Sound in the Arctic, aid in giving them a much milder climate than their northern location would indicate.

The coast of Bering Sea from the Yukon mouth north to Bering Strait is broken occasionally by rugged cliffs, but, as a rule, is low and undulating, and covered with grass and mosses, interspersed with ponds, where the various species of fresh-water fowl breed. Along the beach is strewn great quantities of driftwood, which comes from the Yukon freshets, but trees occur only along a small portion of the coast extending from the vicinity of Unalakleet north around the coast to near Cape Darby, where the spruces are found in some places within a few yards of tide-water. From this point north not a tree approaches within miles of the coast-line. At the head of Kotzebue Sound a few spruces may be seen on the sides of distant mountains, and beyond this the country has the peculiarly barren Arctic appearance. At the head of the Kotzebue Sound a species of tall grass grows in considerable abundance; but leaving this sound to the north the coast becomes more and more barren, until from Icy Cape north it is a flat or slightly rolling monotonous stretch of Arctic bogs.

At Plover Bay, on the Siberian shore, are low hills or mountains rising to 1,500 feet or more, almost sheer from the bay in many places, and made up of enormous masses of rock, down the sides of which the crumbling talus of splinters and fragments, weathered off, make the slopes difficult to surmount. About here the attractions for the birds are very small, and but few species except water fowl are found. On the north, towards Bering Strait, the coast is somewhat hilly; but only at East Cape, the easternmost point of Siberia, do we find it rising again to a rugged mountainous peak. Thence, again, along the northern coast the shore gradually becomes lower until it finally assumes the low undulating barren character of the Arctic tundra; nor does this last appear much more inviting to land birds than does the harsh faces of the broken and mountainous districts. The islands of Bering Sea, as are most islands frequented by sea-birds in the north, are enormous masses of rock apparently forced up out of the water, with almost precipitous sides, affording innumerable chinks and crevices wherein the birds find shelter and places for rearing their young; but with only a slight amount of vegetation, and much more familiar with cold fogs and icy storms at all seasons, than they are with clear skies or warm sunshiny days.

In conclusion, I have only to express my thanks for the courtesies rendered, first to General W. B. Hazen, Chief Signal Officer, and to the Secretary of the Treasury, through whose kind permission and co-operation I was enabled to accompany the Corwin; and also to Professor S. F. Baird and Mr. R. Ridgway, of the Smithsonian Institution, for aid in the preparation of this report.

E. W. NELSON,
Signal Service, U. S. A.

WASHINGTON, *May 18, 1883.*

ERRATA.

Owing to the absence of the author, and the haste with which this paper has been put through the press, the writer had no opportunity to correct the proofs, and in consequence a number of typographical errors are present—the most important of which are detailed in the following list.

Page 59, in place of "seneica" read "suecica."
Page 60, in place of "sylvai" read "sylvia."
Page 63, in place of "clata" read "celata."
Page 64, in place of "myrodioctes" read "myiodioctes."
Page 66, in place of "encoptera" read "leucoptera."
Page 70, in place of "alaudinus" read "alaudinus."
Page 72, in place of "P. iliaca" read "No. 14 Passerella iliaca townsendi."
Page 74, in place of "alaudidae" read "alaudidae."
Page 76, strike out one "a" in "virginianums."
Page 77, in place of "swinia" read "surnia"; in place of "candicans" read "candicans."
Page 79, in place of "sanctic" read "sancti."
Page 80, strike out one "e" in "Haliaeetus;" for "Tetraenidae" read "Tetraonidae."
Page 81, for "ruspestris" read "rupestris."
Through an error the notes under numbers 78 and 79 were not placed under a single heading.
Page 82, for "occidentalis" read "atkhensis."
Page 85, for "scolopaceus" read "scolopaceus"; for "maritima" read "couesi, Ridg."
Page 87, for "pygraeus" read "pygmaeus."
Page 89, for "flairipes" read "flavipes."
Page 93, for "albifrons" read "albifrons."
Page 103, for "groenlidae" read "graenlidae."
Page 107, "Larus cachinnans" appears under two headings by an error.
Page 112, for "fulmorus" read "fulmarus" and space between this word and the next.
Page 114, for "Polbölli" read "Holbölli."
Page 115, for "septentrionalis" read septentrionalis"; for "corineulala" read "corniculata."
Page 116, for "Simorhynchut cristatelhus" read "Simorhynchus cristatelhus"; for "antiguus" read "antiquus."

THE BIRDS OF BERING SEA AND THE ARCTIC OCEAN.

TURDIDÆ. THRUSHES.

HYLOCICHLA ALICIÆ Baird.

(1.) THE GRAY-CHEEKED THRUSH.

In middle latitudes where our acquaintance is made with this bird we associate it with damp woodlands and sheltered glens, and it would seem almost incongruous to one familiar with it in such surroundings to look for it as an inhabitant of the barren stretches of arctic lands where for many miles not a tree raises its shaft. Such is its northern home, however, and throughout the entire arctic region north of Hudson's Bay to Bering Strait and across into Kamtchatka the bird is found in a greater portion of this range as an extremely abundant species. Wherever clumps of dwarf willows or alder have gained a foothold along the sterile slopes and hillsides in the north, a pair or more of these wanderers may be looked for. Along the entire Bering Sea coast of Alaska, and north around the shores of Kotzebue Sound, it is numerous among the many alder bushes found on these shores, and the record of the bird from Kamtchatka renders certain its presence on the adjoining shores of Northeastern Siberia. It is the most northern species of thrush found in America and its breeding range is limited only by the absence of a bush in which to place its nest. It passes by the groves and farms of the Northern States just as the buds are swelling and the warm, misty rains of spring are quickening into life the sleeping seeds and rootlets; filled with buoyant exultation it pauses now and then to pour forth those strange but pleasing cadences which once heard in their full sweetness will never be forgotten. But it has no time to tarry, and ere long it is already far on its way to the north. The strange, wild song which arose but a short time since in pleasant woodland spots and quiet nooks in southern groves is now heard by wandering Indians who seek their summer fishing-grounds by the banks of northern streams. Yet a little later and it troops in abundance near to the shores of the Arctic, where the Mackenzie and other rivers pour their spring floods into the icy sea. Down the Yukon these birds pass, using the densely bush grown bank of the river as their highway, raising now and then their song which finds here fittest surroundings. Reaching the mouth of the Yukon, many wander along the coast of Bering Sea to the north, and some are said to cross the straits.

They have now reached their summer homes, and in sheltered thickets among many of their kind they choose their mates and prepare for rearing their young. Ere long their joyous song is heard no more, but instead the sprightly bird is busily engaged in caring for its gaping brood. In the course of time the young are fledged, and now the unwary birds fall an easy prey to the untried bows of the native boys, who follow them into their bushy coverts and slay many a helpless victim with their blunt-pointed arrows. The skins of the birds killed by the boys are kept till winter and hung in rows as trophies of the young hunters' skill, to be brought out at the great midwinter hunting festival.

As the cold storms of autumn arise the birds, which have escaped the various dangers, and which are easily affected by cold prepare to return, and retracing their way along the course pursued in spring they pass again to the south, now shy and silent, awakening the echoes no longer with joyous melody, but apparently imbued with the saddening spirit of autumn they pass quickly by and are gone.

HYLOCICHLA NANUS Aud.

(2.) THE DWARF THRUSH.

The presence of this species in my list is owing entirely to the identification of Gmelin's Ounalaskan Thrush as this bird by Mr. Ridgway. If Gmelin's bird was one of these thrushes, as the imperfect description may be interpreted to affirm, it occurs there merely as a straggler, for since the original record not a specimen has been obtained at Ounalaska, or elsewhere on the Aleutian Islands, by any of the numerous naturalists who have visited them. The description is so vague and imperfect as given by Gmelin that absolute identification is impossible, and from the geographical position of the original locality the chances are equally as favorable for H. *aliciæ* to occur as for the Dwarf Thrush.

MERULA MIGRATORIA Linn. Sw. & Rich.

(3.) THE AMERICAN ROBIN.

The breeding limit of this bird is restricted to the wooded part of the interior, but it occurs as a straggling migrant on the coast of Norton Sound and Bering Straits and a wind-bound visitant to the Seal Islands. It is present as a summer resident on Kodiak Peninsula, as shown by skins brought me by the Esquimaux. No doubt it is a straggler thence to Northeastern Asia or Chukchi land. It also visits the shores of Kotzebue Sound in the course of its migrations, but I do not know of its nesting anywhere near tide-water on this coast.

It is a pleasant experience for one in a far-off region like this to come across the familiar forms known in other days. The sight of this bird gleaning its food about the houses on a frosty spring morning in May, carries one's mind back from sterile arctic scenery to the blossoming orchards, the hum of bees, and such other pleasant sounds and sights of nature as go to make up a beautiful spring day in lower latitudes. One misses, however, the warbling strain of the blue bird, and the cheerless surroundings soon bring the stern reality too closely home. The birds too seem impressed with the gloomy surroundings, and I have never heard them utter their notes during the time of their visits to the sea-coast.

In the wooded interior, however, they regain their spirits and rear their young even north of the circle, and here their cheering notes enliven the wooded river courses during the long summer days, in striking contrast to the silence of a few months earlier when a deathly hush made the shadows of the forests a fitting haunt for the wolf and wolverines.

There is no record of the occurrence of the robin in Northeastern Asia, that I have found, although as before mentioned it undoubtedly is a casual visitant to that region. Elliott found a single bird wind-bound upon the Seal Islands, beyond which there is no record of its occurrence on any of the islands in Bering Sea.

HESPEROCICHLA NÆVIA (Gmel.) Baird.

(4.) THE VARIED THRUSH.

This handsome bird equals the robin in its northern range in Alaska, and quite a number of skins have been brought me from the northern shore of Norton Sound and from the Kotzebue Sound region. The Eskimo have assured me of its range considerably beyond this district, and Richardson found it on the Mackenzie River, within the Arctic Circle, where he tells us it arrives very soon after the Robin and the Yellow Warbler. It, like the Robin, prefers to nest in the wooded country, but unlike the latter it nests at times in the alder clumps close to the shore of Norton and Kotzebue Sounds. It is unknown from the islands and Asiatic shore of Bering Sea.

I have not had the pleasure of studying the life habits of this bird, so have nothing to add in this particular, but may say that its habits during the breeding season are but little known, very few naturalists having had opportunity to study its nidification.

CINCLIDÆ. WATER OUZELS.

CINCLUS MEXICANUS Swains.

(5.) THE AMERICAN WATER OUZEL.

Throughout the year, along the sparkling streams which descend in a series of cascades from the summits of the mountains on the Aleutian Islands, the cheerful presence and strange habits of this odd little bird animate the silent and otherwise lifeless gorges and ravines furrowing their steep slopes. It braves the wild tempestuous winters of this part of the North Pacific and Bering Sea, and is found farther north wintering even on streams flowing into the Arctic Ocean.

This half aquatic thrush is found about open spots on streams flowing into the head of Norton and Kotzebue Sounds, where it braves the severest temperatures of the harsh winters, regardless of the intense cold prevailing for weeks at a time. It searches busily for its food in the icy waters of the swiftly running streams by whose mossy banks, overhung with stunted pines and willows, it rears its young in summer.

It is unknown whether this or its closely allied Asiatic relatives is found in Chukchi Land. But neither form is found on the islands of Bering Sea, except in the Aleutian Chain, nor were any seen at Plover Bay or East Cape, where, however, the conditions are scarcely favorable for their presence.

SAXICOLIDÆ. STONE CHATS.

CYANECULA SENCICA (Linn.) Boehm.

(6.) THE BLUE THROATED WARBLER.

The presence of this oddly marked songster here is owing solely to the occurrence of several specimens at Saint Michael's, Norton Sound, where several were taken by Dr. Adams in June, 1852.

The various authorities who have written on the habits of the Swedish nightingale, either as seen in Northern Europe or Siberia, agree in giving it rare powers of song, especially in mimicking the notes of other birds. So varied and peculiar are its capabilities in this respect that we can but regret that its presence on American shores is due to mere accident.

The bird, though quite distinct in several characteristics, especially of color and pattern of body, is closely allied to *saxicola*, as it possesses the peculiar distribution of color on the tail feathers almost precisely as in this later genus, and other marks of resemblance. I do not know of its occurrence in Northeastern Siberia, although its summer distribution is subarctic, and it has been found on the Lower Lena and in various parts of Middle Siberia.

SAXICOLA ŒNANTHE (Linn.) Bechst.

(7.) THE STONE CHAT.

The Wheat Ear, although long known as a rather common summer resident in the northeastern corner of America and in Greenland, has but recently been found in Alaska, where Mr. Dall was the first to find it. He obtained a number of specimens in the middle Yukon region, since which time Dr. T. H. Bean has found it not uncommon on the Arctic Coast from Kotzebue Sound to Cape Lisburne, and the writer has taken it in the fall and spring on the shores of Norton Sound at Saint Michael's, and a native brought a skin of one of these birds on board the Corwin at King Island the summer during one of our visits there.

This list of occurrences shows that the bird is to be considered a somewhat regular visitant to some parts if not all of Northern Alaska. It is very erratic in its occurrence, however, and where quite common one season may not be found at all the next.

In the summer of 1880, Dr. Bean found the bird not uncommon in the range just given, whereas in the summer of 1881 I visited the same shore in the Corwin and failed to find a single individual, although keeping a sharp watch for birds wherever we landed. Strangely enough this bird has not been taken anywhere in Eastern Siberia, so that its presence in Alaska must be supposed to result from its passage westward along the northern shore of America from Greenland and its adjoining habitat, evidently entering Northern Alaska and perhaps Northeastern Asia from Europe by way of the Northwest Passage.

SYLVIIDÆ. OLD-WORLD WARBLERS.
SYLVAI EVERSMANNI.
(8.) EVERSMANN'S WARBLER.

Flocks of this small bird came during the middle of June and settled on the Vega at Tapkan, her winter quarters, northwest of the Straits. This was before the ground was free from snow, and the birds appeared to be much exhausted.

PHYLLOSCOPUS BOREALIS (Blas.) Dresser.
(9.) KENNICOTT'S WARBLER.

The first American specimen of this Siberian Warbler was taken by the naturalist of the Western Union Telegraph Expedition at Saint Michael's, Norton Sound, in 1866. Since then no others have been secured until the three specimens I had the good fortune to obtain at the same locality during my residence at that place. Its recurrence appears to be very irregular, as it was found only in two seasons out of four, during which I kept a sharp lookout and had native collectors searching for them, but obtained and saw only the examples mentioned. It has never been taken on the Siberian shore of the region covered by this paper, but further towards Middle Siberia it is known to be common, extending its summer range to the vicinity of the Arctic Circle, passing south through Eastern and Central Asia in its autumnal migration. In the region of Lake Baikal it is a common migrant, as well as further east in Siberia. How general its range in Northeastern Siberia is can only be determined when the numerous ornithological problems of that country are solved by the work of some ornithologist.

PARIDÆ. TITMICE.
PARUS ATRICAPILLUS SEPTENTRIONALIS (Harris.) Allen.
(10.) THE LONG-TAILED CHICKADEE.

An irregular visitor to the Alaskan shore of Bering Sea, mainly about Norton and Kotzebue Sounds, where it is not a rare bird in the fall and at times also in the spring. But it is never resident here, owing to the lack of suitable shelter.

PARUS CINCTUS GRISESCENS. Sharp & Dresser.
(11.) THE SIBERIAN CHICKADEE.

Though to be accounted a Siberian species by right of general distribution and priority of discovery, yet this little Chickadee makes its home among the spruce and paper-birch forests of Northern Alaska, and like the preceding makes occasional excursions to the adjoining coasts and comes familiarly about the houses, where it enlivens the gloomy opening of the long cheerless winter or breaks into the monotony of the silent frosty days later in the season.

Although Mr. Ridgway identified the original American specimens of this bird as typical *Parus cinctus*, a more careful examination of a much larger series made by myself shows that it is really referable to the much grayer and somewhat larger Eastern Siberian form, described in "Dresser's Birds of Europe," and to which all American specimens should be referred.

PARUS HUDSONICUS Forst.
(12.) THE HUDSONIAN CHICKADEE.

This bird is the third and last of a band of active, cheerful wood-sprites, whose busy notes and amusing motions while playing at gymnastics, as they rove in merry troops through the woodlands of the interior, holding their own against the inclement winter with its cold and famine, render them the most interesting of the winter inhabitants of northern forests. Their odd self-assertion and seeming importance render them noticeable and attractive wherever one goes.

Like its relatives, a few of the more adventurous of this species also pay flying visits to the sea-shore, where for a short time they flit about searching the crevices of the log houses, climbing about the fences, and making themselves thoroughly at home for a short season and then betake themselves to more suitable quarters again.

TROGLODYTIDÆ. WRENS.

ANORTHURA ALASCENSIS (Baird) Coues.

(13.) THE ALASKAN WREN.

This sturdy representative of the common winter wren of the Eastern United States makes its permanent home on the foggy, storm-beaten Aleutian and Fur Seal Islands. Here, in spite of inclement weather and the harsh, cheerless form assumed by nature on all sides, this plain but interesting Wren passes its life. All about snow-clad hills or rugged, rock-strewn cliffs and steep mountain slopes rise against a cloud-hidden sky. Masses of sleet and rain dash down the slopes and ravines, sending sheets of spray across the water and driving all else to seek shelter; yet this bird holds its own on some partly sheltered slope or grassy flat, and if spring be at hand its clear notes may be heard breaking forth during a lull in the storm as the hardy songster holds by a firm grasp upon some small bush beaten back and forth in the wind, or perhaps from some jutting rock.

The ravines are still bedded with snow in many places, when he has already chosen a partner and is deep in the mysteries of family life. In autumn he is found sprightly as before, but less musical, as he flits about the grassy flats and hilly slopes, generally in pairs, so that it may be possible he is paired for life.

What its habits are during winter I cannot say, but so brave a heart in so small a body, that bids its owner endure this long, cheerless season, with its weeks of tempests raging over the snow-covered mountains and through the narrow valleys, commands one's admiration. Though the smallest of the birds found on these islands it seems capable of enduring as much as the hardiest of them. It is one of the peculiar forms, limited to these forbidding islands, whose influence upon their inhabitants is not alone shown by the peculiar character of their bird life, but also in their people as well, the language and customs of the latter having their insular peculiarities as striking as those distinguishing this wren from its mainland kin, though in some customs our little troglodyte has varied less than his human fellow-inhabitant, and he still makes his snug nest in some cosy nook in the rocky cliffs bounding the grim faces of the many surrounding mountains, or a cleft in a rocky ledge becomes the chosen spot.

While the Corwin lay at Oonalaska, the last of September and first of October, 1881, these birds were common in pairs, as if permanently mated. They kept among the tall grasses, ferns, and small willows formed on the flats at the heads of the inner bays, but were remarkably silent; and though their movements were active and they were frequently seen balancing on the tops of the tall plants, not a note was heard, and their movements can only be described as similar to those of any wren in such a position.

Mr. Elliott tells me that during exceptionally severe winters on Saint George Island large numbers of these birds perish. A few seasons, however, suffice to bring the number up to its original stand-point.

Another curious point in the history of this bird is the fact, as ascertained by the same observer, that although one of the commonest birds on Saint George Island it is totally unknown on the adjoining island of Saint Paul. This is a remarkable instance of the strange and often unaccountable limitation to the distribution of birds. Saint Paul Island is only about thirty miles from Saint George, where the wren is abundant, but not one is known to pass from one island to the other. One hundred and eighty miles separate Saint George Island from the nearest of the Aleutian, which latter islands must be considered as the birds' original habitat.

MOTACILLIDÆ. WAGTAILS.

BUDYTES FLAVA (Linn.) Gray.

(14.) THE YELLOW WAGTAIL.

As a summer resident on the shores of Bering Sea, in Alaska, this handsome bird makes its appearance the last of May or the first of June, according to the season, and very soon after is mated and performing its summer duty of nesting and rearing its young, in all the suitable portions of the low, open country, from the Yukon mouth on the south to the southern shore of Kotzebue Sound on the north. Saint Michael's may be taken as the center of abundance of this bird in Alaska. At the Yukon mouth, I found it rare in the spring of 1879 and during the summer of 1880. I only found two or three specimens at the various landings made in Kotzebue Sound; it was, also, found sparingly at Plover Bay, where nearly every naturalist who has landed there has also found it. It was not seen on the Arctic shore of Siberia visited by the Corwin, nor does Nordenskjöld mention it as being found at his wintering place. As autumn approaches, towards the last of August, these gentle birds prepare to return to their winter quarters in Southeastern Asia and adjoining islands. One by one they leave our shore, and unless some waif is caught, like the one Mr. Dall secured at sea, off Saint Matthew's Island, nothing more is heard of them in America until they recross the sea again in spring. Meanwhile they have twice passed the strange scenes of China, Japan, and other adjoining lands of the Orient, and penetrated the countries of Southeastern Asia and the adjoining islands, joining meanwhile in pleasant fellowship with many a strange feathered companion, whose experience wots not of the wide lands roamed over by his jaunty, tip-tilted friend, whose air of complacent impertinence speaks of much sight seeing in foreign parts; and who knows but he even affects a slight Eskimo lisp as the result of his voyage across the seas? However, he is a very welcome summer visitor to the cheerless bogs of Northwestern Alaska and makes a pleasant addition to the slightly varied character of the bird life in this portion of the far north.

ANTHUS LUDOVICIANUS (Gm.) Licht.

(15.) THE AMERICAN TITLARK.

During the early spring the Titlark is found sparingly along the entire Alaskan coast of Bering Sea, but does not breed to my knowledge south of the straits, except perhaps on the mountains back from the coast, and I have not found it numerous at any season, though it is said to be common in the interior. It also occurs on the Chuckchee peninsula and Aleutian Islands. The first of August it comes straggling slowly back from its breeding ground in the north, bringing its young in train, and after lingering for a short time about favorite spots in the vicinity of Saint Michael's passes on to seek winter quarters far to the south.

ANTHUS PRATENSIS (Linn.) Bechst.

(16.) THE EUROPEAN TITLARK.

This widely-spread Old World bird has been taken but once within the region treated of in this paper. A single specimen was secured at Saint Michael's by Mr. Dall, during the Russian-American Telegraph Expedition, and remains the only evidence of its presence on either shore of Bering Sea.

MOTACILLA OCULARIS Swinhoe.

(17.) THE SIBERIAN WAGTAIL.

All the later naturalists who have visited Plover Bay, Siberia, have secured specimens of this handsome bird, Dall, Bean, and myself in succession finding it there. The two former took it late in the season in imperfect plumage, while during the second visit of the Corwin to this bay, the last of June, 1881, I secured a fine adult male in perfect breeding plumage, the handsome plate

accompanying this volume showing the bird mentioned. They are found on the grassy flats which cover the spit making out at the mouth of the bay, and are very unsuspicious, if my single example is to be taken as typical. It was close to the Eskimo huts and lighted upon a stone as I drew near, allowing me to approach very closely. I thus obtained the prize without the slightest difficulty. Mr. Turner states that he observed one of these birds on the island of Atka, the westernmost of the Aleutian Chain, in the spring of 1881. And one of the most remarkable facts in connection with the history of this species is the fact that a specimen has lately been received at the National Museum, obtained by Mr. L. Belding in Southern California, where it was obtained in the early winter of 1881–1882, thus introducing it as a member of the fauna of North America. It is a common and pretty well-known bird in collections from Eastern Siberia. Its life history, however, still remains to be worked out. The accompanying plate represents it in the act of darting at an insect in the characteristic manner of this and allied birds.

The specimen of this bird, which I obtained June 26, 1881, at Plover Bay, Siberia, is an adult male in full spring plumage, of which the following is a description:

Back nearly uniform ashy, changing on upper tail coverts to blackish, with an ashy wash on edges of feathers. All but two outer tail feathers black; the two outer feathers white, each having a narrow longitudinal band of black from base along the edge of inner web, which runs out towards the end of the feathers an inch from tip of first and close to tip of second. A black line extends along near the shaft of outer web of the next to outer feather, breaking and disappearing near the middle of the feather. Wing light brown; tertiaries much darker and edged with white. The greater and lesser coverts are so broadly edged with white as to overlap and conceal the dark brown centers, the two thus forming a large, uniform white patch on the upper surface of wing. A broad frontal patch of white extending from bill back on crown to a line drawn across the posterior edge of orbits and continuing back nearly to the occiput as a supraocular stripe. A nearly black line extends from gape back through eye, uniting the neck with the nearly square black patch which occupies the crown and nuchal region and extends partly down on sides of neck. From the base of lower mandible on each side a widening band of white extends back under the eye and down the side of neck, separating the black crown patch from the large black patch which extends from the base of lower mandible down over the throat and breast. The rest of under surface white, tinged with a wash of ashy on sides and flanks. Bill and feet black. Iris dark hazel. Dimensions: Wing, 3.65; tail, 3.75; tarsus, .95; middle toe and claw, .71; culmen, .50 inches.

SYLVICOLIDÆ. AMERICAN WARBLERS.

HELMINTHOPHAGA CLATA (Say) Baird.

(18.) THE ORANGE-CROWNED WARBLER.

This is quite a common breeding bird of the interior of Northern Alaska during each summer, but does not usually appear along the sea-coast until its young are fledged and are on their way south. This takes place during the first half of August, at which time these birds are quite numerous for one or two weeks, especially along the shore of Norton Sound. They are not known to occur on the adjoining shore of Siberia, nor on any of the islands in Bering's Sea.

DENDRŒCA ÆSTIVA (Gmel.) Bd.

(19.) THE YELLOW WARBLER.

A common summer resident in every alder and willow patch along the American mainland, and more numerous on the shores of Norton and Kotzebue Sounds than elsewhere, owing mainly to the abundance of its favorite shelter on these shores. Its familiar notes and bright plumage render it one of the most attractive summer visitants. It is one of the few species of this group extending its range within the Arctic Circle, and has, perhaps, the prettiest plumage of its kind reaching this high latitude in America.

DENDRŒCA CORONATA (Linn.) Gray.

(20.) THE YELLOW-RUMP WARBLER

Occurs as an occasional, but not rare, visitant along the American shore, perhaps most numerous along the shores of Norton Sound. It is, however, a woodland species, and makes but very short stops along the inhospitable coast, but hastens to more congenial locations in the interior, where it rears its young. In the autumnal migration it hastily seeks its more southern haunts, and rarely lingers along the bare coast of the north, as do some of its relatives.

DENDRŒCA STRIATA (Forst.) Baird.

(21.) THE BLACK-POLL WARBLER.

Like the Yellow Rump, this is a rather scarce bird, and is found along the shore of Norton Sound merely as a spring and fall migrant. It also occurs upon the shores of Kotzebue Sound at the same season. Like other small birds, it frequents the vicinity of houses during its passage, where it apparently finds the best foraging grounds. The small garden spot close to the kitchen at Saint Michael's seems to be the great rendezvous and point of attraction for such of these small species as pass that way in spring and fall. Like some of the other small birds mentioned, this is a common interior species; it is unknown on the islands and Asiatic shore of the sea.

SIURUS NÆVIUS (Bodd) Coues.

(22.) THE SMALL-BILLED WATER THRUSH.

Rather common about the shores of Norton Sound during the fall migration, which continues during the month of August. Although not numerous every season, yet from three to a dozen may be taken about the muddy spots in the immediate vicinity of the houses at Saint Michael's. It has not been taken on any of the islands in Bering Sea. These birds breed in the bushy islands of the Lower Yukon in great abundance as well as in some of the more favorable thickets along the coast of Norton Sound, ranging as high up at least as Kotzebue Sound. Their clear, rich notes rise from the dense clumps of willows or alders in their favorite haunts in spring, enlivening the river banks with their wild full tones and dividing the musical honors with the larger Fox-colored Sparrow.

MYRODIOCTES PUSILLUS (Wils.) Bp.

(23.) THE BLACK-CAPPED YELLOW WARBLER.

In companionship with the Yellow Warbler, this pretty little bird makes its summer home among the bushy patches along the coast, especially from the Yukon mouth north to Kotzebue Sound. Both this and the species just mentioned extend their summer haunts even to the confines of the Arctic Circle. Both make pilgrimages in the winter to Mexico and Central America, where they hob-nob and catch flies with the stay-at-home warblers and fly catchers of the tropical forests, and after a season of recreation and plenty they betake themselves over the thousands of miles intervening and arrive a merry, restless party at their nesting grounds early in June or the last of May. They are unknown beyond the Alaskan mainland and are more plentiful in the interior than on the coast.

LANIIDÆ. SHRIKES.

LANIUS BOREALIS Vieill.

(24.) THE GREAT NORTHERN SHRIKE.

The Northern Shrike is a very rare visitant to the coast of Bering Sea, and except at the mouth of the Yukon and along the shores of Kotzebue and Norton Sounds its occurrence is very unusual. In the places mentioned it must be classed as rare. The mouth of the Yukon is apparently the point of most frequent occurrence, while elsewhere it is a mere straggler.

LANIUS CRISTATUS.

(25.) THE CRESTED SHRIKE.

As the last boat came off from Wrangel Island and the captain began to prepare for getting clear from the ice that the strong tide was bringing about us with too much force for safety, a sailor came up to me in a shamefaced manner and held out a dried specimen of this bird which he said he had picked up on the hillside and wished to know if I cared for it. As might be supposed the mummy was taken in hand and is among the prizes secured during the cruise of the Corwin. By the aid of alcohol it came safely to Washington, and Mr. Ridgway has carefully reproduced it in the accompanying plate. It has been represented as perching upon a fragment of drift-wood frozen in the ice, with the shores of Wrangel Island in the distance, the latter being from sketches taken by myself as we were leaving that place. I may refer to the fact that we found fragments of drift-wood, not only upon this island but in the water about it, as several who have seen the drawing have supposed that the perch must necessarily have been introduced solely by a flight of the artist's imagination. This is strictly an Asiatic bird, and its occurrence here upon the hillside far above the tide-mark shows that it must have reached here alive, probably during some storm, and died subsequently of starvation or exposure. Although the bird was obtained the 12th of August, yet it is a young of the year in its first plumage, of which the following is a description:

The crown and upper part of the back is slightly dull rufous or chestnut; back lighter toward rump where it is grayish and yellowish brown with dark bars. The upper tail coverts are russet or reddish brown with dark barring near the end and tipped with grayish. The feathers of crown and back are edged slightly with grayish, showing the immature plumage. The wings are brown with color of the back extending over the shoulders, but with the coverts brown, edged with dull buffy and grayish and becoming reddish in some instances. The tertiaries are edged broadly with pale brownish yellow. The tail is reddish brown, nearly uniform, except the outer feather, which is lighter than the inner. Belly nearly a uniform yellowish white, marked on breast and sides with fine, wavy, and irregular bars of brownish or blackish, giving a loosely vermiculated appearance to the lower surface. The throat is immaculate yellowish white. The lores are grayish white, shaded with buffy, which color extends back as an imperfect supraorbital line, and the cheeks and auriculars are yellowish white or pale buffy, finely maculated with dark edges to the feathers.

The measurements of the bird are:

	Inches.
Wing	3.40
Tail	3.70
Culmen	.50
Depth of bill at base	.28
Tarsus	.98

The graduation of the tail is nearly seventy-hundredths of an inch.

HIRUNDINIDÆ. SWALLOWS.

HIRUNDO ERYTHROGASTRA Bodd.

(26.) THE BARN SWALLOW.

One of the most pleasant sights that meet the traveler's eye on landing at Saint Michael's is the large number of common Barn Swallows which make their homes about the buildings. These birds extend their range to the shores of Bering Sea and the Arctic Ocean. Their cheerful twittering and graceful motions as they circle and glide in wayward flight about the small collection of log houses recall scenes of a far different character than those which fill the eye at this place. Here they nest in deserted native houses or under the eaves of the few frame or log houses, and in some instances seek the shelter of rocky caves and hidden spots on the faces of the cliffs, as was seen on the north shore of Kotzebue Sound, where two nests were found placed far inside of a deep cleft extending into a rocky cliff reaching out into the sea. The nests were in close proximity upon a rocky shelf, while below them the waves dashed back and forth, breaking into spray within a few inches of the nests. In the Aleutian Islands the swallow is scarce, and is said not to occur west of Ounalaska. At this latter place its occurrence is governed largely by the character of the season; a pleasant spring brings them to nest about the village, while an inclement season prevents a single one from making its appearance.

The *Hirundo Unalascæ* Gmelin refers without question to this species, as there is nothing else to which it can be referred occurring at Ounalaska. As before remarked, in some seasons not a swallow is seen at Ounalaska, again they are common; but thus far the researches in that region have revealed no species of swallow except this which visits this chain of islands.

TACHYCINETA BICOLOR (Vieill.) Cabun.

(27.) THE WHITE-BELLIED SWALLOW.

The present bird occurs quite commonly along the shores of Norton Sound during moderately pleasant days the last of May, and coincident with the main flight of the Blackbrant it hunts back and forth through the marshy flats and over the bare hillsides, but is rarely found in the settlements. After a very short stay it leaves for the wooded country in the interior, or on the lower parts of the larger streams where it breeds. In August it is again seen like various other species straggling along the coast. It haunts the vicinity of settlements at this season and may be seen generally in companionship with its cousin, the Barn Swallow, for a day or two, but rarely remains until the latter starts in its southern migration. I find no record of either this or the preceding extending its range to the Asiatic coast, nor are they known, to my knowledge, on any of the islands in the Bering Straits region.

FRINGILLIDÆ. FINCHES.

PINICOLA ENUNCLEATOR (Linn.) Vieill.

(28.) THE PINE GROSBEAK.

An extremely rare straggler to the unwooded shore of Bering Sea. About the head of Norton Sound, however, where spruce forests reach the shore, they are not uncommon. Here, as elsewhere, in the wooded country it is resident. For a discussion of the geographical variation of this bird I must refer those interested to the more general work I am preparing on the birds of the Territory of Alaska, as lack of space forbids taking up the subject here.

LOXIA CURVIROSTRA AMERICANA (Wils.) Coues.

(29.) THE AMERICAN CROSSBILL.

An excessively rare species on the shores of Bering Sea, I know of its occurrence there in but a single instance; this was a specimen taken at Saint Michael's in winter by Mr. Turner. It is of excessive rarity in the Yukon region. The Saint Michael's specimen is identical with others obtained at Sitka and in the surrounding region, which appear to average considerably smaller than the birds of the interior and eastern portion of the continent. Its occurrence to the north of the Alaskan Peninsula can be looked upon as very exceptional.

LOXIA CUCOPTERA Gm.

(30.) THE WHITE-WINGED CROSSBILL.

Although this species is seen much more frequently on the coast than the former, yet it is also a rare bird there except where, as about the head of Norton Sound, the forest of the interior approaches the coast. In the interior, however, this is one of the commonest and most familiar birds, and is one of the few hardy species which braves the rigorous winters in this region. During this latter season they may be found moving in small parties through the tree-tops, or in scattered pairs during the summer attending to the duties of incubation and rearing their young. Neither this nor the preceding species is known to occur upon any of the islands of Bering Sea or upon any part of the Siberian shore. This might be anticipated from a knowledge of the unsuitable character of these portions of the region in question.

LEUCOSTICTE GRISEINUCHA (Brandt) Baird.

(31.) THE ALEUTIAN ROSY FINCH.

Along the entire Aleutian chain of islands, from Kodiak on the east to Atkha and Attou on the west, and including Saint Matthew's and the Seal Islands on the north, this beautiful bird is found to be one of the most frequent species. The delicately blended grays and browns, with the lovely roseate wash over nearly all the body, renders it the richest in color and most attractive species found in this region. In addition to being the northernmost of its limited number of congeners, it is also the giant among its relatives; as well it may be to endure the harsh climate where it has made its home. Much to the writer's regret, although he made special effort to find this bird during both his visits to Ounalaska, a hasty glimpse of a single individual flitting along the rugged face of a cliff near the shore in May, 1877, was the only one seen. Nearly every other naturalist who has visited this locality has secured specimens and records it as one of the commonest birds. Even the long, harsh winter is not able to make these elegant finches seek a milder climate, but amid the whirling snows and desolate scenes of these forbidding islands they make their permanent home. In summer, among the long grasses and other plants, this bird is to be found rendering pleasant the scenes where in winter it alone breaks the dull, cheerless monotony. It is totally unknown on the mainland of either continent, but has near relatives on the American shores, and it appears to be a form strictly limited to this peculiar chain of islands. Although it winters on the Aleutian islands it is only known as a summer resident to the north on the Seal and Saint Matthew's Islands.

ÆGIOTHUS CANESCENS EXILIPES (Coues) Ridgw.

(32.) THE WHITE-RUMPED RED POLL.

All along the coast of Bering Sea, on the Alaskan shore, from the Peninsula of Alaska north to Point Barrow, as well as upon the islands in Bering's Strait and across to the adjoining shore of Asia, this is perhaps the most abundant of all the land birds. Their nests are placed indifferently in bushes and tufts of grass, or a hole in a piece of drift wood on the barren shore serves as a building site. This and the following species intergrade in many instances, so that it is difficult to separate them accurately. My reasons for keeping the two forms separate are given in full in a complete list of the birds of the territory now in preparation. Over all the polar lands of America, Europe, and Asia, as well as in Greenland, we find both forms of this handsome little bird giving animation to many of the otherwise lonely and barren spots. In summer he is usually engaged in rearing his one or two broods of dull-plumaged young and preparing them for the trying experiences they will necessarily face a few months later, when the sun draws his short bow across the southern sky, and long, frosty nights make the very earth crack under the lowering temperature. At this season the stars seem each to hang from the firmament by an invisible cord and twinkle clear and bright overhead. The sharp, querulous yelp of the white fox alone breaks the intense stillness. A white, frosty fog hangs in the air—the chilled breath of nature—which falls silently to the ground in the lovely crystal handiwork of northern genii. In the north a pale auroral arch moves its mysterious banners and the rounding bosom of the earth, silent and chill under its white mantle, looks dreary and sad. After such a night the sun seems to creep reluctantly above the horizon, as though loath to face the bitter cold. The smoke rises slowly and heavily in the fixed atmosphere, and warm rooms are doubly appreciated. Soon small troops of these little red polls come silently about the houses, their feathers puffed out and looking gloomy enough as they search silently among the dead weeds for food. An hour or two later they catch the fuller rays of the sun and become more cheerful and flit busily about, though they are far from showing the character which becomes them so well and which later in the season they reveal under the brightening rays of the sun in early spring-time, towards the last of March and first of April. Then indeed we learn the true worth of our happy companions. They come flitting about the houses on all sides, examining the bare spots on the ground, searching the old weeds and fences, clinging to the eaves, and even coming to the window sills, whence they peer saucily in, making themselves continually at home and receiving a hearty welcome for their cheering presence. The breast is now a beautiful peach blossom pink and the crown shining scarlet. How this bird came to bear these beautiful colors is told in one of the Indian myths which is deemed of sufficient interest to relate; and, after the manner of the tales of our childhood, it begins thus:

Very long ago the whole of mankind were living in cheerless obscurity. Endless night hid the face of the world, and men were without the power of making a fire, as all the fire of the world was in the possession of a ferocious bear living in a far-off country to the north. This bear guarded his charge with unceasing vigilance, and so frightful was his appearance that no man dared attempt to obtain any of the precious substance. While the poor Indians were sorrowing over their misfortunes, the Red Poll, which at that time was a plain little wood sparrow, dressed in ordinary dull brown, heard their plaint—for in those days men and beasts understood one another—and his heart was touched. He prepared himself for a long journey and set out toward the lodge of the cruel bear. After many adventures on the long road which he traversed between his starting-point and the object of his journey, he at length reached the place and by a successful ruse stole a living ember from the perpetual fire which glowed close under the breast of the savage guardian and flew away with it in his beak. The glow of the coal was reflected from his breast and crown, while his forehead became slightly burned. Far away he flew and finally arrived safely at the home of mankind and was received with great rejoicing. He gave the fire to the thankful people and told them to guard it well; and as he did so they noticed the rich glow on his breast and brow, and said, "Kind bird, wear forever that beautiful mark as a memento of what you have done for us;" and to this day the Red Poll wears this badge in proof of the legend, as all may see, and mankind has ever since had fire.

ÆGIOTHUS LINARIA (Linn.) Caban.

(33.) THE COMMON RED POLL.

This, like the preceding bird, is found along the entire shore line of Bering Sea, with the exception of the Seal Islands and a portion of the Aleutian chain. It breeds in abundance wherever found, but is especially numerous along the shore from Norton to Kotzebue Sound; and wherever we landed from the Corwin, like the preceding, this bird was also found. The former, however, appears to be the predominating form, but the two occupy the same breeding range in this portion of their habitat, thus undoubtedly arguing for the distinctness of the two species. We found it with the preceding at East Cape, Siberia, Point Barrow, and at nearly every place where we landed. In winter they band together in flocks and seek the sheltered woodlands toward the interior, where in bushy ravines and on sheltered hill-sides they are found on every hand. During mild weather they make excursions to the coast and more exposed portions of the country, ready to disappear at the approach of an unfavorable change. Some of them, like the preceding, remain to winter along the sea-coast, but only a small proportion of the number which is found in summer. Many doubtless migrate to more southern localities, as they are nowhere found so abundant at this season as during summer. Although not mentioned by Nordenskiöld as occurring at his winter quarters, yet this bird is known to exist throughout the range of the entire circumpolar mainlands of both continents and many of the adjacent islands, rendering it certain that it is found in that portion of Siberia as well as elsewhere. On Herald and Wrangel Islands none of them were seen, owing doubtless to the scanty vegetation on these barren islands not affording requisite shelter and hospitality to tempt them to cross the icy sea and remain on these forbidding shores.

PLECTROPHANES NIVALIS (Linn.) Myer.

(34.) THE SNOW BUNTING.

In the north, the range and abundance of this species in summer is to a great extent complementary to that of the succeeding species. Along the more rugged parts of the coast, on rocky and barren islands and the bare and desolate shores of the Arctic Ocean, wherever explorers have gone they have found these birds before them. The desolate hill-tops of Saint Lawrence Island, the bare weather-worn sides of the mountains surrounding Plover Bay and East Cape, Siberia; the rocky wind-swept islands in Bering Strait, as well as the lonely shores of Herald and Wrangel Islands, and the shingle-strewn beaches along the north coast of Asia and Alaska all appear to be chosen as the favorite summer homes of this bird. When we landed at any of these places we were certain to be greeted by the clear, sharp note of the Snow Bunting, which would be seen running busily a'bout searching for food or wheeling about from place to place, its sharply contrasted black and white plumage quickly attracting the eye and usually the first sign of life. On the mountain sides at Plover Bay its mellow note was heard on June 26, uttering the long, clear, and rather hard song, full of a wild and exhilarating melody fitted to the surroundings. This song consists of four or five clear whistling notes, shorter than the song of the Long Spur, and uttered from a rocky point or the top of some jutting ledge. At Saint Lawrence Island, on June 24, we found them common and nesting, and some native children showed us a nest about 100 yards back of their huts. This nest contained one egg, which was obtained, with the female. After the latter was shot the male kept flying about our heads, or from rock to rock close by, and continually uttering a loud p-cher, p-cher, p-cher, in such a plaintive tone that I was glad when we were out of ear-shot. As long as we remained in the vicinity this bird followed us from place to place, hovering about, not taking the slightest notice of his rifled nest after the female was shot. He showed by his actions that he was fully aware of our having his mate in our possession. I do not remember ever having seen a bird show such affectionate solicitude for his mate as was exhibited on this occasion.

As we landed upon the shore of Wrangel Island, on August 12, were found a pair of these birds, with their full-grown young, upon the beach, and a number of others we found nesting upon Herald Island. This bird arrived at Tapkan on April 23, 1879, according to Nordenskiöld, and it is known to breed commonly on Spitzbergen and Nova Zembla, as well as throughout the Aleutian Islands and wherever the Arctic coasts to the north of Continental America have been visited.

CENTROPHANES LAPPONICUS (Linn.) Caban.

(35.) THE LAPLAND LONG SPUR.

One of the most numerous among the summer residents of the Alaskan mainland, but occurs more sparingly on the adjacent islands and along the shores of Asia. This bird generally frequents portions of the coast least sought by the preceding. Its northern range appears to be limited, and we do not find it either on Wrangel or Herald Island, although on the mainland of Alaska it extends to Point Barrow, where full-grown young were seen in August. It is much more numerous on the Alaskan shore than on the adjoining Asiatic coast. It breeds commonly upon Saint Lawrence Island, but is uncommon at Plover Bay, on the Asiatic shore, only about ninety miles distant. There are flats and other places there which appear suitable as local habitations, yet the birds were not found.

The Long Spur occurs in the greatest numbers on the grassy and moss-covered stretches of level or rolling tundra along the American coast. It was found sparingly along the north shore of Asia, where grassy flats afford suitable retreats; but everywhere along the American coast the bird appears to be a very common summer resident, and most plentiful where the full harshness of the arctic summer was not felt. Along the shores of Norton and Kotzebue Sounds, where the seasons are comparatively mild, it is found in greatest abundance. Thousands of the birds appear on every hand as one strolls about during the breeding season, and in early spring, at the commencement of mating, the air is filled with music. During the winter the Long Spur is not found in the country north of the Aleutian Islands, in which latter region, however, the bird is a permanent resident. Although the Long Spur apparently favors a milder or subarctic portion of the continent, it ranges far to the north, as is shown by being found nesting upon Spitzbergen, southern portions of Nova Zembla, and other far northern lands. Its southern breeding range in Alaska appears to be along the Aleutian chain, where it has been found raising its young, by Mr. Dall and others.

PASSERCULUS SANDWICHENSIS (Gmel.) Baird.

(36.) THE SANDWICH SOUND SPARROW.

On the Aleutian Islands this is a common summer resident, and thence east and south along the Alaskan shore it is also common. It has not been recorded from the Seal Islands, hence its northern range appears to be limited to this chain of islands and the adjoining coast as given. During the migrations it is found along the coast as far south as Oregon and Washington Territories, but its breeding limit in this region is still unknown. Throughout the northern part of its range it is known to breed, and we found it as late as October, 1881, at Ounalaska, and it arrived at this place the first of May, 1877. Some probably remain the entire winter, but the majority pass farther south. Its habits are like those of its congeners, keeping to the grassy flats and the shore close along the water's edge, where a portion of its food is gleaned. This also is one of the several cases in which the Aleutian Islands and adjoining region furnish a stouter, longer billed bird than is found in the closely allied forms of the mainland. Among these may be named *Melospiza cinerea, Leucosticte grisienucha*, and the Kodiak Aegiothii and Pinicola, in addition to the case in hand, as showing some of the most striking instances of this peculiarity.

PASSERCULUS SANDWICHENSIS ALANDINUS (Bp.) Ridgw.

(37.) THE WESTERN SAVANNA SPARROW.

All along the coast of Bering Sea, at least to Point Hope and probably to Point Barrow, this is a common bird, especially along the coast between the Alaskan Peninsula and Kotzebue Sound. Wherever the open moist stretches of comparatively level country afford suitable haunts, it is found in large numbers. Although *anthinus* has been recorded from Saint Michael's and the Yukon region, it is owing to an erroneous identification, as is shown by an examination of the specimens upon which this claim was based, all of which are referable to *Alandinus*. *Anthinus* is strictly limited to the coast of California and is unknown to the north of this region. On the contrary *alandinus* breeds far to the north, extending its breeding range inside the Arctic Circle, and its southern range in summer does not appear to encroach on that of *anthinus*. In winter, however, it is found passing south and mingling with its relatives in the coast region of California.

ZONOTRICHIA GAMBELI INTERMEDIA Ridgw.

(38.) THE INTERMEDIATE WHITE-CROWNED SPARROW.

Along the Alaskan Coast, north of the Aliaskan Peninsula to Kotzebue Sound, the White-crowned Sparrow is a rather common summer visitor and nests in many places. It is one of the most musical birds that reaches these high latitudes along the coast. With the opening spring and appearance of the first flowers comes this handsome songster, whose charming notes and familiar presence about the houses render it an agreeable accompaniment of spring. The last of May, it appears in the vicinity of Saint Michael's, and, taking the wood pile or some other convenient spot for its stage, sings at intervals during the entire day. Pleasant frosty mornings particularly are enlivened by the notes of this bird, and I recall with pleasure the feeling of exhilaration always produced by its song which seemed to form a part of the clear, fresh, frosty atmosphere and the brightening face of nature. For a week or so after the bird's arrival its familiar presence is joyfully proclaimed by notes from the places mentioned, after which it quits the vicinity of man for the sheltering thickets on the hillside, where it performs the duties of the season. A few weeks later, during the last of July or the first of August, it is ready to come about the houses again, a memory of the good things found there early in the season serving to draw the bird from all sides. The weed patches and grassy knolls in the vicinity of the Fort or the native village are filled with these birds, and with their young they wax fat and saucy upon the fare before them. The young frequently come into the court yard and make themselves thoroughly at home; and, if the truth be told, now and then one falls a victim to misplaced confidence, and, in the shape of a dried mummy, travels to distant parts of the world, where, among a host of his ilk, he reposes as a specimen. In autumn old and young alike have but the ordinary chirp common to a host of their kind at this season, and they carry with them but little of the interest attending their spring advent. In the lower Mackenzie River region and to the east these are abundant birds, and are said to render the twilight hours of night during the short summer melodious with their songs. Richardson often complained of their disturbing his rest by their persistent singing while he was journeying down this river. On the Aleutian and other islands of Bering Sea and the Asiatic Coast this is an unknown bird. It is the only form of white-crowned sparrow found in the territory of Alaska and throughout the North. The common bird of the Eastern United States does not reach these high latitudes.

ZONOTRICHIA CORONATA (Pall.) Baird.
(39.) THE GOLDEN-CROWNED SPARROW.

A rather rare summer visitant on the shores of Norton Sound, where it breeds. Its favorite haunts are the same as those of the preceding species. In the fall young and old consort with *intermedia* again on the feeding ground about the houses. Upon the Aleutian and other islands in Bering Sea this bird is unknown, nor have I any record of it along the coast north of Norton Sound.

SPIZELLA MONTANA (Forst.) Ridgw.
(40.) THE TREE SPARROW.

This is perhaps the commonest species of Sparrow frequenting the bushes along the Northern Alaskan Coast. It arrives early in May, or even the last days of April, upon the shores of Norton Sound, and, like the White-crowned Sparrow, announces its presence by first appearing about human habitations. At this time it especially favors such weed patches as have withstood the storms of winter; the convenient shelter thus formed making a favorite gathering place, where the lisping chirp of the Tree Sparrow can be heard at all times, and from which they make excursions to the garden spot by the kitchen or come into the yard. They are always timorous, however, and ready to dive into the fastnesses of their lurking place at the first alarm. Before the snow has left the thickets where they make their nests, they have taken possession as if in anxiety to commence their housekeeping. In the course of time the snow disappears; the sturdy alders begin to open their buds and take on a shade of green, while about their roots busy family groups are at work upon the soft grassy nest, which soon contains their pretty complement o eggs. All goes well, unless some wandering naturalist breaks rudely in upon the happy pair and leaves a scene of ruin behind.

Early in July the parents have a brood of full-grown young, which they straightway introduce to the vicinity of the houses, where we soon find them in full possession of the outworks of the Fort and ready to join in friendly companionship with the White-crowns and young Lapland Long Spurs. The motley crew associate in the most congenial way during this season of plenty, and a plebeian crew they make, all clad in dingy browns and dull buffy grays, each apparently without an object in life but to gorge himself on the abundance of food which the plants begin to shower down. Ere long, however, the cold storms of autumn announce the approach of winter and send many of the more sensitive off to a milder climate. September passes, the frosts and cold are more severe, and as this month ends and October begins the last of the gormands pass on to a sunnier clime.

This species breeds on the shores of Kotzebue Sound, as far north as bushes are found. I have no record of its occurrence on the adjacent Siberian shore, although it is undoubtedly found on the Chukchi Peninsula. It can scarcely be expected to occur upon any of the islands in Bering Sea from their bleak and unsuitable character.

JUNCO HYEMALIS (Linn.) Scl.
(41.) THE BLACK SNOW BIRD.

This is perhaps the most uncommon sparrow found upon the American shore of Bering Sea, and can be noted merely as a straggler from the interior of pretty regular occurrence in spring.

It is rarely seen more than two or three times during the season at Saint Michael's, although at the Yukon mouth it is rather more common. It breeds at this latter location in small numbers, and is also found sparingly in the vicinity of Kotzebue Sound and Norton Bay, as specimens brought me from those localities by natives indicate. It is unknown from the Asiatic shore to the islands of Bering Sea.

MELOSPIZA CINEREA (Gm.) Ridgw.

(42.) THE ALEUTIAN SONG SPARROW.

Among the several peculiar birds found on the Aleutian Chain this is one of the most remarkable. It forms the giant among its kin, and would scarcely be connected with its eastern relative by one not familiar with the links in the chain which unite them. It extends its range from the westernmost of the Aleutians east to Kodiak Island. It has been described under various names by the older naturalists, who secured it during the Russian occupation of the territory; but, as in many other instances, the most of our knowledge of its life history and distribution is mainly the result of work done since the country changed owners.

During a brief residence at Ounalaska, in the Aleutian Islands, in May, 1877, I became somewhat familiar with the habits of this bird at that season, and during the stay of the Corwin at the same place, in the fall of 1881, I was pleased to renew the acquaintanceship at another season. They were common in both seasons, and frequented in autumn, as in spring, the vicinity of the shore, with a preference for jutting craggy points, where great masses of rock lie at the water's edge or the rugged slope of the cliff reaches out into the bay. It is the habit of this bird to hop from rock to rock and scramble about along their inclined faces searching for their food close to the water's edge, where it feasts on the small marine animals stranded by the falling water or living there between the tide-lines. The male frequently mounts to the top of some convenient point and utters his short, rather hard, but pleasant song. This song consists of several loud, hard notes, the first two the clearest and most musical, the others rather harsh. As might be expected from the size of the bird, the song is stronger and louder than that of its eastern relative, the familiar song sparrow. During the entire time of our stay at Ounalaska, in September and October, 1881, the males showed their appreciation every pleasant day by passing a considerable portion of their time upon the roof of the warehouse at the wharf or other conspicuous position elsewhere, uttering their song at short intervals. This warehouse stood beside the wharf to which we were moored, and the passing to and fro of the men handling cargo or attending to other duty made a scene of bustling activity. In spite of this the bird was sure to be found whenever the weather favored. At other times he could be found, with one or two companions, searching the sandy beach close by for food.

PASSERELLA ILIACA (Merrem) Gm.

(43.) THE FOX-COLORED SPARROW.

Common in summer along the coast of Norton Sound, and extends its range north to the shores of Kotzebue Sound. Its loud, clear song rises from every patch of alders of any size along this stretch of coast, and the birds upon their first arrival, about the last of May, come boldly about the dwellings, uttering their loud, clear song from the roofs of the outhouses and other convenient stand-points. At the Yukon mouth it is very common, and I found its song one of the most musical and striking among the very scanty feathered choir which announces the advent of summer at that remote place. It is unknown from any of the islands in Bering's Sea, as well as from the Asiatic shore. Its range extends within the interior of the Arctic Circle, although the lack of bushes along the coast limits its occurrence except on the shores of the two sounds named.

PASSERELLA ILIACA (Gm.) Ridgw.

(44.) TOWNSEND'S SPARROW.

This species is admitted here solely by reason of the identification of Gmelin's *Emberezia a oonalascensis* as this bird. One thing is certain, and that is that since Gmelin's type no specimen of this bird has been secured at Ounalaska, although numerous naturalists have visited that locality and paid special attention to its ornithology. Neither has the bird been found on any of the eastern islands of the chain, which renders its occurrence here still more improbable. *Melospiza cinerea* occurs here, however, in three distinct plumages, one of which answers fairly to the very insufficient description given by Gmelin. The nearest place where *Passerella townsendi* has been taken is on the Shumagin Islands, south of the Peninsula of Aliaska. Of necessity the question of the exact application of Gmelin's name must remain a matter of individual opinion; but in view of the bird in question not having been taken on the Island of Ounalaska or any of the neighboring ones, it seems but fair to consider the chance of his description applying to one of the plumages of *M. cinerea*. I allow the name to remain, as Mr. Ridgway proposes, from the fact that there is little possibility of proving the question for one side or the other, but deplore the utilizing of old names, as in this instance, where there is such opportunity for error.

ICTERIDÆ. BLACKBIRDS.

SCOLECOPHAGUS FERRUGINEUS (Gm.) Swains.

(45.) THE RUSTY BLACKBIRD.

Along the eastern shore of Bering Sea, both in the spring and autumn migrations, this bird is frequently seen. It nests commonly at the mouths of the Yukon and Kuskoquim, as low down as the growth of bushes affords proper shelter. It is a common summer resident in suitable places about the Kotzebue Sound region, extending its nesting area far within the circle. It arrives at Saint Michael's about the middle of May and leaves the coast region about the last of August or first of September. It is unknown on the islands of Bering Sea and on the Asiatic coast.

CORVIDÆ. CROWS, RAVENS.

CORVUS CORAX CARNIVORUS (Bartr.) Ridgw.

(46.) THE AMERICAN RAVEN.

This bird is found abundant in many places, and is more or less common everywhere on the islands and about the shores of this region. On the Aleutian Islands it is perhaps in its greatest abundance, and is remarkably familiar, frequenting the roofs of houses and the open ground immediately in front of them, with as little regard for the presence of man as might be expected from the ordinary barn-yard fowl. Even in this place, however, it keeps its weather eye out for the deadly gun, and the moment one appears with this implement in his hand the ravens become remarkably scarce in that immediate vicinity. Their curious evolutions high in the air, preceding and during a storm, are curious to witness, and they are one of the most striking features to a new-comer in the islands. Upon the Seal Islands the crow is unaccountably absent, though it is familiar on all the other islands of Bering Sea. The Siberian and American coast alike are frequented by it both summer and winter. Nordenskiöld found crows wintering in the vicinity of the Vega, on the Arctic coast, and during my winter journeys along the Alaskan coast I found them everywhere, though less numerous at this season than during the summer.

PICA RUSTICA HUDSONICA (Scop.) Baird.

(47.) THE BLACK-BILLED MAGPIE.

At the head of Bristol Bay this bird has been taken on a few occasions, and this, so far as my knowledge extends, limits the range of the bird on the coast of Bering Sea, although it is found in the interior much farther north.

PERISOREUS CANADENSIS FUMIFRONS Ridgw.

(48.) THE SMOKY-FRONTED JAY.

In the interior this bird is one of the most common residents, and stray individuals wander to the shore of the Arctic and Bering Sea from Aliaska Peninsula north to the shore of Kotzebue Sound.

They are generally found about the mouths of streams, whose bushy borders afford them the sheltered highway which their skulking instinct leads them to favor. The only specimen I ever saw close to salt water was on the shore of Bering Sea, at Cape Romanzoff. We had camped at this cape the night before and were just leaving it as a heavy sea began to run. Pushing off, we had gained a few yards from shore when an odd note caused us to look back, and there, perched on a small bush, close by the remains of our camp fire, stood one of these birds uttering his ludicrous cries, as if making sport of us for not finding him earlier. The waves rendered the landing so dangerous that we were obliged to leave the bird in possession, and whenever I recall the scene at this camp the foreground in the mental picture is occupied by the serio-comic attitude of this bird as he flirted his tail and mocked us from his safe vantage-ground.

ALAUDIDÆ. SKYLARKS.

EREMOPHILA ALPESTRIS LUCOLÆMA Coues.

(49.) THE WHITE-THROATED SHORE LARK.

This bird occurs very rarely on the coast of Bering Sea. I secured a single specimen at Saint Michael's—the first of May—and one or two others have been taken in that vicinity, besides which I have no record of its occurrence anywhere within the region under discussion. The numerous visits made by ornithologists to these shores, during the last few years, and the scarcity of this bird in their collections prove it to be a great rarity in this region, both on the American and Siberian shores. Farther to the eastward, in the interior, the bird is more common, but is still rare, until the farther interior of the continent is reached. All the Alaskan specimens examined are referable to the name heading this article, and it is presumable that shore larks from Northeastern Siberia would be referable to the same. It is not known to occur on the Aleutian or any of the other islands in Bering Sea. It has been found nesting as far north of the old world as Nova Zembla and Spitzbergen; but it was not seen by us on the shores of Wrangel or Herald Islands nor on the adjacent Siberian coast.

TYRANNIDÆ. FLYCATCHERS.

EMPIDONAX PUSILLUS (Swains.) Bd.

(50.) THE LITTLE FLYCATCHER.

Two specimens of this bird, obtained by me at Saint Michael's in the spring, are the only ones found on the shore of Bering Sea. They add very considerably to the bird's known range.

PICIDÆ. WOODPECKERS.

PICUS PUBESCENS Linn.

(51.) THE DOWNY WOODPECKER.

The Downy Woodpecker, a common species in the interior of Alaska, makes frequent visits to the sea-shore in the north, especially during the spring and fall. It is then found about the alder patches, and rarely visits the houses. I obtained a number of specimens from the flagstaff and sides of the storehouse at Saint Michael's, during my residence there. It is more numerous at the mouths of the larger rivers, as the Yukon and Kuskoquim. Here the close approach of the wooded interior to the coast renders its presence common, and it even nests close to the sea-coast in the bushes on the lower Yukon. It is not known from any island of Bering Sea nor from the Siberian coast, but is found in the alders about Kotzebue Sound at times.

COLAPTES AURATUS (Linn.) Sw.

(52.) THE YELLOW-SHAFTED FLICKER.

This is a still more uncommon bird on the shore of Bering Sea. It approaches the coast about the head of Norton Sound, and in rare instances on Kotzebue Sound. During the winter of 1878,

I obtained a skin from a native on the coast near Bering Straits, and was informed that the bird occurred there rarely in summer, and that it nested regularly among the scattered forests a short distance in the interior. It is unknown elsewhere in the region under discussion.

ALCEDINIDÆ. KINGFISHERS.

CERYLE ALCYON (Linn.) Boie.

(53.) THE BELTED KINGFISHER.

Although a not uncommon resident in the interior, along the numerous water courses, this bird is extremely rare on the sea-coast. A single specimen was brought in by a native from the shore near the mouth of a small river to the north of Saint Michael's, and I heard of its capture at one or two other places on the shore of Norton Sound. Elsewhere I do not know of its occurrence, although it is likely to be found about Bristol Bay and perhaps the shores of Kotzebue Sound, where several fresh-water streams occur.

STRIGIDÆ. OWLS.

ASIO ACCIPITRINUS (Pall.) Newton.

(54.) THE SHORT-EARED OWL.

Along the entire Aleutian chain and thence north along the mainland of Alaska to Point Barrow this bird is found. As a summer resident on the Aleutian Islands, Dall found it rather common and found it nesting in burrows on the hillsides. In May, 1877, I found a pair of short-eared owls near Unalaska frequenting the hillsides and becoming very active after sunset. Several times while hunting, at this time of day, I disturbed the birds and found them extremely shy, so much so that they would take flight a hundred yards or more in advance, uttering at the same time a loud rolling cry. During the several years succeeding this I found they arrived the last of May or first of June along the coast of Alaska to the north, where they are summer residents and at times quite numerous. There is no record of the bird from the islands in Bering Sea, with the exception of the Aleutian chain, though its well known wandering habits undoubtedly take it to them at times. Neither is it recorded from the adjacent coast of Siberia, but its range extends through this region. On the Alaskan coast of the Arctic it is found nearly if not quite to Point Barrow.

ULULA CINEREA (Gmel.) Bp.

(55.) THE GREAT GRAY OWL.

This fine Owl can be reckoned as a very rare visitant to the shores of Bering Sea, its preference for wooded country limiting its range to those parts of the interior where spruce and other trees afford it congenial shelter. Stray individuals occur at times along the shores of Norton Sound, where the near approach of the forests to the sea along the banks of the various streams flowing into the sound afford it a convenient highway. As might be inferred from the lack of timber, it is a totally unknown species on all the islands of Bering Sea, and I do not think it is found on the opposite Siberian coast, unless by accident, as the following species visits the Alaskan shore.

ULULA CINEREA LAPPONICA (Retz.) Ridgw.

(56.) THE LAPLAND OWL.

But a single instance is known of this bird's occurrence in the region covered by this paper and the only American record as well. This record rests upon a specimen secured some years since by L. M. Turner at Saint Michael's, Norton Sound. It is a well-known species in the wooded parts of North Europe and Siberia and only occurs on the bare, forbidding coast country as a stray wanderer.

NYCTALE TEGMALMI.

(57.) TEGMALM'S OWL.

This old-world form of the Northern Sparrow Owl claims admittance to the North American fauna by the capture of a single individual near Saint Michael's, Alaska, by Mr. L. M. Turner, beyond which there is no other record of it on our shores. It is found throughout Northern Siberia wherever woodland occurs, and like the Lapland Owl reaches the open coast by merest chance, its preference being for the sheltering forests of the interior.

NCYTALE TEGMALMI RICHARDSONI (Bp.) Ridgw.

(58.) RICHARDSON'S OWL.

This Owl, although a bird of the wooded interior, also ranges along the bushy borders of the various water courses and reaches the shores of Bering Sea and Kotzebue Sound at rare and irregular intervals. It is well known to the natives, who called it "The Blind Owl," because it cannot see well during the day-time and is easily caught alive by the hand. In the interior it becomes quite numerous, and on the lower Yukon nests as low down as the vicinity of Kotlik, whence I have a set of its eggs. The bird is found resident here though only a few miles to the sea-coast. But this is exceptional, as elsewhere the surroundings are not favorable for its presence. The natives of the interior (Indians) catch this bird, tie a small piece of dried fish to its back, and and let it go, claiming they will thus secure good fortune in the hunt and in other matters.

BUBO VIRGINIAANUS SUBARCTICUS (Hoy) Ridgw.

(59.) THE NORTHWESTERN HORNED OWL.

Among the Owls which pay occasional visits to the coast of Bering Sea in Alaska, as well as to the southern portion of its arctic shores, this bird may be reckoned as the most common. Scarcely an autumn passes but a number of individuals are seen occupying conspicuous places on piles of drift wood or other prominent places along the shore in the vicinity of Saint Michael's and thence north where it is well known to the natives. Occasionally it becomes bold enough to frequent the vicinity of the houses, but this rarely occurs. Like the preceding owls, with the exception of the first mentioned, this is unknown on any of the Bering Sea islands. It is also unknown from the Asiatic shore, so far as any records which I have seen go to show.

NYCTEA SCANDIACA (Linn.) Newt.

(60.) THE SNOWY OWL.

From the Kuskoquim mouth, north along the entire Alaskan coast, as also on the northern islands in Bering Sea, the Siberian coast of this sea, and on the coast of the Arctic, this is a resident bird, perhaps most numerous in winter along the Arctic coast. It is not uncommon in summer to see this owl perched along the brow of the cliffs fronting the shore to the north of Kotzebue Sound. It is found to be extremely shy even in these far-off regions, and it is almost impossible to approach within rifle shot. As we landed upon Wrangel Island and ascended the slope of the hill rising from the beach one of these birds arose over 200 yards in advance and made off as though his experience of mankind had been anything but agreeable; yet it is certain that his habitation at that time had never before been disturbed by man. During some seasons, when the lemming abounds at any particular point, this bird becomes correspondingly numerous and preys upon this small rodent. At times, however, it attacks and kills the northern hare, and is one of the most dreaded enemies of the ptarmigan. In winter it glides on noiseless wing close along the surface of the snow, its white plumage blending so completely with the white landscape that it is followed with the greatest difficulty by the eye; ever and anon it vanishes and reappears like a shadow, as it takes its course along the shore or over the open country.

SWINIA FUNEREA (Linn.) Rich. & Sw.

(61.) THE AMERICAN HAWK OWL.

Like most of the wood-frequenting birds, this is also a rare visitant to the sea-coast of Bering Sea and Kotzebue Sound, where it occurs at intervals in the fall and spring. I secured a fine specimen from the top of the flag-staff at Saint Michael's, where it sat looking down upon the people moving about and did not show the slightest sign of fear, until it was brought down with a broken wing. When approached it threw itself in an attitude of defense and its unquailing eye commanded one's admiration for bold and undaunted courage. It occurs in about equal frequency with the Horned Owl, and is well known to the Eskimo, who confound it to a certain extent with Richardson's Owl.

SURNIA FUNEREA ULULA (Linn.) Ridgw.

(62.) THE EUROPEAN HAWK-OWL.

One specimen of this bird has been taken on the Alaskan coast, by L. M. Turner, near Saint Michael's, in winter. It is known from the Siberian shore and throughout Northern Siberia, frequenting the wooded portions of the country, with occasional stray visits to the sea-coast. Both this and the preceding are totally unknown on the islands of Bering Sea, and of exceeding rarity, if they occur at all, along the neighboring Arctic coast. The approach of the wooded country along the Bering Sea shore afford the preceding form more convenient opportunities to reach the neighborhood of the sea, yet their visits in these places are few and very short.

FALCONIDÆ. HAWKS.

HIEROFALCO GYRFALCO CANDICANS (Gm.) Ridgw.

(63.) THE WHITE GYRFALCON.

The winter of 1879 I obtained a single skin of this fine Falcon from a native on the Alaskan coast near Bering Strait. This is the only instance I have ascertained of its occurrence on our coast, although Mr. Dall learned from the people at Saint Michael's, during his residence there, that the bird occurred at rare intervals; and he adds that a little north of Bering Island one of these falcons alighted in the rigging of their vessel and remained with them for some time.

HIEROFALCO GYRFALCO SACER (Forst.) Ridgw.

(64.) MACFARLANE'S GYRFALCON.

Although the previous variety is of such rarity on the coast of Bering Sea, the present form is one of the most abundant birds of prey found in this region. A single specimen obtained by Elliott on the Seal Islands forms the only record from that group. But Dall found it on 'the Aleutian chain and from the Peninsula of Alaska north to Point Barrow on the American shore and across the straits, occupying the islands of that region and the coast of Northeastern Siberia.

This Gyrfalcon is common and is a resident throughout the year. It nests along the cliffs bordering the sea-shore, or in the interior occupying the bluffs along the river banks. It is most numerous in autumn, when the young are found about almost every rocky cliff on the coast, and it carries destruction among the migrating ptarmigan at this season. It has been claimed that this Falcon has a heavy and slow flight, but after one watches the great ease with which it overhauls a ptarmigan in full flight its power of wing is readily proved.

FALCO PEREGRINUS NÆVIUS (Gm.) Ridgw.

(65.) THE AMERICAN DUCK HAWK.

A very rare species in the interior of Northern Alaska. This Hawk is of still greater rarity on the coast of Bering Sea, where it is found only as an excessively rare visitant in the spring and autumn. It is unknown from the islands and Siberian coast of Bering Sea and from the adjacent coast of the Arctic on either side.

FALCO PEREGRINUS PEALEI Ridgw.

(66.) PEALE'S FALCON.

Along the Aleutian Islands Dall found this bird rather common and nesting at various points In his "List of Birds West of Ounalaska," he heads the list with this species, having it identified as *Falco gyrfalco*. Mr. Ridgway informs me that this bird, of which he has examined the specimen obtained by Dall and upon which the erroneous identification was based, is in reality a typical *Falco pealei*. On September 22, 1881, as the Corwin approached Ounalaska from the north six or seven of these birds were seen, one after the other, approaching from the east, and, after a circuit about the vessel, frequently coming within thirty or forty yards, they would make off to the west. At this time the island was nearly twenty miles distant. This was the only time that the bird was observed during the ten days spent at Ounalaska. It is unknown north of the Aleutian Islands, although it undoubtedly extends farther north along the Alaskan shore.

ÆSALON COLUMBARIUS (Linn.) Kaup.

(67.) THE PIGEON HAWK.

This well-known Hawk occurs along the entire Alaskan coast north beyond the shores of Kotzebue Sound. Across Bering Sea it has been taken at Plover Bay and several other points on that coast. Of the woodland birds of prey this is one of the most common species to visit the barren coast region, and may be looked for as a rather frequent and regular visitant along the shores of Norton Sound, Bering Strait, and Kotzebue Sound in spring, summer, and autumn. A skin was brought on board the Corwin from one of the islands in Bering Strait in the summer of 1881. Although numerous in the portions of this region named, it is yet unknown from the Aleutian and Seal Islands, the bleak, rugged character of their shores probably proving unattractive to this small but bold Falcon.

PANDION HALIÆTUS CAROLINENSIS (Gm.) Ridgw.

(68.) THE AMERICAN FISH-HAWK.

In the interior the Fish-Hawk is a not very uncommon bird as far north as the wooded country extends; thence it occasionally visits the shores of Bering Sea. Two were seen the last of May at the Yukon mouth in 1879, and two specimens were brought me from the head of Norton Sound during the summer of 1878. These records include all the information I possess regarding this bird on the coasts herein treated. Whether it is found on the Siberian shore or not in these high latitudes I have no information, although its presence to the south in the Kurile Islands and southward render it probable that it does.

CIRCUS HUDSONIUS (Linn.) Vieill.

(69.) THE MARSH HAWK.

A common migrant along the Alaskan shore of Bering Sea, occasionally found on the Aleutian Islands and extending its range north beyond Kotzebue Sound. It undoubtedly occurs upon the adjoining coast of Siberia, although I do not possess any record of its having been observed there.

ACCIPITER FUSCUS (Gmel.) Bp.

(70.) THE SHARP-SHINNED HAWK.

Like the Pigeon Hawk, the Sharp-shinned Hawk occurs during the entire summer season, from spring to fall; but, unlike the former, it is of considerable rarity and found, as far as my information goes, only along the Alaskan coast, including the shores of Bering Sea and Kotzebue Sound, but not extending to the islands of this sea nor to the adjoining coast of Siberia.

ASTUR ATRICAPILLUS (Wils.) Bp.

(71.) THE AMERICAN GOSHAWK.

Wherever the Ptarmigan is found in the vicinity of the wooded country, and frequently far distant from a tree or bush, this bold, hardy bird is found as its unwelcome companion. In spring the Goshawk is occasionally seen passing over Saint Michael's as the first warm, sunshiny days begin. Then on, until the breeding season is over, it is seen no more. But in autumn it returns to the sea-coast in considerable numbers; about equaling the Gyrfalcon in abundance for a time, and like that species preying upon the migrating Ptarmigan.

Among the many records of this bird's boldness, I possess an additional one obtained during the visit of the Corwin to Kotzebue Sound in September, 1881. I had winged a Ptarmigan on the top of the famous ice cliff of Escholtz Bay and the bird fell just beyond a small knoll from me; the instant the Ptarmigan struck the ground, I was surprised to see a Goshawk dart out from a small alder patch near at hand and with a graceful inclination pick up the bird and make off with it; which so surprised me that I stood watching the performance until the hawk had made good its escape. As it flew away a second bird, evidently its mate, joined it, and the two passed over the hill and disappeared from view.

By a careful comparison of specimens in the Smithsonian Institution with the considerable series obtained by me in the north, I have reached the conclusion that Mr. Ridgway's variety *Striatulus* is nothing but the plumage assumed by the older birds, as is readily shown by several specimens in which the change made from the immature plumage to that of the adult is taking place. Mr. Ridgway has examined the same series and concurs with me in this conclusion.

ARCHIBUTEO LAGOPUS SANCTI-JOHANNIS (Gmel.) Ridgw.

(72.) THE AMERICAN ROUGH-LEGGED HAWK.

Along the entire Alaskan coast of Bering Sea and the Arctic, including at least the eastern portion of the Aleutian Islands, the Rough-legged Hawk is a common resident in summer. At Ounalaska I found a pair breeding upon a cliff near the village, and secured one of the birds with their eggs in May, 1877. At Saint Michael's it was found nesting upon cliffs on the border of a small lake in the interior of the island, and the bird was among the most common of the migrating birds of prey. The Ounalaskan specimen is indistinguishable in every particular from a European specimen in the Smithsonian collection, and the basis for the separation of the American bird from that of Europe and the northern portions of the Old World generally is merely in the black phase assumed by the American bird in the Hudson Bay and adjoining region. In Alaska this phase is unknown as far as my observation goes, and is totally unrepresented in the considerable series of specimens obtained by myself and various others in that region. This being the case, and various Alaskan birds which I have examined being so closely related to the old world form, it appears necessary to recognize them under the name of the old world bird. Thus limiting the geographical variety, *Sancti-Johannis*, to that portion of the continent where it actually occurs.

The Rough-Leg occurs in Siberia, and in China is a species with dark feathers to the thighs, but very similar in other respects to *lagopus*.

AQUILA CHRYSAETUS CANADENSIS (Linn.) Ridgw

(73.) THE GOLDEN EAGLE.

This is one of the rarest among the birds of prey on the shores of Bering Sea and the adjoining portion of the Arctic Ocean. I know of no record of its occurrence on the Asiatic shore nor on the islands of Bering Sea, but in the winter of 1879 I saw portions of one of these birds in a native village near Bering Strait, and fragments of their skins were brought to me in one or two instances from the shore of Norton Sound during my residence at Saint Michael's. The quills and tail of this bird, like those of the Bald Eagle, are highly prized by the Eskimo for use in their religious festivals.

HALIAEETUS LEUCOCEPHALUS (Linn.) Savig.

(74.) THE BALD EAGLE.

Among the Aleutian Islands this eagle is very abundant, and frequently as many as ten or fifteen may be seen in a single day over a limited area. It is a denizen here, finding an abundance of high cliffs and crags upon which to rear its young, and about which it soars in fine weather. North, along the coast, this eagle is rather uncommon, owing mainly to the very low, flat character of the country. Wherever the coast becomes mountainous or cliffs abut on the seashore one is pretty certain to find one or more pairs of these birds in the vicinity. It ranges considerably within the Arctic Circle wherever the mountainous character of the country is such as to attract. The abundance of reindeer and other game has its influence as well. During my residence at Saint Michael's a number of birds were seen passing over, and quite a number of skins were brought me by the Eskimo from various points along the coast to Bering Straits and Kotzebue Sound.

The great Sea Eagle of the Kamtchatkan coast and Bering Islands has been reported from the Aleutian chain, but the Bald Eagle was undoubtedly mistaken for it.

TETRAONIDÆ. GROUSE.

CANACE CANADENSIS (Linn.) Bp.

(75.) THE SPRUCE PARTRIDGE.

This, one of the handsomest of our grouse, occurs from the Northern States through British America to the shores of Bering Sea, at the head of Norton Sound, where the spruce forests approach and directly border on the shore. It is not abundant here but is a sparing resident and breeds. Further in the interior it becomes more numerous. Its range may approach the sea-shore again about the head of Bristol Bay, where the forest reaches within a short distance of the coast; but we have no data from that region. In the wooded interior of Siberia this fine grouse is represented by a closely related form, *falcipennis*, which is not known to approach any of the shores under discussion. The Spruce Grouse from the vicinity of Bering Straits is identical in every way with specimens from Maine and New Brunswick, and thus shows less sensitiveness to climatic influence than the following species.

BONASA UMBELLUS UMBELLOIDES (Dougl.) Baird.

(76.) THE GRAY RUFFED GROUSE.

In the same localities as the preceding is found occurs this bird, which forms the northern variety of the familiar Partridge, or Ruffed Grouse, of the entire eastern North America. I had no opportunity to learn anything of special interest concerning the habits of either this or the preceding species along the coast region mentioned. With the exception of the wooded country at the head of Bristol Bay there is no portion of the Bering Sea coast where either the Spruce or Ruffed Grouse would occur, as the remainder of the shore and all the islands are destitute of trees.

LAGOPUS ALBUS (Gm.) Aud.

(77.) THE WHITE PTARMIGAN.

The White Ptarmigan, or Willow Grouse, occurs in greater numbers in Northern Alaska than all the other species of grouse combined. Along the northern portion of the country wherever open country occurs it is found in abundance, and especially along the shores of Bering Sea and the Arctic Ocean, where it breeds in great numbers. The last of April and first of May throughout this region, from the mouth of the Kuskoquim River north to Point Barrow, the loud notes and peculiar movements of the males form one of the most characteristic features at this season, and render the birds very conspicuous. It is found on the adjoining coast of Siberia as well as on the American shore, but does not occur on the Aleutian Islands, with the single exception, perhaps, of the easternmost island adjoining the peninsula of Aliaska, where two species of Ptarmigan are said to occur. To the west of the island on the Aleutian chain it is not found, being replaced by the species mentioned below. Neither is it found on the fur seal nor any of the other islands in Bering Sea, with the possible exception of Saint Lawrence. In the autumn, just previously to the severe winter storms, there is a partial migration of this Ptarmigan from the Arctic coast south to the valleys of the Yukon and Kuskoquim, where the sheltering thickets of willow and alder afford it refuge during the winter. As spring re-opens it passes to the north and regains its breeding grounds. Some of the hardier among these birds, however, remain during the entire winter in the extreme north. On September 8, 1881, while the Corwin lay in Kotzebue Sound, these Grouse were gathering in considerable flocks, preparing for their southern migration. They were found along the shore where the abundant supply of berries afforded them food. They were attended as usual by numerous Goshawks, and several Gyrfalcons were seen in the vicinity. In spring, while the males are paying court to the objects of their choice, they select some slight elevation, such as a prominent knoll or a snow bank, upon which they take their stand and utter their loud, harsh note of defiance, or do battle with some roving free-lance of their kind.

LAGOPUS RUSPESTRIS (Gm.) Leach.

(78.) THE ROCK PTARMIGAN.

Along the eastern shore of Bering Sea and the Arctic Ocean in Alaska, wherever the mountains or high hills approach the sea, this grouse occurs. It is found in the immediate vicinity of Saint Michael's, frequenting the hill-tops in summer and seeking the shelter of the willows and alders about their bases in winter. On the coast to the north, reaching the vicinity of Bering Strait, I found them numerous in the winter of 1879. They are much more unsuspicious than the preceding species, and will allow a very close approach, standing with their heads raised inquiringly and a pretty air of wonderment about them. In winter their beautiful milk-white plumage, with the sharply contrasted jet-black bill and bar through the eye, renders them very handsome objects, particularly when seen in life. Their shape and movements on the ground are also much more graceful and elegant than those of the ordinary Ptarmigan. They exist in far smaller numbers than the White Ptarmigan, and their range is more restricted, owing to the low and little varied character of the northern coast country. Wherever low mountains or hills occur throughout the northern portion of the territory, however, this bird may be confidently expected to occur. On the Aleutian Islands it is represented by forms which are mentioned below, and the Siberian shore has a form perhaps identical with this; but, as Professor Nordenskiöld records those taken by the Vega party at their winter quarters as *L. subalpinus*, this name is accepted as applying to the Northeastern Siberian bird, since there are no specimens at hand from that region.

LAGOPUS RUPESTRIS (Gm.) Leach.

(79.) ROCK PTARMIGAN.

On the Island of Ounalaska, thence to the eastward and also to the westward for an uncertain distance, occurs the handsome Ptarmigan designated above. Of this form there are but two specimens in existence in the summer plumage. These are a male and female obtained by me on the hills back of Ounalaska in the spring of 1877. The winter bird, of which the Smithsonian possesses a single example obtained by Mr. Dall, is indistinguishable from the winter plumage of the ordinary Rock Grouse. This specimen lacks the black border through the eye, but this character appears to be merely individual. This is the species which in Mr. Dall's papers on the birds of the Aleutian Islands he designated as the White Ptarmigan, *Lagopus albus*, and in the Bulletin of the Nuttall Ornithological Club for 187 I recorded the capture of the two specimens previously mentioned under the name of *Lagopus rupestris*.

Beyond the mere capture of the bird there is little known of its habits, the only data which I can furnish being that it frequents the mountain tops and slopes among the Eastern Aleutian Islands, and is common there, breeding during June.

The detailed description of this form will be given in the account of the Birds of Alaska, now in course of preparation.

LAGOPUS RUPESTRIS OCCIDENTALIS Turner.

(80.) ATKHAN PTARMIGAN.

At the western end of the Aleutian chain occurs another form of Ptarmigan, as is shown by specimens secured on the Island of Atkha by Mr. L. M. Turner during his residence at that place. This form differs in several important respects from the Oonalaskan birds, as it does also from the bird of the mainland. Mr. Turner has designated his interesting variety as given at the head of this paragraph, and describes it in his Contributions to the Ornithology of Alaska, which at the present writing is being prepared. Concerning the habits of this form I possess no information. Its distribution, however, must be limited, since it is found only on the western extremity of the Aleutian chain, and very probably forms merely a local race peculiar to the island where obtained, perhaps extending its range to the few adjoining islands.

LAGOPUS ALPINUS

(81.) SUBALPINE PTARMIGAN.

On the north coast of Siberia occurs this form, according to the narrative of the Vega's voyage, in which Nordenskiöld records finding this species resident at their winter quarters on the Siberian coast to the northwest of Bering Straits. In the middle of December he found a flock of fifty of them at Tapkan. Still farther to the west along the shore occurs this or an allied species, as Hedenstrom records, a species of Ptarmigan wintering upon the New Siberian Islands, which is the same as is found on the adjacent coast of Siberia. It seems remarkable that these birds should be able to sustain life during the intense cold and fierce storms which sweep over these desolate Arctic islands. Nordenskiöld, in his Voyage of the Vega, states that they found a "fell" in the winter of 1872, just south of the eightieth parallel, on Spitzbergen, where about 1,000 of these birds wintered. He thinks some of these at times hybernate in crevices among the rocks or pass the winter "in a kind of torpid state." Whether this hybernation theory is justified by the facts or not, it certainly appears very curious that these grouse are able to winter in 80° north latitude, passing safely through the several weeks of continuous total darkness which occurs there in midwinter, and be found fat and vigorous as soon as the sun appears above the horizon; yet such are the recorded facts. Just how the bird manages to exist during this time remains to be satisfactorily accounted for. The species found in Spitzbergen, to which this relates, is the *Lagopus Hyperboreus*. Just what the relationship is which the Rock Grouse of Northeastern Siberia bears to those found on the adjacent coast of North America and to the Aleutian Islands races remains a question to be solved only when a sufficient series of the birds from the various regions in question may be brought together. At present the material in this puzzling group is entirely insufficient to make any definite statement on the matter, and it will remain for some future explorer to solve the problem. It is to be hoped that some of the present parties now in that region will bring material which will aid in settling this interesting subject.

HÆMATOPODIDÆ. OYSTER CATCHERS.

HÆMATOPUS NIGER PALL.

(82.) THE BLACK OYSTER CATCHER.

The Black Oyster Catcher, although one of the most robust of the waders found in the North, does not extend its range beyond the shores of the Aleutian Islands, and thence across to the Kurile Islands and adjoining Asiatic coast, where it is recorded by Pallas.

STREPSILAS INTERPRES (Linn.) Illig.

(83.) THE COMMON TURNSTONE.

Along the entire Alaskan coast, from the Aleutian Islands north to Point Barrow, this bird is a summer resident, although it does not occur in abundance at any point. Its habits are very similar to those of the other small waders with which it associates during this season. In autumn it passes to the south, and is found on the various islands of Bering Sea, except perhaps the Aleutian chain, where it is yet to be recorded; although, as it has been found abundant during the migrations on the Seal Islands by Elliott, there is no doubt whatever that it also visits the Aleutian chain. In addition to migrating along the west coast of America it also passes along the Asiatic coast, by way of the Kurile Islands, to Japan and southward, where it has been recorded in winter, and the Smithsonian has recently received spring birds in breeding plumage from Japan. To the north along this coast it occurs as far as Bering Strait, if not beyond. A number of pairs were seen mated and with nests on Saint Lawrence Island the last of June, 1881; and while the Corwin was coaling in the vicinity of Cape Lisburne, during the first of August, 1881, I found these birds quite numerous on the hills back from the coast, where they had been breeding earlier in the season. The young were on the wing at the time of our visit, and were found with their parents seeking their food about the dry, hilly portions of the country in preference to their usual haunts along the sea-shore or low grassy flats. They were seen afterwards near Point Barrow and at Kotzebue Sound.

STREPSILAS MELANOCEPHALA Vig.

(84.) THE BLACK TURNSTONE.

This species is far more numerous on the coast of Alaska during the summer than is the preceding. It breeds abundantly about the coast of Norton Sound, and its familiar form is met everywhere on the flat, grassy marshes and about the borders of brackish pools in this region.

As the Corwin approached Wrangel Island, during the first of August, on her several attempts to reach that land, small parties of these birds came off and circled about the ship, with wistful curiosity, as if to inquire the cause and purpose of this invasion into these heretofore unapproached shores. They were also observed once or twice in the vicinity of Herald Island.

On shore at Wrangel Island we did not see a single example of these birds, although our hasty visit might readily account for this. They occur on both coasts of Bering Sea. Their winter home, so far as recorded, appears to be confined to the west coast of America, as no instance is known to me of its capture during this season on the southeast coast of Asia. It may be remarked here that among the very large collection of these two species of Turnstones obtained by me in the North and compared with the extensive series from that region which exists in the Smithsonian collection, there does not appear to be the slightest intergradation of the characters showing an approach of the two forms; so there is every reason for agreeing with Mr. Ridgway and terming the Black Turnstone a distinct species. The common Turnstone of the Bering Sea coast and Eastern Asia, perhaps including those which are found on the islands of the South Pacific, appear to show an average much darker plumage than birds from middle and northeastern America, and it is possible that it may be necessary to separate it from its eastern relative as a geographical race, in which case the varietal name *pacificus* is proposed for the new form.

CHARADRIIDÆ. PLOVERS.

APHRIZA VIRGATA (Gmel.) Gray.

(85.) THE SURF BIRD.

During several successive autumns at Saint Michael's, I had the good fortune to secure specimens of this widely spread and interesting bird. It had previously been taken along the coast of the North Pacific, reaching the southeastern shore of Alaska and thence southward, but the present record is the first of its occurrence in Bering Sea and places its range beyond 63° north latitude, and it undoubtedly reaches the vicinity of Bering Strait, which lies but a short distance farther to the north. In the vicinity of Saint Michael's it frequents the rocky shores of the small outlying islands and the capes, whose rugged beach lines afford them congenial haunts. Their habits and feeding grounds are exactly those of the Wandering Tattler, and both species occur in autumn or during the entire month of August, which answers in this latitude to the beginning of autumn in more southern latitudes. They are never common, but appear as stray individuals and are not shy.

SQUATAROLA HELVETICA Linn. Cuv.

(86.) THE BLACK-BELLIED PLOVER.

This handsomely plumaged Plover reaches the shores of Bering Sea in May, and remains to breed at various points, frequenting the vicinity of the larger river mouths by preference, although it occurs at various other points along the coast. Its range also extends to the Asiatic Shore, where it is not numerous, and north to Point Barrow, in Alaska. It has not been recorded from any of the islands of Bering Sea, although from its known range on the mainland it undoubtedly occurs on many of them.

CHARADRIUS DOMINICUS Mull.

(87.) THE AMERICAN GOLDEN PLOVER.

The large form of the Golden Plover, which is so familiar to all in the Eastern United States, extends its summer range north and northwest to the shores of the Arctic Ocean and thence to the entire Alaskan coast of Bering Sea, ranging occasionally to the adjacent Siberian shore and the islands in this sea, whence specimens have been obtained. Along this portion of its range, including the Bering Sea islands and the North Alaskan coast, its habitat intermingles with that of the small Asiatic form, which also comes to these northern latitudes in summer to rear its young. The Golden Plover is one of the handsomest as well as most interesting of the waders occurring in the North, and its gentle habits and sweetly modulated notes make it a very welcome visitor. During the mating season the males have a rich liquid song of the most musical character, and their beautifully blended black, white, and golden plumage renders them very conspicuous.

CHARADRIUS DOMINICUS FULVUS (Gmel.) Ridgw.

(88.) THE PACIFIC GOLDEN PLOVER.

The first record of this form on American territory was in Elliott's "Condition of Affairs in Alaska." Here is described a single specimen of typical *fulvus* which he obtained upon Saint Paul Island. During my residence in the North I gathered a large series of Golden Plover, mainly from the coast of Norton Sound, and among these I found every step of gradation between the large Eastern American and small Eastern Asiatic form. A strange fact to be noted here is that the adults taken on the Bering sea-coast of Alaska average large, and show characteristics which render them more closely allied or identical with the Eastern American form, whereas the young birds taken in the same localities are so covered with rich golden spots and shading that they would be unhesitatingly referred to the variety *fulvus*. Along the entire Asiatic shore of Bering Sea this form occurs as a summer resident, wherever the country is sufficiently level to afford it proper feeding ground and breeding places. It was also one of the few birds we found on Wrangel Island, a single specimen in breeding plumage being seen when we made our landing on the 12th of August. As in the case of the Turnstone, the Golden Plover is yet to be recorded from the Aleutian Islands, although it must necessarily visit them during its migrations. While midway between Ounalaska and California, the 1st of October, 1881, a small flock of these birds were seen passing overhead, steering their course directly for the Sandwich Islands, which were about one thousand miles distant at the time. They make this long flight twice annually, passing to and fro across the entire North Pacific, and winter upon the Sandwich Islands, summering north of the Aleutian chain.

ÆGIALITES SEMIPALMATUS Bonap.

(89.) THE SEMI-PALMATED PLOVER.

On both shores of Bering Sea, extending on the Alaskan coast from the peninsula of Aliaska north to Point Barrow and along the entire northeastern Asiatic coast. To the northwest of Bering Strait, wherever we landed from the Corwin during the summer of 1881, these birds were found, although sparingly. It was not seen abundantly in any locality, but a pair of adults were found in almost every instance where we made the land except on Wrangel and Herald Islands. It was found on Saint Lawrence Island, in Bering Sea, and I noted it as a regular but not numerous summer resident on the shore of Norton Sound.

ÆGIALITES MONGOLICUS.

(90.) THE MONGOLIAN PLOVER.

There is a single record of this bird's occurrence in Alaska.

Two specimens were obtained on Choris Peninsula, in Kotzebue Sound, during the summer of 1849, by the English search-ship Plover, and were for a long time in Sir John Barrow's collection, presented a few years since to the University Museum at Oxford, where the examples are to be found at present. The record of this is in the "Proceedings of the Zoological Society" of 1871, page 110, where Mr. J. E. Harting makes various interesting remarks concerning the different birds in this collection.

SCOLOPACIDÆ. SNIPE.

GALLINAGO MEDIA WILSONI (Temm.) Ridgw.

(91.) WILSON'S SNIPE.

This bird is abundant in the interior of the fur countries, where it breeds. It is among the most uncommon of the waders found along the shores of Bering Sea, where, however, it breeds in small numbers. It also occurs on the Arctic coast, especially about Kotzebue Sound, but is unknown at any of the Bering Sea islands or the Northeastern shore of Siberia, although its range undoubtedly includes this latter region, as we found the following species there.

MACRORHAMPHUS GRISEUS SCOLOPACENUS (Say) Coues.

(92.) THE RED-BELLIED SNIPE.

The present species largely replaces the latter on the shores of the American coast of Bering Sea and is extremely abundant. Its peculiar habits and odd notes in spring make it one of the most conspicuous waders found along our shores. In fall it is silent, but abundant in flocks everywhere along the flat coast wherever brackish pools and shallow tide creeks afford it suitable feeding ground. It is also found about the shores of Kotzebue Sound and still further north, and breeds throughout this range. We found it common at Cape Wankarem, on the North Siberian coast, on August 6, 1881. But there is not a record of it from the islands in Bering Sea.

ARQUATELLA MARITIMA (Brünn.) Baird.

(93.) THE ALEUTIAN SAND PIPER.

Along the entire Aleutian chain this Sand Piper, lately described by Mr. Ridgway, is a common resident, breeding throughout its range and straying northward along the entire Bering Sea coast during the autumn. Although it does not breed anywhere in the region about Norton Sound, yet during August and September, up to the closing of the sea by ice in October, it is very numerous. The Purple Sand Piper, mentioned by Pallas as occurring on the Kurile Islands, answers to this species, and this being the case, the range of this bird must be extended to these islands and the adjoining coast of Asia. The present bird is known to have been captured on the Asiatic shore, in the vicinity of Bering Strait, and the record of Nordenskiöld of *Tringa maritima*, occurring at his winter quarters to the northwest of Bering Strait, must refer to the present bird, since the true Purple Sand Piper is replaced in this region by the present form. This record of Nordenskiöld is the first one we have of the presence of this bird in the Arctic, though on the American coast it also occurs in autumn on the shores of Kotzebue Sound. It is exclusively a shore bird, and if it occurs at all in any region may be confidently looked for wherever the coast is most rugged and strewn with rocks to the water's edge. Most of the former records of *Tringa maritima* in Bering Sea and the adjoining regions refer to the present bird, with an occasional reference to the following species when speaking of the Seal Islands. This species, *couesi*, winters on the Aleutian Islands as well as along the shores of the mainland in the Sitkan region and south.

ARQUATELLA PTILOCNEMIS (Coues) Ridgw.

(94.) THE PRIBYLOV SAND PIPER.

This curious Snipe is limited in summer to the Fur Seal Islands, and thence extends north to Saint Matthew's and to Saint Lawrence Islands, the first and only record of its occurrence on the latter island being a pair observed by us on the southern shore June 24, 1881, when we landed from the Corwin during a gale. The male was seen keeping close to the native huts, and was very unsuspicious, allowing us to approach within a few paces; he kept rising on vibrating wings in the face of the fierce wind blowing over the summit of the hill on which we found him, and uttering a sharp, metallic, trilling note, much louder and harder than the somewhat similar note of *Tringa semipalmata*.

Thus far, although this bird is known to be a migrant, leaving its summer home on the islands mentioned at the approach of winter, its habitat during the cold season is unknown. Whether it is confined to the southern shore of the Aleutian chain or passes to some portion of the American or Asiatic coast yet remains to be ascertained.

ACTODROMAS ACUMINATA (Horsf.) Ridgw.

(95.) THE SHARP TAILED SAND PIPER.

The first knowledge of this bird's occurrence on the coast of America was obtained by me at Saint Michael's, where it is an abundant species every autumn, coming during August and remaining until the sharp frosts of the approaching winter cause it to hasten away. Following my capture of the species comes its capture on the coast of Kotzebue Sound, at Hotham Inlet, the 1st of September, 1880, by Captain Hooper, on the Corwin, during his first cruise in the Arctic; and on the 9th of September the same season Dr. Bean, on the Coast Survey schooner Yukon, secured a second specimen at Port Clarence, Bering Strait, and this concludes our present knowledge of the distribution of the species on the American coast. During the summer of 1881, on the 1st of August, we landed from the Corwin on the northeast coast of Siberia, in the vicinity of Cape Wankarem, and found these birds numerous, feeding on the flats which were closely bordering the shores of the Arctic Ocean and sparingly grown up with fine grass. From the actions of the birds at this time it was evident that they had nested in the vicinity, and this region is probably the true summer home of this handsome species. During the migration it has been taken in Japan and along the east coast of Asia, and is known to winter in Australia and Southern India.

ACTODROMAS MACULATA (Vieill.) Coues.

(96.) THE PECTORAL SAND PIPER.

On the American coast of Bering Sea, as also at Kotzebue Sound, this bird is a common if not abundant summer resident. It is perhaps most numerous about the Yukon mouth, where it was preparing to breed in considerable numbers early in June, 1879. It is unknown from any of the Bering Sea islands, but on the north coast of Siberia, during the summer of 1881, we found them numerous in company with the Sharp Tailed Sand Piper. At several points where we landed it was found wherever grassy flats occur affording it proper feeding grounds. In a recent letter to the New York Herald, received from Mr. R. L. Newcomb, the Naturalist of the Jeannette, we learn that on the 18th of August, 1880, while their vessel was frozen in the ice to the northwest of Wrangel Island, a pair of these birds came on board. This extends their known range north to about 76° of latitude, and renders it probable that they breed on the islands of the Arctic Ocean in this region.

EURINORHYNCHUS PYGRANUS (?)

(97.) THE SPOONBILLED SAND PIPER.

This peculiarly marked bird has recently had several very interesting additions made to its known history by the observations made by Nordenskiöld in the spring of 1879, by Dr. Bean in the summer of 1880, and myself in 1881. On the northeast coast of Siberia Nordenskiöld records this bird as occurring in such numbers that on two occasions in spring it was served upon their mess table on board the Vega while they were lying frozen in at their winter quarters. It arrived in spring at Tapkan, with the first bare spots, early in June, and disappeared in July. To the westward, in the same vicinity, during the summer of 1881, I saw several of these birds, and at Plover Bay, on the Bering Sea shore of the same coast, secured a fine adult female in breeding plumage, taken on June 26. Nothing peculiar was observed in its habits, and I approached the bird without difficulty or its showing the slightest concern as it stood on the flat at that place. The bird was first seen feeding in the shallow water at the edge of a pool, and then stood with its head drawn back and without paying the slightest attention to me until it was shot. It is a handsomely plumaged species, as is shown in the accompanying plate by Mr. Ridgway. There is a single known instance of its occurrence on the American coast, and this was at Hotham Inlet, where a specimen was secured by the English ship Plover during the summer of 1849. The record of this specimen is in the proceedings of the London Zoological Society for 1871, page 110, where we learn that this specimen taken on Choris Peninsula, Hotham Inlet, was lately presented to the Oxford Museum, among other birds in the collection of Sir John Barrow.

In the Ibis for 1875, Mr. Swinholm records a specimen killed at Hakodadi, Japan, in September, and it is well known as a winter resident in the south of Asia, its summer home being apparently, from the records we now possess, the northeastern Arctic shores of Asia. There have been various records of the bird in Europe, and especially in France. But Mr. Harting doubts their authenticity, and says: "M. Jules Verreaux has recently informed me that no specimen of *Eurynorhynchus* ever existed in the Paris Museum, and that the bird to which Lessing refers under the head of *Eurynorhynchus Griseus*, and a specimen under *Ecolia euria, Vieillot*, is nothing less than a *Tringa* with the hind toes cut off and bill remodeled with the aid of some warm water."

The proceedings testified to the rarity of this species in French Museums, and the manner in which an artificial evolution may be encompassed. Mr. Harting continues by stating that nothing is known of its nesting, and he refers to the unexplored region of Northeastern Asia as the place likely to afford light on this point as well as upon a number of other little known species, and his surmise has proved correct in this instance at least. A passable figure of this bird in breeding plumage, taken from the specimen secured on the Choris Peninsula by the Plover, is to be found in the Ibis for 1869. Up to October of this year twenty-four specimens were known to Mr. Harting, of which twenty-three were recorded from Southern India, and these were doubtless all in winter plumage.

The description of the specimen secured by me is as follows: Crown feathers with blackish centres edged with rusty reddish approaching chestnut. Back of neck with the dark centres becoming much fainter and the borders rufous, changing to buffy reddish, which, in addition to edging the feathers, appears to wash their surface and the dark central portions. The back and scapulars have well marked black centres edged with rufous buffy and grayish intermixed. The tertials have dark brownish centres edged with grayish and russet. Wing coverts light brown edged with gray. The secondaries largely white, and an imperfect wing-bar formed by the white tips to the secondary coverts. Quills grayish brown approaching black at the tips. The chin is whitish, washed with a pale shade of rufous, this latter shade becoming bright over the sides of the head and entire lower surface of neck, reaching the upper portion of the breast. The forehead and around the base of bill washed with grayish over the rufous bases of feathers. The breast is rich buffy, changing to white on the posterior half of breast and entire abdomen. A scattered band of dark opaque shaft spots cross the breast, and extend back on the sides which are otherwise white. The tail is dark ashy brown; bill, foot, and tarsus black. The wing measures 3.95 inches; the tail, approximately, 1.50 inches. This member was injured by shot to such an extent that the perfect dimensions cannot be secured. Tarsus, .90 inch; culmen, .90 inch; width of expanded tip, .47 inch. The hind toe is perfect but minute. The toes are not webbed.

ACTODROMAS BAIRDI Coues

(98.) BAIRD'S SAND PIPER.

Along the Arctic coast, from Point Hope to Point Barrow, during the summer of 1881, wherever we landed from the Corwin this species was found common, especially at Point Barrow, where forty or fifty were observed scattered about the edges of the pools and sand-spits at that place during our visit. It occurs sparingly on the Siberian shore, and a young bird has been sent to the Smithsonian Institution which was obtained on Arakamacherhi Island, near Saint Lawrence Bay. On the coast of Norton Sound it is a rare bird, occurring only occasionally during the migrations and rarely if ever breeding in that vicinity. It is not recorded from any of the Bering Sea islands, although it is undoubtedly found on Saint Lawrence during the nesting season and visits the others as a stray migrant.

ACTODROMAS MINUTILLA (Vieill.) Bp.

(99.) THE LEAST SAND PIPER.

Like the preceding, this Sand Piper is very rare on the Norton Sound shore of Bering Sea, and thence north along the Arctic coast. It is considerably outnumbered by the last species. There is no record of its occurrence on the Siberian shore, nor is it known from any of the Bering Sea islands.

PELIDNA ALPINA AMERICANA Cass

(100.) THE RED BACKED SAND PIPER.

About the entire Bering Sea shore of Alaska, north of Kotzebue Sound, and across along the adjoining coast of Siberia, wherever we landed during the summer of 1881, this bird was found abundant. A number of specimens were secured at Cape Wankarem, on August 7, 1881, and are identical with specimens secured on the American coast. It breeds wherever found in this region, and is one of the commonest waders, arriving at Saint Michael's early in May, and it appears throughout this region as rapidly as the snow leaves the ground sufficiently bare for birds to secure their food. It was also noted as common on Saint Lawrence Island, in Bering Sea, but it is unknown elsewhere on the islands of this sea, except as an occasional visitant to the Seal Islands during the migrations.

EREUNETES PUSILLUS (Linn.) Cass.

(101.) THE SEMI-PALMATED SAND PIPER.

Along the entire Alaskan coast, from the Peninsula of Aliaska to Point Barrow, as well as on the coast of Northeastern Asia and Saint Lawrence Island, Bering Sea, this small Sand Piper is a common summer resident, breeding wherever the land bordering the coast is level and dotted with pools or lakelets. It is perhaps the most abundant of the waders throughout this region, and its rapid trilling note is heard on every hand during the day in the mating season.

CALIDRIS ARENARIA (Linn.) Illig.

(102.) THE SANDERLING.

In Mr. Dall's list of the birds of Alaska he gives the present species as common at Nulato and thence down the Yukon to the sea-coast. During the time of my residence in the territory, and including the various points visited during the cruise of the Corwin, on both the Siberian and American shores, not a single individual of this bird was seen. It occurs, however, in this region, but is irregular, and I am inclined to think somewhat rare. We learn from a letter in the New York Herald, from Mr. Newcomb, that while the Jeannette party were passing to the mouth of the Lena there was a considerable number of these birds seen upon Thaddeus Island, one of the Liakhov Group, on August 30, 1881, and they secured twelve of the birds. This is not a well-known bird in these regions, but specimens have been seen and procured by nearly every Arctic expedition, and its circumpolar distribution renders still more strange the great scarcity of the bird on the Norton Sound shore, where during the four years I passed there not an individual was seen. It is known, however, from the eastern coast of Asia, on the shores of Japan and China, as well as on the Kurile Islands and along the Pacific coast of America in the middle latitudes.

LIMOSA LAPPONICA NOVÆ-ZEALANDIÆ Gray.

(103.) THE PACIFIC GODWIT.

Occurring during both migrations on the Aleutian Islands and thence north along the other islands of Bering Sea, and abundant on the Bering Sea shore of Alaska during the breeding season. It is not known to nest, however, except on the mainland, merely occurring during its passage to and fro upon the islands mentioned. It is also known from Northeastern Siberia, although no examples were seen during the summer of 1881 at the points we visited in the Corwin. Nor was it seen to the north of Bering Straits, either on the shore of Kotzebue Sound or beyond, and I do not know of its occurrence there. The loud notes of this bird and its large size render it one of the most conspicuous among the waders of the Bering Sea coast of Alaska. Its presence there in considerable numbers makes it a characteristic and important member of the avian fauna. They arrive in the vicinity of Saint Michael's the last of May or first of June, and after nesting leave for the South during August, a few only remaining until September.

LIMOSA HÆMASTICA (Linn.) Coues.

(104.) THE HUDSONIAN GODWIT.

Mr. Dall secured two specimens of this bird at the Yukon mouth during his explorations in that region, beyond which there is no record of its presence on the coast of Bering Sea. I did not see a single individual in that region, and it must be of considerable rarity. Nor is it known from any of the Bering Sea islands and the Asiatic coast.

TOTANUS FLAIRPES (Gmel.) Vieill.

(105.) THE YELLOW LEGS.

This bird is an extremely rare accidental visitant to the coast of Bering Sea in Alaska. It is perhaps more numerous at the Yukon mouth than elsewhere. In the vicinity of Saint Michael's two or three specimens were secured during four summers, mainly in August, after the breeding season was over, when, like many other birds, these appear to wander from their breeding grounds, visiting parts of the country unknown to them in the breeding season.

HETEROSCELUS INCANUS (Gmel.) Coues.

(106.) THE WANDERING TATTLER.

Every summer, as the end of July approaches or August begins, this bird makes its appearance about the rocky islets and coast along Norton Sound, in the vicinity of Saint Michael's. Its habits are very retired, and unless its haunts were visited not a single individual would be seen. In spring it occurs very sparingly, and has been taken at this season even up the Yukon to Nulato and Anvik, and undoubtedly a few breed in this region; but the majority are birds which have wandered from more southern points. It occurs quite frequently on all the islands of Bering Sea, their rocky shores and isolated position apparently rendering them favorite grounds. When disturbed on their feeding grounds these tattlers usually show but little alarm, but fly on easy wings a short distance, and when they alight are readily secured. They are rarely seen except singly, although several may be found at times in the same vicinity. The young birds obtained in fall are less brightly marked than the spring adults. Their note is a loud, ringing whistle, which seems specially fitted to the bird and the haunts it occupies, and as the shrill cry re-echoes from the towering cliffs and ledges at the base of which it feeds its peculiar character and intonation might lead one to fancy some genie of the rocks was uttering its cry. When the birds are approached by boat, as they are feeding along the water's edge, they ascend gradually, with an expression of mild curiosity, and pass from ledge to ledge until they reach a jutting point on the face of the cliff or its brow, where they stand in relief, like beautiful, clear-cut statuettes, and do not utter a sound or move until they are still further alarmed, when they take flight, uttering at the same moment their loud note before mentioned. This bird is as common upon the Bering Sea shore of Siberia as it is upon the Alaskan coast, but it is not known to the north of Bering Strait on either coast.

TRYNGITES RUFESCENS Vieill.) Caban.

(107.) THE BUFF-BREASTED SAND PIPER.

Like the preceding species, this handsomely plumaged bird is a great wanderer. It is found over nearly the entire globe, especially the continental portions, and wends its way regularly in spring to nest in the far northern regions. On the coasts of Bering Sea it is rare, a single pair obtained at Saint Michael's in spring being the only two that I saw during a four years' residence there. On the north side of Siberia, however, it was found quite common in the vicinity of Cape Wankarem early in August, 1881. Although it is so uncommon in the Bering Sea region, it is very abundant at various points on the Arctic coast, and the lower course of the Anderson River in British America may be especially mentioned, as it has been found breeding there in the greatest abundance.

NUMENIUS HUDSONICUS Lath.

(108.) THE HUDSONIAN CURLEW.

This Curlew is mainly known on the shore of Norton Sound as a migrant in the spring and autumn; a few, however, remain to breed there. As the snow disappears in spring towards the end of May, the loud clear whistle of this species is a welcome sound, as it announces the mild weather of early summer. Remaining but a short time at this season, the majority pass still further to the north. In autumn they return early in August or the last of July, and feed upon the various ripening berries until into September, when they depart for the south. It is unknown on the islands of Bering Sea and adjoining shores of Northeastern Siberia. It is, however, found on the Alaskan shore, north to the vicinity of Point Barrow, and undoubtedly visits Saint Lawrence Island and the Siberian coast during the summer.

NUMENIUS BOREALIS (Forst.) Lath.

(109.) THE ESKIMO CURLEW.

Though much smaller than the latter, this bird considerably outnumbers it, and is much more common during all the summer season on the coast of Norton Sound. Its habits and haunts are almost identical with those of its larger relative, except that it breeds more frequently in the southern parts of its range. Both forms appear at the Yukon month in spring, and sparingly during the breeding season. Both reach high northern latitudes, at least to the limit of continental lands. At Wankarem, on the North Siberian coast, August 6, 1881, four specimens of this bird were seen passing over, and were the only Curlews seen upon the Siberian coast during our various visits to that shore. Elliott has recorded its presence on the Seal Islands during the migrations, and it probably visits most of the Bering Sea islands at this time. It occurs all along the Arctic coast of Alaska, wherever suitable lowlands occur.

NUMENIUS TAHITIENSIS (Gmel.) Cass.

(110.) THE BRISTLE-THIGHED CURLEW.

Although this is the largest Curlew found on the Bering Sea coast of Alaska, it is as well the most uncommon. The only record of its presence there rests upon the capture of a single male in the spring of 1880, when I saw a pair feeding upon the last year's berries, which covered the slightly elevated land bordering an extensive series of flats. It had a loud, clear note, very similar to that of the Hudsonian Curlew, and was not shy. I readily approached them, and secured the male, and afterwards severely wounded the female. The only other instance of its capture in the north is the single specimen secured at Kodiak by Bischoff, in 18—

It is a well-known bird on the islands of the South Pacific, where it exists in great numbers, but its presence in the North is rather unexpected, and like that of several other birds, notably the Pacific Golden Plover and Pacific Godwit, which wander to sub-arctic regions in summer, its winter home is among those islands dotting the South Pacific.

PHALAROPODIDÆ PHALAROPES.

PHALAROPUS FULICARIUS (Linn.) Bp.

(111.) THE RED PHALAROPE.

The present handsome species is extremely abundant on the Alaskan and Siberian coast of the Arctic, north to Wrangel and Herald Islands and thence south along both shores of Bering Sea. It breeds from the mouth of the Kuskoquim River, north along the coast of Alaska, and on the Siberian coast, mainly along the northern shore. Throughout the breeding season it is limited rather closely to the shore, but when the young are fledged and able to follow their parents all leave the shore behind or frequent the lagoons and brackish lakes in the immediate vicinity of the sea. The few vessels which break the monotony of these northern waters in summer find dotting the waves on every hand these buoyant and graceful birds, their quick, agile, and elegant movements attracting attention, while their numbers render them conspicuous as they wheel and circle in flocks about the vessel, their wings flashing in the sunlight.

To the whalers in this region they are known with the next species as "bowhead birds," from their habit of feeding upon minute animalculæ which afford the right whale or bowhead its food. Hence a community of interests attracts these pigmies and the largest cetacean of the North to prey upon the same fare. A logical deduction follows, based upon experience, by which the whalers predict the presence of whales wherever this elegant bird is to be found in great numbers. We saw it repeatedly while cruising in the ice off Wrangel and Herald Islands and thence across the Arctic to Point Barrow or the Bering Sea coast. The calm spaces between the large fields and blocks of ice afford favorite resorts for the members of the numerous bands of Phalaropes along the edge of the pack. They are quite plentiful around the entire Arctic Zone and are familiar to fishermen, whalers, and explorers who visit this dreary region. They are among the few species which the forbidding climate of the highest latitudes does not appear capable of deterring from making their summer home there. Nordenskiöld found this bird's eggs laid on the bare ground of Spitzbergen, and reports it as the commonest species along the north coast of Asia.

LOBIPES HYPERBOREUS (Linn.) Cuv.

(112.) THE NORTHERN PHALAROPE.

Like its relative just mentioned, the Northern Phalarope is an extremely abundant bird in the north, although its disposition is perhaps less maritime and less northern than the one just described. On the Bering Sea coast of Alaska the Northern Phalarope is in great excess of its stouter relative. Thence north the Red Phalarope is the more numerous, and especially so in various parts of the Arctic. On the northern coast of Siberia the Northern Phalarope was found sparingly, whereas the other species was in the greatest abundance. Both forms unite in the same flocks and were found throughout the sea as far as the Corwin penetrated during the summer of 1881; but in this part of the range the Northern Phalarope, in spite of its name, was less and less numerous the farther north we advanced, while the other species was in equal number throughout. Both birds occur during the migrations about the Aleutian and other islands of Bering Sea. But the Northern Phalarope appears to be the only species breeding in the Aleutian chain and thence north to Saint Lawrence Island, where the Red Phalarope nests. We learn from Nordenskiöld that the Northern Phalarope breeds on Nova Zembla and at the New Siberian Islands, besides being found all along the North Siberian coast.

GRUIDÆ CRANES.

GRUS FRATERCULUS Cass.

(113.) THE LITTLE CRANE.

From the Peninsula of Aliaska north along the mainland of Alaska to Kotzebue Sound this small northern representative of the well-known Sand Hill Crane is found breeding in abundance, especially towards the northern portion of this range. It also occurs on Saint Matthew and Saint Lawrence Islands, though it occurs in small numbers at these points. During his visit to Saint Matthew's Island on August 9, 1874, Elliott saw a few of these birds, and it has been found on the East Siberian coast, in the vicinity of Saint Lawrence Bay, where Nordenskiöld saw a considerable number of them as he was passing south in July, 1879, after wintering in the Arctic. Until very recently this bird has been confounded with the larger Sand Hill Crane, and various authors who have referred to *Grus Canadensis* from the northern region of America, according to our present knowledge, referred to the present bird, which occupies this territory exclusively. On the coast of Norton Sound it is extremely common, and throughout the summer, from early in May until toward the end of September, its loud, rolling note and tall figure stalking over the flats are among the most characteristic sights and sounds of this region. They are not very shy, and I have frequently approached them within gunshot by merely appearing not to notice them but continuing in a narrowing circuit to walk round their position until within sixty or seventy-five yards, the bird continuing to stare stupidly at me and uttering its long note and appearing as if doubtful whether it was worth while to take wing or not, until its thoughts were accelerated by a shot. They are extremely curious at this season, and I have frequently decoyed them within gunshot by lying upon the ground and waving a hand or some conspicuous article in the air. As the birds approach from a distance they will almost invariably turn and try to investigate the matter before passing on their way. In many cases they only make a slight detour from their course and pass on, but I have frequently had six or eight of the birds circling about until some would approach within thirty-five or forty yards, offering an easy prize. Their food is composed of the various berries which grow so abundantly on the tundra of the north with an addition of whatever other palatable morsels are found, such as a stray lemming or mouse, or even insects and other small fry that chance may afford. They are not very good eating, although crane steak takes its turn in varying the sameness of the fare in the North.

ANATIDÆ. DUCKS, GEESE.

OLOR AMERICANUS (Sharpless) Bp.

(114.) WHISTLING SWAN.

During the cruise of the Corwin this fine bird was observed but once. This occasion was on July 15, while we were at the head of Kotzebue Sound, where it was found with quill feathers molted, as were the geese at that place. Although the swan was seen so rarely during this expedition, yet the bird is to be found in large numbers along the Alaskan coast of Bering Sea. Here it breeds, especially from the Yukon mouth south to the mouth of the Kuskoquim River, where the flat land, dotted with innumerable marshy lakes, affords a favorite resort. It was not seen on the Siberian coast, and I have no record of its occurrence there, but this or an allied species occurs there. On the American shore but a single species of Swan occurs, the large Trumpeter Swan not being known west of Fort Yukon. We learn from Mr. Dall's paper on the birds of the Aleutian Islands that several specimens of this swan were shot upon Sanak Island in September, some years ago, but they are unknown from the Aleutian chain proper and from the other islands in Bering Sea.

CHEN HYPERBOREUS (Pall.) Boie.

(115.) SNOW GOOSE.

On the American coast of the Arctic and Bering Sea this bird is not very abundant. It occurs however, in considerable flocks for a few days during the spring and fall migrations; and each season a few are killed in the vicinity of Saint Michael's on Norton Sound. Its occurrence upon the north coast of Asia is attested by specimens captured by Nordenskiöld's party at Tapkan in the spring of 1879. These birds are, at present, like the Swan, unknown from the islands of Bering Sea, their migration apparently taking an inland course rather than along the shore lines. Although the Snow Geese are known to nest in the greatest abundance in the Anderson River and surrounding region along the northern coast of British America, yet their nesting place in Alaska is unknown. They certainly do not remain to nest anywhere along the Bering Sea coast, and we did not see any of these birds along the Arctic shore to Point Barrow; so that if they nest at all in this region it must be on those flats bordering the Arctic shore east of Point Barrow. In autumn they leave for the South among the last of the migrant geese, finding their way to the vicinity of Saint Michael's towards the end of September, although in some seasons they appear before the middle of this month; they linger here in autumn from ten days to three weeks, depending upon the weather to a great extent.

The great abundance of this bird in California during the winter season would testify to its breeding in great numbers somewhere to the north of this region. But according to my observations on the Bering Sea coast of Alaska the bird must take some other route towards its northern breeding ground, and it must undoubtedly pass north from California, and soon after cross the mountain ranges to reach their eastern slope, after which the geese pass to the Arctic by an inland course; otherwise the Snow Geese would be found in greater abundance on the coasts of this northern territory.

ANSER ALBIFRONS GAMBELI (Hartl.) Coues.

(116.) THE AMERICAN WHITE-FRONTED GOOSE.

This is the most widely distributed and abundant Goose throughout Northern Alaska, extending its habitat across to the Siberian coast of Bering Sea, and nesting as well upon Saint Lawrence Island. We found it in considerable numbers at the head of Kotzebue Sound the middle of July, 1881, and found many of the adults with their wing feathers molted and unable to fly, and the young still in downy plumage at that time. It is extremely common from the mouth of the Kuskoquim River to the head of Kotzebue Sound, nesting everywhere; thence north to the extreme Arctic coast of the territory. Wherever one goes, in suitable places, this bird is certain to be found. During the spring and fall migrations the White-fronted Goose is found occurring rather sparingly throughout the Aleutian chain, having been taken at Atton, Ounalaska, and Sanak; but their visits are only made at this season, as none are known to remain and breed.

BERNICLA CANADENSIS LEUCOPARIA Brandt) Cass.

(117.) THE WHITE-CHEEKED GOOSE.

The distribution of this bird along the shores of Northern Alaska is almost identical with that of the White-fronted Goose, with the addition, however, of the Aleutian chain, which is contained within the breeding range of the present bird. Like the last species, it was found molting at the head of Kotzebue Sound on July 15, 1881, where it was very numerous. It occurs in the greatest abundance in the vicinity of the Yukon mouth and along the adjoining portion of that coast. There is no record of its presence on Saint Lawrence Island, but on the western portion of the Aleutian chain it is a regular summer resident, rearing its young in considerable numbers upon the isolated islands there.

The natives at these western islands have domesticated considerable numbers of these birds, and whether caused by confinement or otherwise, the white collar on the neck, dividing the brown of the body-color from the jet-black of the head and neck, was very conspicuous, and an inch in width in some specimens seen at Ounalaska the autumn of 1881. The small flock of these Geese seen at Ounalaska, with their dark, handsomely contrasted colors and gentle ways, made very interesting and fine-looking pets. They were noted upon the Seal Islands by Elliot, who tells us that they occurred there as irregular or straggling visitants, which remained but a short time before resuming their line of migration. There is no record of this species from the Siberian shore, where, however, it undoubtedly occurs. It reaches the extreme northern coast of Alaska, where it breeds.

BERNICLA CANADENSIS OCCIDENTALIS (Baird) Dall & Bann.

(118.) THE LARGER WHITE-CHEEKED GOOSE.

The present bird, although intergrading with the latter species, differs in ordinary examples sufficiently to be readily distinguished, mainly by its lighter colors and larger size. Its distribution is somewhat different as well. I do not know of its occurrence on the Aleutian chain; and, in fact, its abundance appears to be greatest at the Yukon mouth and thence up this river, and perhaps to the southward. North of the Yukon mouth it is much less common than the smaller form, and at Saint Michael's ten of the smaller birds were secured to every one of the larger form. At the Yukon mouth the proportion of the two forms is about equal. All of the birds seen sufficiently near to ascertain their identity while we were in Kotzebue Sound were of the smaller form, and I doubt if the larger bird (the subject of the present notes) occurs in any considerable numbers north of the Bering Sea coast, except in the interior, where it is found along the course of the Yukon.

The true Canada Goose, so well known in Eastern North America, is unknown anywhere on the lower Yukon and the coast of Alaska, either on the Bering Sea or Arctic shores.

BERNICLA NIGRICANS (Lawr.) Cass.

(119.) THE BLACK BRANT.

On the shores of Bering Sea, including the various islands and Alaskan coast, the Black Brant occurs in large numbers during the spring migrations. During this season it is in such numbers that it affords better sport than all of the other geese combined, and is the bird which recurs most frequently on the fur-trader's table at that season. In autumn it occurs much more rarely, only straggling parties being found along the shore as autumn closes. In Dall's notes on the ornithology of the Aleutian Islands he speaks of securing the eggs of this bird on the Semicki Islands, near Attou, and at Kyska and Amchitka. This note, however, is to be referred to the White-cheeked Goose which breeds on these islands, but the Black Brant is unknown there during the breeding season. Its farthest south breeding point which I have been able to ascertain is the Yukon mouth, where I saw a single bird in June, 1879; thence north it is extremely rare until the vicinity of Bering Strait is passed, after which occasional pairs occur with more or less frequency during the breeding season, until the low northern coast from beyond Cape Lisburne to Point Barrow is reached, and thence eastward the bird breeds in great abundance wherever the flat marshy country affords it suitable grounds. While at Point Barrow in August, 1881, a considerable number of these birds were brought off by the natives, and an examination showed that they were moulting their quill feathers, thus proving conclusively that they were summer residents in the vicinity.

Captain Smith, an experienced whaler and trader in these waters, has assured me of having seen these birds going and coming to the northward of Point Barrow, thus proving the existence of land further north in that direction. They are also known to breed in the greatest abundance along the northern shores of British America, selecting the lower courses of the large rivers which flow into the Arctic in that region. The natives informed me that occasional pairs were found breeding in the vicinity of Saint Michael's, but that they were extremely rare. On the first of June, 1879, a single pair were seen by me a few miles south of that place, and by their anxiety showed plainly that their nest was in the vicinity. This, with the single individual seen at the Yukon mouth, is the only instance which came directly to my knowledge of its occurrence during the breeding season south of the Straits. Although it undoubtedly occurs on the Siberian shore, yet it was not noted by us during our cruising along that coast in the summer of 1881, nor was it seen on Wrangel Island, although on this island we saw evidences of the presence of some species of geese; but our short stay prevented our ascertaining their identity. Mr. Dall tells us that upon his return to the coast of California in the latter part of October enormous flocks of these birds were seen about one hundred miles off shore as they were flying south, frequently alighting in the water near the ship.

PHILACTE CANAGICA (Sevast.; Bannist.

(120.) EMPEROR GOOSE.

This strange and handsome bird has the most limited range of any American species of Goose. It summers and raises its young on the Bering Sea coast of Alaska from the mouth of the Kuskoquim River north to Bering Strait; but north from the Yukon mouth it is found very rarely. From the Yukon mouth south to Cape Vancouver may be taken as the point of its greatest abundance. Here it occurs in thousands every summer. From this point it extends its range to the westward, and occurs in considerable numbers upon Saint Lawrence Island, where we saw considerable numbers of them during June 24, 1881, while we were lying at anchor off the northwest end of the island. During this time abundant flocks of these birds were passing and repassing along this end of the island, apparently on their way to and from some favorite feeding ground.

At East Cape several birds were seen the first of July, and they were found by Nordenskiöld, arriving at his winter quarters at Tapkan on the northern coast of Siberia in the spring as soon as the snow left; and he speaks of them in his account of the Vega's voyage as the "Painted Goose" of Pallas. There is a record of two or three instances of their occurrence in Port Clarence, on the American shore of Bering Strait, and I know of two pairs being taken in Golovnin Bay on the north coast of Norton Sound, and others at Shoktolik, on Norton Bay, with the chain of occurrences continued south by Saint Michael's to the Yukon mouth. But at all these points except the last this bird is very rare. Just how numerous it is on the Siberian coast is still unknown; but from its large numbers along the American shore and its wintering habitat restricted mainly to the Aleutian Islands, where it is found in the greatest abundance at this season on the various parts of the chain, it may be confidently designated as an American species which extends its range during the summer to portions of the northeastern Siberian coast. My first acquaintance was made with this bird on Akoutan Island, just east of Ounalaska, in May, 1877, when a native brought one on board the vessel; and we learned from him that it is more or less common wherever open beaches are found along these islands, and in consequence are called "Beach Geese" by the natives. Those groups of rocky islets to the south of the Aleutian chain, known as the Shumagin and Sanak Islands, and others lying nearer the south shore of the Aliaska Peninsula form the principal wintering ground of this species; thence to the west along the entire Aleutian chain it occurs, but in less numbers than on that portion just mentioned.

ANAS BOSCAS Linn.

(121.) THE MALLARD DUCK.

On the entire Bering Sea coast of Alaska the common Mallard is a comparatively rare duck. It is most numerous from the northern shore of Norton Sound in the vicinity of Saint Michael's, south to the mouth of Kuskoquim River, but is nowhere abundant. It was not seen by us during the cruise of the Corwin, nor is it recorded from the northeastern Siberian coast or the Arctic within the region treated in this paper. Elliot mentions a pair of these birds which reared their young on the Saint Paul Island of the fur seal group during the season of 1872, and several others were seen later in the season. He also noted the bird on Saint George's Island, but not as a regular visitor. It is recorded by Mr. Dall as one of the most abundant winter visitors among the ducks at Ounalaska, occurring in considerable numbers by October 12, 1874, and from then until the succeeding month of April it was very numerous. It is not known to breed on the Aleutian Islands, but only along the coast and islands to the northward.

DAFILA ACUTA (Linn.) Bonap.

(122.) THE PINTAIL DUCK.

This is perhaps the most abundant fresh-water duck found on the coast of Bering Sea and the Arctic shores to the north. It nests yearly in the greatest abundance all along the coast from the peninsula of Alaska to the farthest northern extreme of Alaska in the vicinity of Point Barrow, being perhaps in greatest abundance on the shores of Norton and Kotzebue Sounds. We found them numerous about Kotzebue Sound during our several landings there; and several were seen on Saint Lawrence Island in Bering Sea during our visits there. They also occur on the north Siberian coast, and, in fact, were noted at almost every place we landed where the surrounding country affords them the proper marshy tracts. While at sea, midway between the Aleutian Islands and San Francisco on October 15, 1881, a bird, which at a distance appeared very much like the female of this species, was seen circling about overhead for ten or fifteen minutes, after which it started off toward the south. Whether this was the present species or not it was of course impossible to say, but from its form and motions it was evidently some species of fresh-water duck. In autumn these birds become extremely fat and well-flavored, and they are the finest table Duck afforded in the north, while their abundance renders them easily obtainable and large numbers are secured by the fur traders in autumn and stored for winter use. They move south among the latest of the water fowl, the last ones occurring in October, and they return again in spring when the open spaces begin to appear in the ice along the shore—sometimes by the first of May, or even before in unusually early seasons. I have seen several of them about one of these holes in the ice, caused by several springs on the shore, when the whole country was covered with a deep layer of snow and winter still appeared in full force.

MARECA PENELOPE (Linn.) Selby.

(123.) THE EUROPEAN WIDGEON.

The only record of this species in Alaska is that given by Elliott, who secured specimens upon the seal islands. He tells us that he saw but a few specimens, and these were apparently solitary examples, never in pairs, and the few he observed during his two years' residence on the fur-seal islands were apparently windbound or straggling specimens. This species is also recorded by Dall as obtained at Onnalaska on the 12th of October, 1871, who adds that it is not uncommon among the Ducks brought in by the native hunters at that season, and tells us that it migrates about the 1st of May. It has not been recorded from any other points or islands on the American side of the sea. But the records quoted render it highly probable that its capture on the mainland is a matter of time and further work in that region. In the vicinity of Saint Michael's it must be extremely rare, as I carefully examined all the Ducks brought in during my residence at that place with the hope of securing some of these birds, but failed.

MARECA AMERICANA (Gmel.) Steph.

(124.) AMERICAN WIDGEON.

On the Norton Sound coast of Bering Sea this is a common bird. It is found breeding along the entire Alaskan coast of Bering Sea and north to Kotzebue Sound and the Arctic coast beyond. It was not noted by us upon any of the islands visited in the vicinity of Bering Strait during the summer of 1881, nor on the Siberian shore. But on September 6 of that year, when we visited the shore at Hotham Inlet, in Kotzebue Sound, a number were obtained from the natives, who told us that they were numerous in that vicinity at the time. They leave for the south a little earlier than the Pin-tailed Duck and arrive later in spring.

SPATULA CLYPEATA (Linn.) Boie.

(125.) SPOON-BILLED DUCK.

Along the Alaskan coast of Bering Sea, mainly limited to that portion between the head of Norton Sound and mouth of the Kuskoquim River, this Duck is not uncommon, although it is nowhere abundant. In the vicinity of Saint Michael's it arrives in spring about the middle of May with the majority of other migrating water fowl and nests on the surrounding flats, leaving for the South towards the end of September. It has not been recorded from any of the Bering Sea islands, nor do I know of its having been taken on the northeastern shore of Siberia. It is found, however, on the Arctic shore of Alaska, north to Kotzebue Sound, if not beyond, and a few individuals were observed by us towards the middle of September, 1881, at the head of Escholtz Bay.

QUERQUEDULA DISCORS (Linn.) Steph.

(126.) BLUE-WINGED TEAL.

During the time of my residence on Norton Sound not a single individual of this bird was taken among the many hundreds of ducks secured by the various hunters about the station. It occurs, however, very rarely at this place, and is recorded by Dall as being found sparingly at the Yukon mouth. Mr. Bannister notes it as not uncommon at Saint Michael's in early spring; but there must be some error in this record from the great scarcity of the bird at the same locality during the period of my residence there. Captain Smith saw the bird and obtained its eggs from near Cape Romanzoff; and this completes our record of this teal within the region treated in the present paper. It is mentioned by Mr. Dall as perhaps occurring at Ounalaska in winter, but this was merely surmised, as no specimens were obtained and the habits of this species are such that there is little probability of its occurring there.

NETTION CAROLINENSIS (Gmel.) Baird.

(127.) GREEN-WINGED TEAL.

This handsome bird is the smallest Duck found in the north, and occurs rather frequently along the Alaskan shore of Bering Sea, and ranges north nearly if not quite to Point Barrow, along the shore of the Arctic. It has been found as a summer resident of the Aleutian Islands as far west as Kyska, and is occasionally at Attou, near the western extreme of the chain. Mr. Dall tells us that it was upon this species they relied mainly for supplying their table during their surveying in the western portion of the Aleutian chain, and he found the young ones abundant at Amchitka in July. Further to the north, however, it is less numerous, and although generally distributed, and rather common, yet during a day's shooting one would scarcely see more than a half dozen or so of this species at most localities. They arrive early in the spring—about the middle of May or thereabouts—before the ice and snow have more than partly disappeared. It is not known from the Siberian shore, nor from the islands of Bering Sea, except the Aleutian chain, although it undoubtedly breeds upon Saint Lawrence Island. A number of these birds were bought from the natives of Hotham Inlet in Kotzebue Sound, September 6, 1881, where they were apparently numerous at the time.

FULIX MARILA (Linn.) Baird.

(128.) SCAUP DUCK.

This is one of the most abundant Ducks in the north, being found breeding almost everywhere on the marshy flats and lake-dotted tundra of the mainland, and extending its range to such islands as afford it suitable feeding grounds. Both this and the smaller species, *affinis*, are recorded by Dall as occurring at the Yukon mouth; but according to the observations I was enabled to make at that locality and in the adjoining region, among hundreds of Scaup Ducks seen not a single individual could be referred to anything but the common large-billed species, and I do not think *affinis* reaches the sea-shore of Northern Alaska. The large Scaup, however, as before noted, is extremely numerous and hatches its young on the borders of almost every lakelet and pool along the entire coast. It occurs on Saint Lawrence Island and north about the shores of Kotzebue Sound, and probably beyond to the extreme north coast of the territory. It was not noted by us upon the northeastern shore of Siberia, but undoubtedly occurs there during the summer.

CLANGULA GLAUCIUM AMERICANA (Bp.) Ridgw.

(129.) AMERICAN GOLDEN EYE.

This is a very rare species on the shores of Bering Sea. The only instance where I met with it alive was late in autumn near Saint Michael's, where a party of four was seen in a small pond, three of which were secured. It occurs more commonly along the streams of the interior, but it is rare along the sea shore, and I have no record of its presence about Kotzebue Sound, although it undoubtedly reaches that point. It is unknown from the islands of Bering Sea and the northeastern shore of Siberia.

CLANGULA ALBEOLA (Linn.) Steph.

(130.) BUTTER-BALL DUCK.

This beautiful little Duck is reported by Mr. Dall as not uncommon at the Yukon mouth, where it breeds; but no specimens of it were noted during my residence at Saint Michael's, nor did I see it on my visit to the Yukon mouth in the spring of 1879. Mr. Dall's record is the only one attributing this species to the shore of Bering Sea, and no further records are at hand of its occurrence in that region. It is also unknown from the shores of the Arctic coast of Alaska and Kotzebue Sound in addition to the islands and Siberian coast visited by the Corwin.

HISTRIONICUS MINUTUS (Linn.) Dresser.

(131.) HARLEQUIN DUCK.

This richly-marked bird is found on the shores and islands of Bering Sea, extending into the Arctic, but north of the Straits it is much less numerous. On the Aleutian Islands it is an abundant species, especially in winter and spring. During May, 1877, at Ounalaska they were extremely numerous in large flocks, frequenting the inner harbors, but were too shy to allow close approach. Mr. Dall informs us that they remain later than most other Ducks; and also notes their occurrence in summer on the Shumagin Islands. It breeds along the coast to the northward from these islands; and Elliott records it as being extremely numerous about the fur-seal islands, where it occurred close along the beach in flocks of hundreds, keeping closely bunched together, and comparatively heedless of approach. This author records his total inability to secure any of the eggs of this bird, although they were permanently resident there in summer, and he offered large rewards to the natives. The females appeared to outnumber the males two to one, and he was at a loss to account for not securing its nest. The probability is that these birds were barren females, or young of the preceding year, which for some cause did not pass to their northern breeding ground, but remained here, feeding upon the abundant animal life found in these waters. It haunts the clear cold streams of the interior which flow down the mountains and empty into the Yukon and its tributaries. The bird seeks secluded pools in these waters, and the natives when wishing to hunt them proceed up a considerable distance on the course of the stream in their birch canoes, and then float silently down with the current, gun in hand, and secure the birds before they become aware of being approached; otherwise, if the birds' attention is attracted they are said to dive with such rapidity that it is almost an impossibility to secure them; but by remaining perfectly quiet in the canoe they are easily approached and killed. Around the shore of Norton's Sound this duck is not common in spring, occurring very rarely as a migrant, and nesting only along the streams flowing into this body of water. When the young are ready to take wing—during August, or from the last of July until September—they become more and more common on the rocky portions of the shore, frequenting the same localities and often joining in flocks of the Scoters. I have generally found them thus associated, or sunning themselves upon the projecting rocks and reefs at low tide during this season. They are used by the natives of the interior as toys, the bird being skinned, stuffed with moss and decorated with beads and bright colored threads to serve as dolls for the children, their handsomely variegated plumage attracting the eyes of the savages.

The Harlequin is also found along the northeastern shore of Siberia, and visits all the Bering Sea islands during the summer. It was not seen by us, however, in the Arctic during the cruise of the Corwin, and if it occurs there it must be as a straggler or very rare summer visitant.

HARELDA GLACIALIS (Linn.) Leach.

(132.) OLD SQUAW DUCK.

Everywhere around the islands of Bering Sea and the mainland coast, extending through the Straits and along both the Alaskan and Siberian shores to the farthest limit of land, this peculiar Duck is found in abundance. It is a noisy bird in spring, with a loud and sonorous note, and occurs everywhere on the sea among the drifting ice, or on shore in secluded pools and small sluggish streams. It occurs as a resident on the fur-seal islands, and upon the Aleutian chain. It was also seen about Saint Lawrence Island during our visits there in June and July, 1881, and was common at East Cape, Siberia, as well as along the north coast of this land. It is reported as being a common species at Nova Zembla by Nordenskiöld, and a recent letter in the New York Herald from the naturalist of the Jeannette reports them common August 30, 1881, on Thaddens Island, one of the Liakhov group, as the Jeannette party were making their way to the mouth of the Lena after losing their vessel. Its habits are a strange combination of the salt and fresh water Ducks in Alaska, as it appears to frequent indifferently the rocky islands surrounded by the sea with an entire lack of fresh water, or is found far up the Yukon, where fresh water alone exists. It has a peculiar and rather musical note, making it one of the most conspicuous birds on the ponds and streams of the sea-coast and marshes about the mouth of the Yukon, where in spring its loud cries and lively manners make it a very amusing and interesting bird. It arrives in the sea with the first openings in the ice during April each spring, or in earlier seasons the last of March. These ducks are very much emaciated at this date, but gradually regain their flesh, until in May the ponds open on shore and allow them to seek their nesting grounds. In the autumn they remain until the sea freezes over, and thus closes their only means of gaining subsistence, after which they are forced to depart for the South.

POLYSTICTA STELLERI (Pall.) Brandt.

(133.) STELLER'S EIDER.

The present species is widely distributed over the coasts of Bering Sea, occurring on both the mainlands as well as about all the islands of this water. It was found merely as a straggler upon the fur-seal islands by Elliott, but is extremely numerous on the Aleutian chain in winter where it occurs as a very abundant resident at this season, joining sometimes in flocks with the King Eider. Dall informs us that it pairs early in May and breeds upon the Aleutian chain. The larger number, however, pass farther north at this season. During my visit to Ounalaska in May, 1877, these birds were found in small numbers scattered over the inner harbors, but were extremely shy, and notwithstanding repeated efforts to secure them they invariably took flight long before my approach within gunshot. They have been reported as wintering in great abundance upon Sanakh Island, and as occurring in large numbers on the north coast of Aliaska Peninsula during the summer. North along the coast of Norton Sound they are only known as autumnal visitants. Each fall, just before the inner bays freeze over in October, a number of these birds are found sometimes in considerable flocks feeding about the tide-rips, and at this season I secured a number of specimens; but no adults were ever noted at this locality, and I do not know of the bird's occurrence in spring, although it may be taken as a rare straggler. It was not noted by us anywhere along the coast of Alaska from Saint Michael's north through Bering Strait to Point Barrow; but we found a number of them the first of July in the brackish ponds on Saint Lawrence Island, where they were evidently breeding, and again on the north coast of Siberia they were excessively numerous. Flocks of thousands were found about Cape Wankarem during our stay there the first of August, 1881, and, in company with an equal number of King Eiders and a few of the Pacific Eider, were seen passing out and in each evening to and from the large estuary back of the native village. This village was built upon the spit cutting this estuary from the sea at this place, and lay directly in the track of flight followed by these Eiders as they passed to or from the sea. As these flocks passed back and forth the birds were being continually brought down by the slings thrown into the midst of the passing birds by the natives; yet, notwithstanding this, the birds continued from day to day the entire season to pass and repass this place. Their heedlessness in this respect may be accounted for from the fact that these people were without guns of any kind, and were thus unable to frighten them by the noise of the discharge. The birds were easily called from their course of flight, as we repeatedly observed. If a flock should be passing a hundred yards or more to one side, the natives would utter a long, peculiar cry, and the flock would turn instantly to one side and sweep by in a circuit, thus affording the coveted opportunity for bringing down some of their number. These flocks generally contained a mixture of about one-twentieth of the number Pacific Eiders, and the remainder about equally divided of Stellers and the King Eiders. At times the entire community of these birds, which made this vicinity their haunt, would pass out in a solid body, and the flock thus formed exceeded in size anything of the kind I ever witnessed.

The first night of our arrival was calm and misty, the water having that peculiar glassy smoothness seen at such times, and the landscape rendered indistinct at a short distance by a slight mistiness. Soon after we came to anchor before the native village this body of birds arose from the estuary a mile or two beyond the natives' huts, and came streaming out in a flock which appeared endless. It was fully three to four miles in length, and considering the species which made up this gathering of birds it was enough to make an enthusiastic ornithologist wild with a desire to possess some of the beautiful specimens which were seen filing by within gunshot of the vessel. A little later in the evening the natives brought off a considerable number of the birds which they had killed with their slings, and during our stay at this place, the following day, we saw large numbers of them killed with these implements, and a few were obtained with our guns. This portion of the Siberian coast appears to be the grand summer resort of this Eider, as the Aleutian Islands form its wintering ground. One of the remarkable facts in the history of its distribution, however, is shown in its total absence on the opposite American coast of the Arctic where the surroundings appear to be almost identical with those found on the Siberian shore, yet for all the thousands of these birds seen on this latter coast not one was noted on the American shore, although the King Eider occurs equally numerous upon both sides of the Arctic.

LAMPRONETTA FISCHERI Brandt.

(131.) SPECTACLED EIDER.

Along the Alaskan shore of the Bering Sea, from the mouth of the Kuskoquim River north to the head of Norton Sound, the present bird is a rather common and in some places abundant summer resident, nesting and rearing its young along the borders of the numerous brackish pools which are found so abundantly in the low marshy land of this region. It was not seen elsewhere during the cruise of the Corwin, and it is doubtful if it ever reaches the shores of the Arctic Ocean, although it may occur occasionally about Kotzebue Sound. Dall records it as occuring rarely at Unalaska, and we learn from him that it is a rather rare and very shy winter visitant, migrating early in May to its breeding grounds to the north. The southern limit of its winter habitat is unknown, and from the known range of this species at present it appears to be one of the most narrowly limited of our sea fowl, even having a narrower territory than is covered by the Emperor Goose, which joins with it in a great portion of its range.

September 15, 1881, when we were approaching Saint Michael's and about twenty-five miles off the outer end of Stewart's Island, in Norton Sound, a large flock of these Eider were seen, consisting almost entirely of males. They were in full plumage, with the dark areas much more extended than in spring, and appearing considerably different from the bird as seen then, but readily recognizable by the large velvety white patch surrounding the eye. Unlike the common Eider of the North, *V-nigra*, the males do not pass the most of their time at sea during the breeding season but keep near their mates, frequenting the brackish ponds and tide creeks along the shore until the young are hatched.

SOMATERIA V-NIGRA Gray.

(135.) PACIFIC EIDER.

This species of Eider is found everywhere about the shores and islands of Bering Sea, and nests throughout nearly all this range. While at Samakh Island, near the eastern end of the Aleutian chain, the middle of May, 1877, considerable numbers of these birds were found upon the outlying reefs and exposed rocks. They were then in decreased numbers, as we were told by the residents that they visit this portion of the Territory in greatest abundance during the winter season. As is well known, the nesting range of this bird extends from its highest northern point south to the Farallon Islands, off San Francisco, and perhaps still farther to the south. Mr. Dall reports them as wintering abundantly at Onnalaska and breeding in large numbers along the western portion of the Aleutian chain during the summer. At Plover Bay, on the Siberian shore, June 26, 1881, a few pairs were seen, and again the first of July at East Cape, Siberia. It was found sparingly along the entire northeastern Siberian shore from Plover Bay around through the Straits and nests nearly to Cape North.

As previously mentioned, it was joined with the King Eider and Steller's Duck in the immense flocks of these birds which were frequenting the estuary of the river near Cape Wankarem, but the present species was very decidedly in the minority. A few of these birds were also found at Point Barrow, Alaska, on August 16, 1881, and thence south along the coast they were found much less numerous than the King Eider until Kotzebue Sound is reached; and thence south along the coast of Alaska the King Eider is replaced almost entirely during the summer by the present species.

The last of August, 1881, as we left Point Hope, Alaska, and were midway between that place and Bering Strait, several of these Eiders passed us on their way South, showing that the autumnal migration commences very early in the season with them.

This species is said to be extremely abundant on the north coast of British America, especially between the mouths of the Mackenzie and Coppermine Rivers, where it is said to occur in greatest numbers. From the western limit of that portion of the Arctic bordering the Bering Strait region, west to Spitzbergen and the North Atlantic, the common eider duck is found replacing the Pacific Eider. On Spitzbergen it nests in colonies, and the Walrus hunters of that sea credit the females with stealing eggs from one another. The male bird is said to remain in the vicinity and watches while the female sits upon the eggs, giving the alarm at the approach of any danger.

SOMATERIA SPECTABILIS Linn.) Bois.

(136.) THE KING EIDER.

The King Eider is found in great abundance along the Aleutian Islands during winter, some remaining to breed, and thence north in summer along the Siberian coast of Bering Sea and the northeastern Arctic shore of Siberia. Although so numerous on the Siberian coast in summer, yet on the Bering Sea coast of Alaska it is a very rare bird, occurring only as a straggler. Among the large number of Eiders secured by me during my residence at Saint Michael's not a single individual of this bird was obtained, although it was well known to the natives and reported by them as being seen occasionally while they were seal hunting far off shore. After Bering Strait is passed, however, following along the north Alaskan shore in the Arctic to Point Barrow, the King Eider is found to be very abundant, becoming more and more numerous the farther north we reached, until along the stretch of coast between Icy Cape and Point Barrow we found them in large flocks in the summer of 1881. Off Cape Serdze Kamen, Siberia, northwest of the Strait, large numbers of these birds were seen on July 9, 1881, and they were again found at various points along that coast where we touched. Nordenskiöld reports it as occurring at Spitzbergen, but as being more numerous on the shores of Nova Zemlya.

August 11, 1881, as the Corwin was making her way towards Wrangel Island, a number of these birds were seen sitting upon the ice, and remained gazing stupidly at the vessel until she approached within fifty or sixty yards, when they splashed off into the water and took wing. Again the next morning, as we landed at the mouth of the river on Wrangel Island, a female with her young swam away from the beach and passed out of sight around the adjacent point, thus proving conclusively that the bird nests upon this land.

At Cape Wankarem, Siberia, August 5, the same summer, the natives brought off to us large numbers of these birds, which they killed with slings as described under the Steller's Eider. This latter species, with the King Eider, formed the main body of the great flocks of Eiders which were continually passing and repassing during the time of our stay at that place. At Point Barrow, Alaska, on August 16, they were also in great abundance, and appeared to have the same habit as observed at Wankarem of flying to and from the sea across the low sandy spit separating the bay at the point from the sea.

ŒDEMIA AMERICANA Sw. & Rich.

(137.) AMERICAN SCOTER.

Along the Alaskan coast of Bering Sea this species nests in considerable numbers wherever the low, marshy character of the coast affords it proper ground. It occurs sparingly upon Saint Lawrence Island, and thence north through Bering Strait to the shores of Kotzebue Sound, in the Arctic, and upon the northeastern coast of Siberia mainly south of Bering Strait. In the Aleutian Islands it is a common winter resident, but is not known to breed there.

MELANETTA FUSCA (Linn.) Boie.

(138.) VELVET SCOTER.

Like the preceding, this bird is rather numerous along the coast of Norton Sound, but occurs mainly in autumn after the breeding season is finished. It is not found nesting so commonly as the American Scoter in this region, but probably passes farther to the north. It was seen in the vicinity of Kotzebue Sound during the cruise of the Corwin, and across the Arctic to the Siberian shore, where, at Cape Wankarem, on August 7, 1881, a considerable number of these birds were seen upon the rocks at the points of the cape. Later in the summer, as we steamed south along the shore of Siberia from Bering Strait, quite a number of these birds with the last named species were seen in the sea off shore. A month earlier in the season none had been seen at this point, but these birds were probably those which had nested on shore at these points and were now returning to their usual habits of frequenting the sea. This species is also found at Ounalaska, where Dall obtained specimens in October; and at the last of May, 1877, they were quite numerous there and I secured several individuals during my stay at that place.

PELIONETTA PERSPICILLATA (Linn.) Kaup.

(139.) THE SURF DUCK.

This is perhaps the least common of the Scoters on the shores of Bering Sea, but occurs rather commonly in the vicinity of Saint Michael's, Norton Sound, every autumn, and again in spring. A number of individuals were seen off the northeast coast of Siberia the last of August as we passed out of the Arctic in the Corwin. It was also seen with the preceding species on the rocks at Cape Wankarem the 1st of August, and several times along the American shore of the Arctic in autumn. It was not observed by me during the breeding season at the Yukon mouth in 1879, nor in the vicinity of Saint Michael's, but as its eggs were obtained by Bischoff in the vicinity of Sitka, it undoubtedly includes the entire coast, thence north, in its breeding range.

MERGUS MERGANSER AMERICANUS (Cass.) Ridgw.

(140.) AMERICAN SHELDRAKE.

Dall records several specimens killed on December 20 at Ounalaska in the outer bay after a storm, and states that it cannot be considered as more than an accidental visitor, although it is reported to be common in winter at the seal islands. This is probably an error, as Elliott makes no corroboration of this. I have not observed this species anywhere along the Alaskan or Siberian coasts, and it must be exceedingly rare upon the former coast, as the natives were unable to give me any information concerning it, notwithstanding repeated inquiries made both at the Yukon mouth and in the vicinity of Saint Michael's; nor was it observed anywhere at the various points we landed, both on the Siberian and the American coasts of Bering Sea and the Arctic during the cruise of the Corwin.

MERGUS SERRATOR Linn.

(141.) RED-BREASTED FISH DUCK.

This is the commonest species of sheldrake, occurring upon both shores of Bering Sea. It nests upon Saint Lawrence Island and along both the American and Siberian coasts. On the former coast it is common, and in many places is an abundant bird. It has also been taken upon the Aleutian Islands by Dall, who secured specimens at Amchitka. Along the Alaskan coast of the Arctic to Point Barrow it is also found in varying abundance. Although we did not observe it on the Siberian coast of the Arctic during the summer of 1881, yet its known distribution on the adjoining shores and islands would indicate that it is found there as well.

LOPHODYTES CUCULLATUS (Linn.) Reich.

(142.) HOODED SHELDRAKE.

A single large flock of this handsome bird was seen by Mr. Bannister in the vicinity of Saint Michael's in October, 1865, just before the harbor became frozen over. This is the only record I possess of the occurrence of this bird in the waters of Bering Sea. It was not seen by us during the cruise of the Corwin on either shore, and as not a single example was observed during my residence at Saint Michael's the species is undoubtedly extremely rare on the western coast of Alaska.

GROCULIDÆ. CORMORANTS.

PHALACROCORAX VIOLACEUS (Gmel.) Ridgw.

(143.) VIOLET-GREEN CORMORANT.

This handsomely colored Cormorant is the commonest of its kind along the Aleutian chain and about the shores of the various islands in Bering Sea, visiting both shores in addition wherever the coast assumes a bold, rocky character, affording the birds suitable nesting places. It is found sparingly on the islands in Bering Strait, and thence extends through into the Arctic, being found upon both shores there as in Bering Sea. It is not numerous in the vicinity of Saint Michael's and the Yukon mouth, mainly owing to the low character of the coast, but towards the head of Norton Sound it nests in large numbers upon the bold cliffs fronting the sea in that vicinity.

At Plover Bay during our visits in June and July, 1881, these birds were very numerous, and were noted at various other points along the coast. On June 29, scattered individuals of a species of Cormorant to which I refer this bird were seen in the sea off Cape Serdze Kamen, but none were secured. A species of Cormorant, either this or the following, was seen at Herald Island, and again one or two individuals near Wrangel Island and on the American shore in the vicinity of Cape Beaufort, on July 27; but as they were shy at all these localities no specimens were secured, and it was impossible to ascertain definitely to which species they should be referred.

PHALACROCORAX BICRISTATUS Pall.

(144.) RED-FACED CORMORANT.

Nordenskiöld records the capture of several of these birds at North Cape, Siberia, where they were nesting upon the cliffs in large numbers at the time of the Vega's visit there on September

17, 1879. It was, perhaps, this species in place of the Violet-green Cormorant which was noted by us to the north of this cape about Wrangel and Herald Islands, as well as at Cape Beaufort on the north shore of Alaska and one or two other points along the Arctic shore of this territory.

This species is well known as a resident upon the fur-seal islands, where Elliott found them remaining throughout the winter, despite the severity of the storms and cold at various times. It serves as a dainty morsel for the resident Aleuts upon these islands during the winter, when other kinds of fresh meat are not procurable. According to Elliott it nests some weeks in advance of the other water fowl, and builds a large structure upon a jutting shelf along the face of the cliffs. These birds have from three to four eggs, and the young come from the shell almost without feathers, but grow rapidly under the care of the old birds. He notes the great amount of curiosity possessed by these birds at the appearance of any unusual object which approaches the vicinity of their nesting places or feeding grounds. This appears to hold everywhere. I have rarely visited the haunts of Cormorants without their circling around and around, although sometimes so shy as to keep well beyond gunshot. Their curiosity appears to bring them in the neighborhood of the objects of their suspicion again and again. We found this bird quite numerous in the vicinity of Unalaska Island on our arrival there the last of September, 1881. In the spring of 1877 it was also rather common about the harbors at that place. It is a resident throughout the Aleutian Islands, according to Dall. These birds appear to be a fitting accompaniment of the bleak, barren coast found so frequently along the northern shore of Bering Sea. The dark cliffs, with scarcely a trace of vegetation, and the cold rocks, perhaps relieved here and there by banks of snow in the ravines, are rendered still more wild and inhospitable in appearance by the presence of these large, awkward somber-colored birds, which circle silently back and forth in front of their cliffs, fitting habitants of the remote and cheerless wilds where their home is made.

LARIDÆ. GULLS. TERNS.

PAGOPHILA EBURNEA (Phipps) Kaup.

(145.) THE IVORY GULL.

There is no record of this bird's occurrence anywhere in Bering Sea, but Nordenskiöld found this gull quite frequent during the time of his stay on the northeastern shore of Siberia at Tapkan, and noted them at various points around the northern shore of Asia during his voyage through that region. It is found quite commonly about Spitzbergen and Nova Zemyla, where it keeps in the vicinity of the shore, and in winter is frequently seen standing near the seal-holes in the ice waiting for the seal to appear, the cause of this being its habit of devouring that animal's excrement. It is abundant in this region and off the high northern latitudes of America, but very few of its nests have been found thus far, one by McClintock, at Cape Krabbe, in North America, in latitude $77° 25'$ north, and again by Malmgren, at Murchinson Bay, in Spitzbergen, in latitude $82° 2'$ north. The two nests found by Malmgren consisted of a depression from twenty-five to twenty-six centimeters in diameter in a heap of loose gravel on a ledge of a sloping limestone wall. Each nest contained one egg, which on the 30th of July already contained a down-covered bird. Murchinson Bay was covered with ice at the time these nests were observed. On September 4, 1879, this bird was seen off Herald Island by the naturalist of the Jeannette, and again in the middle of June; and in July, 1880, a number of these birds were seen, and at various other times during the drift of this ill-fated vessel. In the vicinity of Bennett Island on July 29, 1881, they were again seen, and were probably nesting there.

There is no North Pacific coast record of this species, and it appears to be a winter resident in high latitudes, not passing south beyond the ice limit, except very rarely, when, as in a few instances, it has been taken along the coast of Maine, in eastern North America, and perhaps as far south as Massachusetts. On the west coast of America we possess no such southern records, and it is doubtful if it ever passes south of the Aleutian chain, although as yet we do not possess a record of the bird south of Bering Straits. It is one of the most beautiful of the gulls, and any addition to our knowledge of its biography will be a welcome contribution to northern ornithology.

RISSA TRIDACTYLA KOTZBUEI (Bp.) Coues.

(146.) PACIFIC KITTIWAKE.

About the shores of Bering Sea everywhere that rocky cliffs or bold islands rise from the water this elegant Gull may be found, usually occurring in the greatest abundance. During our visit to a rocky islet in Escholtz Bay, Kotzebue Sound, on September 7, 1881, the young were seen perching upon the ledges and jutting points of this precipitous island. Although the approach to the nesting places was difficult, yet the young stood gazing stupidly at us as we drew near until, though they were able to fly, several were knocked from their perches with stones before they would take wing, and one was caught in my hand without its showing the slightest alarm until seized. Elliott found them breeding in greatest abundance at the fur-seal islands, and we found them about the shores of Saint Lawrence Island the last of June, 1881. On Herald Island they were nesting in large numbers, and although seen in less abundance about the shores of Wrangel Island, yet they were common there. On May 1, 1880, during the drift of the Jeannette, they were seen by Mr. Newcomb, the naturalist of this vessel, and were quite common from that date on during the remainder of the summer. At Bennett Island they were found more numerous than elsewhere by the people from this vessel. It is a common bird over all parts of the Arctic, extending along both the Alaskan and Siberian shores from Bering Strait. During our cruising in the summer of 1881 I had repeated occasions to notice the graceful motions and powers of flight possessed by this handsome Gull. Its buoyancy during the worst gales we met was fully equal to that possessed by the Rodger's Fulmar, with which it frequently associated at these times. These birds were continually gliding back and forth in graceful curves, now passing directly into the face of the gale, then darting off to one side on a long circuit, always moving steadily, with only an occasional stroke of the wings for long periods if there was a strong wind. The closely-allied form, the well-known Kittiwake of the North Atlantic and adjoining portion of the Arctic Ocean, is found breeding upon Spitzbergen and Nova Zemlya, as well as upon the Preobraschrine Islands on the North Siberian shore. It is more common in the very high northern latitudes than the Glaucous Gull, according to Nordenskiöld, and occurs far out to sea, where it follows vessels for days at a time, circling around the tops of the masts, sometimes, according to the walrus hunters of the seas north of Europe, pecking at the end of the pendant before a storm. This latter habit was noticed by us in the Pacific Kittiwake as we approached Wrangel Island during our several attempts to land there. One evening it was nearly calm and clear, but the appearance of the sky indicated that foul weather was preparing to descend upon us, and as we worked in through the ice, attempting to reach the shore, several young Kittiwakes came off towards us, and circling about approached close to the pendant flying from the mast-head with their bills almost touching the point of this streamer. They moved up and down, following the sinuous movement of the pendant in the most curious manner, apparently trying to satisfy themselves as to the cause and appearance of this strange phenomenon. The common Kittiwake of the North Atlantic is said to make an elaborate nest of moss, mud, and grass, which harbors innumerable insects, of which the naturalist on board the Vega obtained twelve species from a single nest. The Bering Sea bird constructs a nest of moss and sea-weed, or other material in a like manner, but the parasites from this source have not been examined.

RISSA BREVIROSTRIS Brandt.

(147.) RED-LEGGED KITTIWAKE.

The present handsome species of gull is limited in the region covered by this paper to the Aleutian Islands and to the fur-seal group. It nests in great abundance about the latter islands, where, according to Elliott, it comes by tens of thousands to breed. This author testifies to its elegance of coloring and grace of movement; and its handsomely contrasted plumage and bright red feet certainly render it one of the most attractive of its kind in these northern waters. The last of May, 1877, while I was at Onnalaska, these birds were quite numerous for two or three days, when they all disappeared as suddenly as they had come, and passed north to their breeding ground about the seal islands. This gull is also found north at Saint Matthew Island, but there is no record of its occurrence beyond this. No examples have been obtained either upon Saint Lawrence Island or the adjacent American and Asiatic shores of Bering Sea. It is, however, recorded from the Kamtchatkan coast, and undoubtedly occurs about the shores of Okhotsk Sea, north of which it is doubtful if it is ever found.

LARUS GLAUCUS Brunn.

(148.) THE GLAUCUS GULL.

This is one of the most widely spread and common Gulls of Bering Sea and the adjoining coast of the Arctic. It is largely outnumbered, however, by the Kittiwake Gull, which has a nearly similar distribution. At the fur-seal islands Elliott records this large fine bird as restricted in its breeding ground to Walrus Islet, although it frequents the larger islands throughout the season, and feeds upon the carcasses of the seals left on the killing ground. It was numerous, and preparing to nest about the bold headlands and cliffs at Oonalaska, towards the end of May and first of June in 1877. During my residence at Saint Michael's it was found as an abundant species, arriving with the first open water in spring, and only retiring when the sea was closed by ice in autumn. During the cruise of the Corwin, the summer of 1881, it was found at nearly every point visited, among which may be named Kotzebue Sound, Cape Lisburne, Herald Island, the northern shore of Siberia, Bering Strait, and Plover Bay, in nearly all of which places it was in abundance, or at least a common bird. Its loud, harsh notes and large size render it one of the most conspicuous birds of the North. The chosen surroundings of this Gull in Bering Sea, where it breeds on all the islands and shores, would scarcely necessitate the well-known name of ice gull, which this bird has earned on the North Atlantic coast and adjoining Arctic Sea, where it is so well known as the accompaniment of the ice-pack of that region. Here, however, it is content to remain farther south, breeding even south to where the fragments of ice rarely, if ever, find their way, and from some time in June until the commencement of winter no ice is seen anywhere south of Bering Strait. We learn from Nordenskiöld that it breeds upon Bear Island, Spitzbergen, and Nova Zemlya, as well as upon the new Siberian Islands, which, with its known range in the North Atlantic, shows that the bird seeks a home indifferently either in the high north, where the ever present ice-pack covers the sea, or south, where a milder climate and less grim surroundings are found, as about the shores of Bering Sea. The Burgomaster, as this bird is sometimes termed, in its North Atlantic range was found nesting upon Herald and Wrangel Islands during our visits there, and it would be difficult for one to visit any part of the Arctic shores around the entire circumpolar region and not meet this gull. It is bold and voracious among its kind, and ruthlessly robs the breeding waterfowl of their eggs or young, which it greedily devours whenever opportunity affords.

LARUS LEUCOPTERUS Faber.

(149.) GLAUCUS WINGED GULL.

This species was found with the preceding, and perhaps outnumbering the Glaucus Gull upon the Aleutian Islands, in the spring of 1877. They were extremely abundant about the various headlands there, and were afterwards found to the north at Saint Michael's and in Bering Strait. Their distribution covers all the shores of Bering Sea, main-land and islands, and extends through the Straits along both coasts of the Arctic; but they are less common north of the Straits than to the south. At Plover Bay they were quite numerous on June 26, 1881. During the explorations of the Western Union Telegraph Company specimens were secured at Sitka and others at Kodiak; and the bird is found along the entire west coast of America from California north, being of common occurrence along the entire sea coast of Alaska and the various islands of Bering Sea, besides on the Siberian coast. It was found on the shore of the Arctic north to Cape Lisburne and Icy Cape, on the American side, and to Cape Serdze Kamen and the vicinity of Herald Island on the Siberian side. None were seen at Point Barrow, although they undoubtedly occur there. Its habits are almost identical with those of the Glaucus Gull, but it may usually be distinguished when in company with the latter by its smaller size.

LARUS MARINUS (Linn.)

(150.) GREAT BLACK-BACKED GULL.

Although the present species has been recorded from the coast of Japan, there was no record of its occurrence in Bering Sea or the adjoining portion of the Arctic until during the summer of 1880. During this season Captain C. L. Hooper, of the Corwin, secured a specimen at the Greater Diomede Island, in Bering Strait, and the same season Dr. T. H. Bean, of the National Museum, obtained a young bird at Chernooskie, on Ounalaska Island, making the only two records of this bird's capture in Alaska, although Dr. Bean afterwards found it at Port Clarence, on the Alaskan shore of Bering Strait, and saw numerous other specimens during his summer cruise.

It is a little strange that this conspicuous and well-marked bird should have escaped attention so long in this part of its range, but it must be somewhat localized in its distribution here, since during my residence at Saint Michael's I kept a continual lookout for rare species of Gulls, and among the large numbers of these birds obtained and examined not a single individual could be referred to this species.

LARUS AFFINUS Reinh.

(151.) THE SIBERIAN GULL.

During the various visits made to the northwest Siberian coast by the Corwin in the season of 1881 these birds were found to be numerous at Plover Bay, and thence around the shore through Bering Straits along the coast to the northwest, the last ones being seen in the vicinity of Cape Serdze Kamen and Waukeram, just west of Kolinchin Bay. At all these places the bird was common, and was quite frequently seen some miles off shore as we were passing along this coast. It was not observed, however, on the American shore, where it is almost certain to occur, although there is no definite record of its presence there up to date. On June 26, 1881, these gulls were preparing to breed about the headlands of Plover Bay, and on the 29th of this same month were found to be abundant off Cape Serdze Kamen, where they were evidently nesting or about to prepare for this duty.

LARUS CACHINNANS Pall.

(152.) THE SIBERIAN HERRING GULL.

This Gull is occasionally observed about the Yukon mouth and about the entire coast of the territory, although it is among the rarest of the laridæ to occur on the shore of Norton Sound. It is not known from the islands of Bering Sea, where it undoubtedly occurs. The record given of *Larus argentatus* by Mr. Dall in his paper on the birds of Alaska refers to this bird. He records it as plentiful at Plover Bay, and it is a common species along this coast. Just what its range is to the north of Bering Straits I have no data upon which to base an opinion.

LARUS CACHINNANS Pall.

(153.) PALLAS'S HERRING GULL.

Although this species is recorded from the northeast coast of Siberia, by Pallas, it was not observed during the cruise of the Corwin, but might easily have been overlooked from the cursory manner of our survey there. The close similarity of the two shores of Bering Sea render it extremely probable that any species of gull found in the vicinity of Bering Strait on either shore is almost certain to be taken sooner or later upon the opposite coast.

LARUS BRACHYRHYNCHUS Rich.

(154.) SHORT-BILLED GULL.

The present species of Gull is extremely abundant along the eastern coast of Bering Sea, from the head of Norton Sound to the Peninsula of Aliaska. It was not observed on any of the Bering

Sea islands or the Siberian shore during the cruise of the Corwin, nor was it seen north of Bering Strait, although specimens were brought me from the Kotzebue Sound region during my residence at Saint Michael's. It is very numerous along the course of the Yukon and other rivers in the interior of Alaska, and breeds throughout the range given.

LARUS PHILADELPHIÆ (Ord.) Gray.

(155.) BONAPARTE'S GULL.

This is a very rare bird along the Alaskan coast of Bering Sea, being found there during the migrations merely as a straggler from its breeding grounds in the interior. There is no record of either this or the preceding species from any of the Bering Sea islands, but the latter is far less numerous and widely spread on the shores of this sea than the former. I found Bonaparte's Gull numerous only in one instance in the vicinity of Saint Michael's. This was towards the end of September, 1880, when for a few days they were abundant along the canal which separates Saint Michael's Island from the mainland. There is no record of its presence along the shore of the Arctic, although it may possibly occur at the head of Kotzebue Sound.

RHODOSTETHIA ROSEA (Macgill.) Bruch.

(156.) ROSSE'S GULL.

During my residence at Saint Michael's I secured a single specimen of this bird. It was a young of the year, and although it was taken the first of October, yet it still retained, nearly complete, its imperfect mottled plumage. This was the first specimen of this rare and beautiful bird taken in the region about Bering Strait. Since this capture, however, we have still further knowledge of this bird's distribution. Nordenskiöld obtained a beautiful adult specimen which was shot from the vessel while frozen in on the Siberian shore near Bering Strait on July 1, 1879; and the naturalist of the Jeannette, Mr. Newcomb, writes in a recently published letter to the New York Herald that "In the middle of October, 1879, a pair of these birds came along the lead where I was sitting, and when within range I fired, tumbling one down into the water; the other turned and I got it. They proved to be Rosse's Gulls (*Rhodostethia rosea*), an exceedingly rare species, very buoyant and graceful on the wing; beautiful pearly-blue on the back, vermilion feet and legs, and lovely tea-rose on the breast and underpart, the rosy tint being scarcely a color; then blending in exquisite harmony with the pearly blue of the upper parts. They were in full feather. I afterwards got three more in adult and immature plumage."

While the Jeannette party were on their way toward the Siberian coast, after the loss of their vessel, a number of these Gulls were seen, but were not obtained. Eight specimens of this beautiful bird were secured by Mr. Newcomb during the drift of the Jeannette, but during the retreat of this party toward the coast all but three specimens in the most interesting states of plumage were abandoned, with many other results of their long captivity in the ice. These three specimens are now preserved in the Smithsonian collection, and with the one obtained by me at Saint Michael's form a series of four birds the only ones at present in any American collection, and representing each a different state of plumage. The richness of the rosy tint on the breast is incomparable with that on any other gull which I have ever seen. One of the specimens brought by Mr. Newcomb still retains the color, and is of an extremely rich peach-blossom pink, much richer even in this faded condition than is usual in life upon gulls which are ornamented with this rosy suffusion during the breeding season. It is to be hoped that some of the several American expeditions now in the north may secure other specimens of this interesting and lovely Gull, which is the most beautiful of its kind, and add still more to its history. And now that the range of the bird is known to extend around the entire circumpolar regions, the next point to ascertain will be its breeding ground, and peculiar habits during the nesting season. Notes upon its habits are particularly desirable, as thus far the naturalists who have obtained specimens of this variety have only recorded the facts of their capture.

XEMA SABINEI (J. Sabine) Leach.

(157.) SABINE'S GULL.

From the Peninsula of Aliaska, north, along the Alaskan shore to Kotzebue Sound, this is a very common Gull. It is especially numerous during the breeding season on the low marshy coast between the Yukon mouth and Saint Michael's, where it breeds. It is common, however, at various other points along the American coast, and across to Saint Lawrence Island and the Siberian shore of Bering Sea, whence specimens have been secured by various parties visiting that coast. It was seen at Saint Lawrence Bay by the naturalist of the Jeannette on August 29, 1879; and when we neared Wrangel Island the 1st of August, 1881, two young gulls about the size of this bird came off and kept about the vessel for some time. They were in dark, mottled, immature plumage, and kept at such a distance that it was impossible to be positive of the species. From the frequent occurrence of Rosse's Gull to the north of this land, as noted by the naturalist of the Jeannette, and the fact that no adult Sabine's Gulls were seen either along the adjoining shore of Siberia or in this vicinity, the chances are that these two young birds were Rosse's Gulls; but at the time I identified them as being the young of Sabine's Gull, as their size and the general appearance of their coloration as seen at a distance indicated. It was not noted by us during the cruise of the Corwin anywhere around the shore of the Arctic, unless the two immature birds seen off Wrangel Island belong to this species.

STERNA CASPIA Pall.

(158.) CASPIAN TERN.

This large Tern is extremely rare in the north. It was only observed by me at the Yukon mouth on two occasions, both times escaping without injury in spite of my attempts to secure it. The natives were well acquainted with the bird, however, but always insisted that it was very uncommon. They have a name for the common Arctic Tern which they also apply to this large species with the termination "puk," meaning great or large, showing that there is little doubt as to the bird's correct identification. There is no record of its occurrence to the north of Saint Michael's, which is the most northern point whence I have any information of its occurring; nor is it known from the islands of Bering Sea or the Siberian shore.

STERNA MACRURA Naum.

(159.) THE ARCTIC TERN.

Along both shores of Bering Sea and upon both shores of the adjoining Arctic waters this bird is very common. It was noted in the vicinity of Point Barrow during our visit there in August, 1881, and along all of the north Siberian coast visited, and is a well-known resident of the Bering Sea shores. It nests wherever found in this region, and occurs indifferently either in the interior along the courses of the rivers, or on the salt marshes and barren islands on the sea coast. This is one of the circumpolar species, which is familiar to all voyagers in these northern regions. It nests on some of the sterile islands of the North, in flocks, upon the bare sandy or pebbly ground, with no trace of any artificial nest. It is common upon Spitzbergen but scarce on Nova Zemlya, and was noted in the vicinity of the New Siberian Islands by Nordenskiöld. On the eastern shore of Bering Sea I have only found it nesting singly, in pairs scattered here and there over the marshes, and in one instance three pairs were found occupying the same small island in a lake, which is the largest number I found nesting in close proximity. In this, however, as in many other instances, the birds' habits vary greatly with the locality.

STERNA ALEUTICA Baird.

(160.) THE ALEUTIAN TERN.

This handsome Alaskan Tern has an extremely limited distribution, being found from Kodiak Island north to Bering Strait on the American mainland shore, and occasionally crossing to the

Siberian coast. As noted by the naturalist of the Jeannette, who saw several of these birds at Saint Lawrence Bay the last of August, 1879, it is very irregular in its distribution, as the coast for a hundred miles may not have a single pair, and again they may occur in the greatest abundance. Rather low rocky islets appear to be their choice for breeding places, as shown by their habits in the vicinity of Saint Michael's, where they nest among the low vegetation covering the rocks, making no artificial nest, or but a slight attempt at one, usually depositing their eggs in a slight hollow made in the dead grasses and moss. The nests were difficult to find from the close resemblance of the eggs to the ground upon which they are placed. The birds hover overhead when disturbed, but become very shy after a little persecution in the way of shooting, so that although I made repeated efforts to secure a considerable number of specimens I was able to get but comparatively few. They are far more suspicious than the Arctic Tern, which abound in the same localities and may be killed by hundreds if desired.

STERCORARIUS POMATORHINUS (Temm.) Vieill.

(161.) POMARINE JAËGER.

During the summer season these birds are found breeding around the northern coast of Bering Sea from the vicinity of the mouth of Kuskoquim River to Bering Strait, and among the northern islands of this sea, and along the Siberian shore. They extend their range at this time through the Straits, and are found scattered over the entire part of the Arctic navigable for vessels, breeding upon both shores. During this season they reach south to the Aleutian chain, and it is possible that some remain there to breed; but as these birds have a northerly distribution in summer the probabilities are against the supposition. A few were seen at Plover Bay and then scatteringly throughout the Arctic, generally near shore, during the cruise of the Corwin. They were more numerous on the Asiatic coast than on the American side, except when we reached the vicinity of Point Barrow, where a considerable number of these birds were seen among the drift ice. On June 29 they were very numerous off Cape Serdze Kamen, on the Siberian shore. About Nova Zemlya, Nordenskiöld informs us, this species is much less numerous than the parasitic Jaëger; but like this latter species the present bird has a circumpolar distribution. As we approached Herald and Wrangel Islands on our various visits to that vicinity these Gulls were seen at times, and were very numerous near Herald Island the day we made our landing there, July 30.

STERCORARIUS CREPIDATUS (Banks) Vieill.

(162.) RICHARDSON'S JAËGER.

On the coast of Bering Sea, having there almost precisely the same range as the large Jaëger just mentioned, this bird is found in about equal numbers. It is confined to the vicinity of the shore more closely than the large species, and during the breeding season, at least, prefers the brackish pools and marshy land along the low portions of the coast, such as that from the Yukon mouth north along the shore of Norton Sound. It was seen at nearly all the points visited by us both in Bering Sea and the adjoining portions of the Arctic. As we passed north to the vicinity of the ice it became much rarer or was entirely absent; none were seen in the vicinity of Wrangel or Herald Islands, nor were any noted north of Icy Cape on the Alaskan shore, although they probably reach Point Barrow at times. This bird is said to breed on Spitzbergen and Nova Zemlya, where it lays two eggs upon the bare ground on low, unsheltered, and often wet islets or headlands. It is very greedy, and in its haste will frequently swallow so much as to be sometimes unable to fly until it has disgorged.

According to Nordenskiöld, when it is disturbed in the vicinity of its nests it creeps along the ground with odd motions and flapping wings to draw attention from its eggs. This same habit is possessed by the birds on the Alaskan shore, as I have frequently observed during the breeding season.

STERCORARIUS PARASITICUS Linn., Saunders.

(163.) LONG-TAILED JAËGER.

The present species is the most elegant of the Jaëgers in its general make-up, and especially when on the wing. At this time the bird shows all the grace and ease of movement which characterize such birds as the Swallow-tailed Kite and other species with very long wings and slender bodies. It appears to delight in exhibiting its agility, and two or more frequently perform strange gyrations and evolutions during their flight as they pass back and forth over the low, flat country which they frequent. It is like the parasitic Jaëger, found more plentifully along the low portions of the coast than at sea, and is very numerous along the coast of Norton Sound. It was noted but a few times by us during the cruise of the Corwin north of Bering Strait, but was seen at Saint Lawrence Island and various other places visited along the shores of this sea, especially on the American side. Toward Spitzbergen these birds are said to be rare and to increase in numbers toward Bering Strait. It is one of the species noted during the drift of the Jeannette in the ice to the north of Wrangel Island, but was very rare.

PROCELLARIDÆ. PETRELS. ALBATROSSES.

DIOMEDEA NIGRIPES Aud.

(163 a.) BLACK-FOOTED ALBATROSS.

The "gony," as this bird is called on the North Pacific, is an abundant bird over this entire stretch of the ocean. It takes company with a vessel on its leaving San Francisco, and follows it to the neighborhood of the Aleutian Islands where it disappears; and, as we noted, in October, 1881, soon after we left Oonalaska these birds appeared and were with us continually in pleasant or stormy weather until we approached San Francisco. The majority seen were young, the light-colored birds being observed only at intervals. Nearly all are dark smoky-brown, but here and there may be seen one with a ring of white feathers around the rump, at the base of the tail; and all have a marked line of white surrounding the base of the bill. Those with the white on the tail almost invariably have a white spot under each eye. The graceful evolutions of these birds afford one of the most pleasing sights during a voyage across the North Pacific, and they are a source of continual interest during the otherwise monotonous passage.

DIOMEDEA BRACHYURA Lemm.

(164.) SHORT-TAILED ALBATROSS.

On July 11, 1881, at Cape Rome, Alaska, just south of Bering Strait, was seen a young Albatross of this species in the dark plumage. It had a bright yellow bill, with a bright ring around the base, evidently produced by the white feathers surrounding the base of the beak. Later in the season adults of this species were seen between Saint Lawrence Island and Plover Bay, Siberia; and the mandibles of two specimens were obtained in the ruined villages on Saint Lawrence Island. As we passed the Diomede Islands, in the middle of Bering Strait, in July, a young Short-tailed Albatross was observed circling back and forth over the rising sea, which was being covered with foam by the gale which was rising at that time.

These records are the most northern which we possess of this bird, and extend its range, as noted, to the middle of Bering Strait; and we can infer from this that the bird occasionally wanders into the Arctic Ocean. To the south among the Aleutian Islands, reaching the vicinity of the seal islands occasionally, this bird is very abundant, in some instances fifteen or twenty being in view at one time while a vessel is sailing through some of the passes. In May, 1877, many of these birds were seen by me while passing from Oonalaska Island east to Samakh, and again upon the return trip. They rarely approached the vessel, however, and it was impossible to secure one of them.

FULMORUSGLACIALIS RODGERSI (Cass.) Coues.

(165.) RODGER'S FULMAR.

This is an extremely abundant bird over all the deep-water portions of Bering Sea, extending into the Arctic Ocean to the vicinity of the ice pack. It rarely visits the eastern shore of the sea, however, from the mouth of the Kuskoquim north to the head of Norton Sound, the shallow and muddy character of the water here apparently not being suitable for the presence of food upon which this bird exists. On the western shore of the sea in the vicinity of Plover Bay and Saint Lawrence Island, thence north through Bering Strait, the bird was found in the greatest abundance during the visit of the Corwin to that region. It was also abundant north beyond the Straits along the Siberian shore. The shallow character of the water on the American coast north of the Straits had the same effect in not presenting suitable foraging ground for these wide-ranging birds.

Nordenskiöld tells us that the common Fulmar, which is the North Atlantic representative of the bird under consideration at present, is much more common on Bear Island and Spitzbergen than it is upon Nova Zemlya. It breeds abundantly on Bear Island on some of the sloping cliffs not difficult of access. One case is mentioned where on May 26, 1876, the eggs were seen deposited directly upon the bare ice which covered the rocks at the time. In one place a bird was found frozen fast by one leg as it sat upon the eggs, in August, 1596, as recorded by one of the old Dutch expeditions which touched that coast. On the northern part of Nova Zemlya, Barents found some Fulmars nesting upon a piece of ice covered with a little earth. In both of these cases the underpart of the egg during hatching could not be warmed above the freezing point.

During the cruise of the Corwin in Bering Sea and the Arctic, it was observed that on some days Rodger's Fulmars would be seen in large numbers; and again in passing over the same area not a single individual would be noticed. These birds breed on the precipitous islands of Bering Sea, and I am inclined to think some nest upon Herald Island in the Arctic Ocean. Although in our hasty visit to that island none were seen, yet the cliffs on the side opposite our landing were eminently suitable for nesting places such as these birds delight to choose, and the abundance of the bird up to within a comparatively short distance of this land, rendered the supposition probable. Elliot found them breeding in greatest abundance upon the fur-seal islands, where he secured their eggs.

As we approached the harbor of Onnalaska on September 22, 1881, hundreds of these birds were seen in the ordinary light-colored plumage, which were in company with about an equal number of birds either of the same species or a closely related one of exactly the same size, which were clad in a sooty-brown or blackish-brown plumage. Both birds were sitting in the water in immense flocks, covering acres, and as we steamed among them they appeared totally unable to rise, the vessel almost running down numerous individuals as they flapped clumsily along the surface of the water trying to rise; the perfectly calm sea at the time apparently rendered the birds almost helpless.

Mr. Ridgway suggests that the dark-colored birds seen at that time were the Slender-billed Fulmar, which may be the case, but if so it shows that these birds exist in large numbers in the North, although they have not been secured by the numerous naturalists who have visited that region. A number of these dark birds were also seen north of Bering Strait on two occasions, and should undoubtedly be referred to the same species as those seen in the vicinity of Onnalaska, of which unfortunately no specimens were secured.

PRIOCELLA TENUIROSTRIS (Aud.) Ridgw

(166.) SLENDER BILLED FULMAR.

There is but a single record of this bird's capture on the coast of Alaska. This was at Kotzebue Sound, whence Mr. Dall secured a single skin during his explorations in the Territory. Several times during our cruising in the Arctic in the summer of 1881, a dark-colored Fulmar was seen in company with the common species and of about the same size. This may perhaps be the Slender-billed species, although it was impossible to identify them positively, since no specimens were secured.

As we approached Oanalaska in September, large numbers of dark plumaged Fulmars were also seen in company with the common species (*rodgersi*), but then, as before, it was impossible to secure specimens. The intensity of the dark coloring in many of these specimens seemed to preclude the idea of their being referable to Rodger's Fulmar, and it is to be hoped that any naturalist visiting the Territory hereafter may pay especial attention to securing some of these birds, and thus settle the point; for if these dark colored birds were the slender-billed species it must be a very common bird, notwithstanding its having escaped the notice of every naturalist who has visited the Territory within the last ten or fifteen years.

CYMOCHOREA LEUCORRHOA (Vieill.) Coues.

(167.) LEACHE'S PETREL.

These birds are very numerous in the vicinity of the Aleutian Islands, but are soon lost sight of when these islands are left in passing to the north. South from these islands they occur over the entire Pacific, from the Aleutian chain to San Francisco. They are yet unknown, even north to the fur-seal islands, although they undoubtedly reach that group occasionally.

CYMOCHOREA MELÆNA (Bp.) Coues.

(168.) THE BLACK PETREL. !

As we left the Aleutian Islands on our way to San Francisco in October, and thence on for several hundred miles, a large Black Petrel was repeatedly seen. The size of this bird would indicate that it was the species mentioned above, although no specimens were secured. It was repeatedly seen in company with Leache's Petrel and the Forked-tailed species, and excellent opportunities were afforded for judging of its relative size.

OCEANODROMA FURCATA (Gmel.) Bp.

(169.) FORKED-TAILED PETREL.

This elegant Petrel is found over all Bering Sea, reaching Saint Michael's, and about the head of Norton's Sound, as well as Bering Strait. It was found nesting on some islets in the middle of Unimak Pass, near Oanalaska, by Mr. Dall, and is numerous along the entire Aleutian chain. To the north the bird is less and less abundant the farther one goes, and perhaps never penetrates to the Arctic side of Bering Strait. Several specimens were secured in the vicinity of Saint Michael's during my residence there, and they are well known to the natives, who find them while they are seal hunting, far off shore, the birds rarely coming close to the coast. These are among the most beautiful of the Petrels. The delicate shade of the entire plumage and the bird's graceful motions are marked even among this group of birds, proverbial for their grace and elegance upon the wing.

FREGETTA GRALLARIA (Vieill.) Bp

(170.) WHITE-BELLIED PETREL.

From the time we left the Aleutian Islands in October, until we were eight or nine hundred miles distant to the south, scarcely a day passed but a Petrel with the belly white, and answering closely in all its markings to the description given of this bird, was seen circling about. They were frequently quite close to the vessel, and were carefully examined with glasses, and the peculiar markings were such as to distinguish them from the other Petrels almost as far as they could be seen. They were in company with other Petrels and appeared less numerous than any of the other species.

PODICIPIDÆ. GREBES.
PODICEPS POLBÖLLI Reinh.
(171.) AMERICAN RED-NECKED GREBE.

These Grebes are quite numerous, occurring along the entire American coast of Bering Sea, and breeding from the Peninsula of Aliaska to the vicinity of the Straits. They are most numerous, however, in autumn, when they are found frequenting the sea; and some years from ten to a dozen specimens may be secured, while in others but one or two will be seen. It is unknown from the islands and the Asiatic shore of this sea, and the only portion of the Arctic coast of which I have proof of its occurrence is in Kotzebue Sound, where it also nests in summer.

DYTESAURITUS (Linn.) Ridgw.
(172.) HORNED GREBE.

Like the preceding, this bird is found all along the mainland shore of this sea, where, however, it breeds very sparingly, being mainly an inland species. It is found quite frequently in the interior, where it nests and visits the sea-coast during the autumnal migration. It is also found on the shore of Kotzebue Sound, but is not known from the islands of this sea nor the Asiatic coast.

COLYMBIDÆ. LOONS.
COLYMBUS TORQUATUS Brünn.
(173.) THE LOON.

This bird is found along the Bering Sea coast, on both sides, and also upon the shore of the Arctic, breeding wherever found. It is not abundant in this region, neither is it rare. There is no record of its occurrence upon any of the islands of this sea, although, as noted, it occurs on both shores.

COLYMBUS ADAMSI Gray.
(174.) GREAT WHITE-BILLED LOON.

This bird, the largest of the Loons, has a circumpolar distribution, although it is not known to occur in abundance at any locality. It is found breeding about Kotzebue Sound, whence the natives brought me several specimens, and reported the bird to be rather common there in summer. I secured a young bird at Saint Michael's in autumn, and it is known to occur on the Asiatic shore. There is no record of its presence about the Bering Sea Islands, but, like the other species of Loons, it undoubtedly visits these islands, during the migrations at least. The difficulty of studying the birds which frequent the sea about these storm-beaten islands is apparent, and accounts for the little progress which can be made in determining the full number of species which are found in their vicinity.

COLYMBUS ARCTICUS Linn.
(175.) BLACK-THROATED LOON.

This bird is found everywhere along the shore of Bering Sea on the American coast, and is very abundant, nesting along the shore from the Peninsula of Aliaska north to Kotzebue Sound. It was also seen in Bering Strait the first of July, and noted on several occasions along the Asiatic shore, where it also breeds. It has not been recorded from the islands of this sea, although undoubtedly occurring there in the migrations.

COLYMBUS PACIFICUS Lawr.
(176.) PACIFIC DIVER.

This bird is very rare on the coast of Bering Sea. Among the large number of Black-throated Loons secured by me, only one proves to belong to this bird, and the same proportion is found to hold good with other collections which have been brought from that country. This specimen was taken at Saint Michael's. The predominance of *arcticus* probably holds good for all the Bering Sea localities.

COLYMBUS SEPLENTRIONALIS Linn.

(177.) RED-THROATED DIVER.

This bird is present in about equal numbers with the black-throated species, and is extremely familiar, its loud note and peculiar habits, like that of the other Loons, rendering it well known to any one who becomes familiar with the marshes of the North. It nests abundantly all along the coast from the Peninsula of Aliaska to Kotzebue Sound, extending across the sea to the Siberian shore, but is not known from the islands of this sea, although it undoubtedly occurs there.

ALCIDÆ. AUKS.

FRATERCULA CORNICULALA (Naum.) Gray.

(178.) HORNED PUFFIN.

This is one of the most common birds found in Bering Sea. It nests abundantly all along the Aleutian chain and upon all the rocky islets of this sea, as well as almost every rocky cape which projects along the coast line. It was seen by us in small numbers off Cape Serdze Kamen on June 29, 1881, and a few were noted at East Cape the first of July. At Herald Island a single specimen was seen, and in the vicinity of Cape Thompson and Cape Lisburne, on the American shore, a few were seen, but they were not abundant. Puffin Island, a small rocky islet in Escholtz Bay, Kotzebue Sound, is literally alive with these birds, which cover the rocks as they perch along the slope of the rocky shore. While visiting this islet a bird was seen coming in from the sea, carrying four sticklebacks in its mouth. The fish were placed crosswise in the bill, and the bird looked very odd as it came swiftly along with the fish so held. It flew directly to a crevice in the rocks and disappeared. While walking over the island the growling and grunting noises made by the birds is distinctly heard, and the entire ground appears to be alive with them. The representative of this bird in the North Atlantic, the Large-billed Puffin, breeds in small numbers about the northeast end of Spitzbergen and on Nova Zemlya, which, with the record from Herald Island, forms the northernmost data we possess concerning their distribution.

LUNDA CIRRHATA Pall.

(179.) TUFTED PUFFIN.

These birds are very common all along the Aleutian chain, and thence north to Bering Strait. They are, however, much less abundant in nearly every place than their relative, the Horned Puffin, which has the same distribution. A few of the present species were seen at Cape Thompson, on the Alaskan coast of the Arctic, July 19, but they were far more scarce than the other species. They were also seen off Cape Serdze Kamen the last of June, and again at East Cape the first of July. The same proportion was found to hold in Kotzebue Sound, so it is evident that this bird is a more southern species than its relative.

PHALERIS PSITTACULA (Pall.) Temm.

(180.) PARROT-BILLED AUK.

These odd birds are very common in Bering Sea, from the Aleutian Islands north, breeding in great abundance upon the fur-seal group and all the other islands of this sea. They also swarm by thousands about the Diomedes and other islands of Bering Strait, besides along the Siberian shore, where, at Plover Bay, we found them in the greatest abundance. They were also seen off Cape Serdze Kamen on June 29, 1881. It rarely extends its range beyond the Straits, however. On August 26, while on an excursion to the head of Plover Bay, we secured quite a number of these birds, and in every case found them gorged with the small crustaceans which swarmed in the water there. They were extremely numerous here, as well as all along this portion of the coast. Their oddly shaped bill is well adapted for capturing the minute crustacea with which the waters abound in this region, though it would not answer the purpose for opening bivalves, as suggested by some of the older authors. Early in July it was found nesting upon the Diomede Islands, and its eggs were secured. It lays but a single one, which is white and about the size of that of a pigeon.

SIMORHYNCHUS CRISTATELLUS (Pall.) Merrem.

(181.) CRESTED AUK.

Like the preceding species, this bird is extremely numerous in Bering Sea, but like the latter prefers those portions of the sea in which the water is very deep and cold. Hence along the Alaskan shore the birds are rare, but upon the Aleutian Islands and the fur-seal group, the Diomedes, in Bering Strait, and the Asiatic shore north through the Straits they are very numerous, swarming like bees around a hive over the steep rocky islands which are found in these waters. Several of these birds were seen in the vicinity of Herald Island during our visit there, but they appeared to be very rare, as compared with the Guillemots and Murres. At Wrangel Island also, on August 11 and 12, others were seen, but only two or three individuals in all.

SIMORHYNCHUS PYGMÆUS (Gmel.) Ridgw.

(182.) WHISKERED AUK.

These birds are found along the Aleutian chain, but are not known from the islands to the north of that, and were not observed by us during the cruise of the Corwin. The habits and distribution of this species are little known, and it did not fall under my observation during the time of my residence at Saint Michael's nor upon either of my visits to the Aleutian Islands.

CICERONIA PUSILLA (Pall.) Ridgw.

(183.) LEAST AUK.

These birds are extremely abundant, breeding by millions along the Aleutian chain and upon all the other islands of Bering Sea, thence north to Bering Strait, occurring rarely, however, upon the American mainland coast, but found very commonly along the Siberian shore. A pair were seen August 15 off Icy Cape, on the Arctic coast of Alaska, which is the farthest northern record known of this small species. A few were seen off Cape Serdze Kamen on June 29, 1881, and these two records are all we have of their presence in the Arctic.

PTYCORHAMPHUS ALEUTICUS (Pall.) Brandt.

(184.) CASSIN'S AUK.

This is another species occurring on the Aleutian Islands, which, however, was not noted by us during the cruise of the Corwin, and whose range does not extend far, if any, into Bering Sea beyond the immediate vicinity of these islands.

SYNTHLIBORHAMPHUS ANTIQUUS (Gm.) Coues.

(185.) BLACK-THROATED GUILLEMOT.

This is also a species occurring in the Aleutian Islands, which did not fall under our notice, occurring, however, more or less commonly there.

BRACHYRHAMPHUS MARMORATUS (Gm.) Brandt.

(186.) MARBLED GUILLEMOT.

This is an extremely abundant species throughout the Aleutian Islands, where it breeds and extends its range northward along the west coast of Bering Sea to Bering Strait. It was found very numerous during our visits to Plover Bay, and thence along the shore to the Straits; but was not observed to the north of this latter point.

BRACHYRHAMPHUS KITTLITZI Brandt.

(187.) KITTLITZ'S GUILLEMOT.

This extremely rare bird was observed by me at Unalaska in the spring of 1877, where I secured a single specimen in the breeding plumage. It was also taken towards the western end of this chain by Mr. Turner a few years later, and with these two specimens ends the known history of this species on these islands up to the present date.

URIAGRYLLE (Linn.) Bruun.

(188.) BLACK GUILLEMOT.

These birds occur throughout Bering Sea and are numerous. They extend their range also well into the Arctic, reaching Herald and Wrangel Islands, and specimens were noted by the naturalist of the Jeannette, who records them in the vicinity of those islands, discovered during the explorations made by the people of that vessel.

In that portion of the Arctic north of the Atlantic the Black Guillemot is found breeding north to 80° in some cases, although it is more numerous south of this. It was found nesting with Brunnich's Guillemot in longitude 113° east by Nordenskiöld during his voyage. During the drift of the Jeannette it was seen passing to the westward on May 1, 1880, and at various other places was observed. Upon Bennett Island it was found nesting in great numbers the 20th of July, 1880. On April 6, 1881, it was found in about latitude 76°, longitude 161° east. During its residence in these high latitudes it is reported to feed upon the small Arctic tom cod, which the naturalist of the Jeannette reports to have seen the bird kill by beating them upon the water and shaking them in their bills. These birds were quite numerous at Herald Island. As we approached through the ice on the 30th of July flock after flock of them, joined with the Murre came off towards the Corwin. When we were making a landing large numbers of them were seen bringing fish, from three to four inches in length, to their young, and as the waters surrounding this island were seen to swarm with crustaceans, there appeared to be an abundance of food.

URIA COLUMBA (Pall.) Cass.

(189.) PIGEON GUILLEMOT.

This is the most abundant of the small Guillemots throughout the North, from the Aleutian Islands to those of Wrangel and Herald, where we found it breeding abundantly during our visit there on the Corwin. We found it near Cape Serdze Kamen, where it was nesting, and also in great abundance upon Herald Island, where it was perhaps the most abundant bird present, far outnumbering the Murre. It was also nesting upon East Cape, the Diomede Islands, and along the entire portion of the Siberian coast wherever cliffs and mountainous slopes occurred fronting the sea. None was observed on the western portion of the New Siberian Islands by Nordenskiöld, but the Chukchees reported it to him as wintering at Tapkan, wherever open water was found during that season.

LOMVIA TROILE CALIFORNICA (Biyant) Coues.

(190.) CALIFORNIA GUILLEMOT.

These birds are found along the Pacific coast, reaching to the Aleutian Islands, beyond which it is uncertain how far their range extends. They were not observed by us during the cruise of the Corwin in the Arctic, although among the millions of Murres which breed upon the cliffs on the shores of this sea, both north and south of Bering Strait, it is very probable they may occur.

LOMVI ARRA (Pall.) Bp.

(191.) THICK-BILLED GUILLEMOT.

This bird occurs in greatest abundance throughout Bering Sea and the adjoining portions of the Arctic, reaching Herald and Wrangel Islands, where we found it breeding by thousands.

The bird also occurs along both shores of Bering Sea in the greatest numbers wherever cliffs afford proper nesting sites. At Cape Serdze Kamen, northwest of Bering Strait, we found it in large numbers just off shore, and again at East Cape on the rocky faces of the cliffs, as well as upon the islands in the middle of the Straits. It was rather scarce, however, among the islands in Kotzebue Sound. On July 30, 1881, as we drew near Herald Island on the Corwin this bird became more and more abundant, circling about us or alighting in small parties and singly among loose blocks of ice, sometimes standing upon the ice or sitting upright near its edge. Flocks came swinging about us in circles, apparently filled with curiosity at the strange apparition breaking in upon their quiet. As we drew still nearer myriads of Guillemots and these birds, with large numbers of the Kittiwake Gull, came swarming down from the cliffs until the air was filled with their moving forms, and occasionally the awkward shape of a Cormorant was seen as it passed back and forth and then returned again to its home among the ledges.

On two occasions one of the Murres was seen perched upon the edge of an ice cake a few yards in diameter and staring at us intently until the bow of the vessel struck the opposite sides of its support, when the bird would plump into the water with ridiculous haste.

As we climbed the steep faces of the island many of them dropped off their perches here and there and circled back and forth above our heads, uttering at the time a peculiar low growling note. The Guillemots had a fine piping note, which they also uttered during our ascent of the island. Both birds were extremely unsuspicious, and allowed us to pass within a few yards without showing any signs of fear.

LOMVIA ARRA BRUNNICHI (Sch.) Ridgw

(192.) BRUNNICH'S GUILLEMOT.

There is no record of this bird from Bering Sea, but it breeds on Spitzbergen and Nova Zemlya and islands of that region north to 80° at least. Nordenskiöld found half-grown young on the Preobrae Islands, August 24, during his voyage. It was also seen by him east of Cape Cheljuskin.

This bird, like the Black Guillemot, is reported by him as wintering in the Arctic wherever open places occur during that season.

The naturalist of the Jeannette observed it the first of May, 1880, as it was flying to the westward by their vessel, and it was seen again at various times during the drift of that vessel, and was breeding upon Bennett Island in greatest abundance. It is upon this last record that the bird is included within the present list, since we have no record of its occurrence nearer Bering Strait.

LIST OF FISHES KNOWN TO OCCUR IN THE ARCTIC OCEAN NORTH OF BERING STRAIT.

[Prepared for Capt. C. L. Hooper, United States Revenue Marine, by TARLETON H. BEAN.]

The following list, based exclusively upon the collections of the United States National Museum, is incomplete; but the material upon which it is founded is in the Museum and constitutes a voucher for the names employed. Many other fishes certainly exist in this portion of the Arctic, but, as this does not profess to include all recorded species, it is unnecessary to compile additional names:

1. GASTEROSTEUS PUNGITIUS L. subsp. BRACHYPODA Bean.
   Elephant Point, Escholtz Bay, September 2, 1880. Dall & Bean.
   Near Icy Cape, Arctic Ocean, August 25, 1880. T. H. Bean.
2. PLEURONECTES STELLATUS Pallas.
   Anderson River, *fide* Prof. S. F. Baird.
   Hotham Inlet, Kotzebue Sound, 1880. Capt. C. L. Hooper.

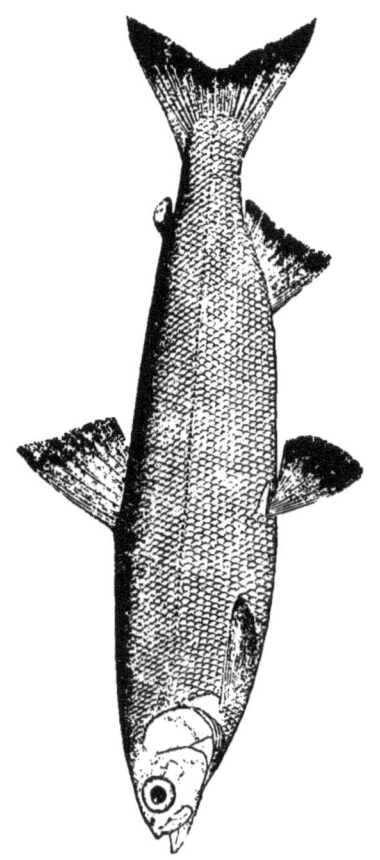

3. PLEURONECTES GLACIALIS Pallas.
    Hotham Inlet, Kotzebue Sound, 1880. Capt. C. L. Hooper.
    Chamisso Island, Kotzebue Sound, September 2, 1880. Dall & Bean.
4. BOREOGADUS SAIDA (Lepech.) Bean.
    Cape Lisburne, Arctic Ocean, August 21, 1880. Dall & Bean.
    Latitude 66° 45′ north, longitude 166° 35′ west, August 19, 1880. Herendeen & Bean.
5. GYMNELIS VIRIDIS (Fabr.) Reinhardt.
    I have identified a specimen of this species from the far north, but it does not belong to the collection.
6. LYCODES COCCINEUS Bean.
    Big Diomede Island, September 10, 1880. T. H. Bean.
7. NOTOGRAMMUS ROTHROCKII Bean.
    Cape Lisburne, August 21, 1880. Dall & Bean.
8. LUMPENUS ANGUILLARIS (Pallas) Girard.
    Point Belcher, Arctic Ocean, August 27, 1880. Dall & Bean.
9. PODOTHECUS ACIPENSERINUS (Pallas) Gill.
    Cape Lisburne, Arctic Ocean, August 21, 1880. (No barbels.) Dall & Bean.
10. COTTUS TÆNIOPTERUS Kner.
    Point Belcher, Arctic Ocean, August 27, 1880. Dall & Bean.
11. COTTUS HUMILIS Bean.
    Chamisso Island, Escholtz Bay, August 27, 1880. Dall & Bean.
    Point Belcher, Arctic Ocean, August 27, 1880. Dall & Bean.
12. GYMNACANTHUS PISTILLIGER (Pallas) Gill.
    Point Belcher, Arctic Ocean, August 27, 1880. Dall & Bean.
13. GYMNACANTHUS GALEATUS Bean.
    Off Cape Sabine, Arctic Ocean, August 24, 1880. Dall & Bean.
14. AMMODYTES AMERICANUS De Kay.
    Point Belcher, Arctic Ocean, August 27, 1880. Dall & Bean.
15. OSMERUS SPIRINCUS Pallas.
    Kotzebue Sound, September 2, 1880. E. P. Herendeen.
    I am not certain that this species is distinct from O. dentex Steind.
16. MALLOTUS VILLOSUS (Müller) Cuv.
    Bering Strait. Wm. Simpson.
    Cape Lisburne, Arctic Ocean, August 21, 1880. Dall & Bean.
    Point Belcher, Arctic Ocean, August 27, 1880. Dall & Bean.
17. COREGONUS LAURETTÆ Bean.
    Point Barrow, Arctic Ocean, 1880. Capt. C. L. Hooper.
18. COREGONUS MERCKII var.
    Hotham Inlet, Kotzebue Sound, 1880. Capt. C. L. Hooper.
19. SALVELINUS MALMA (Walb.) Jordan & Gilbert.
    Hotham Inlet, 1880. Capt. C. L. Hooper.
    Hotham Inlet, 1880. Capt. C. L. Hooper.
    Hotham Inlet, 1880. Capt. C. L. Hooper.
    Cape Lisburne, Arctic Ocean, August 21, 1880. Dall & Bean.

20. ONCORHYNCHUS GORBUSCHA (Walb.) Gill & Jordan.
   Colville River, *fide* Capt. E. E. Smith. Abundant in Plover Bay.
21. ONCORHYNCHUS KETA (Walb.) Gill & Jordan.
   Bering Strait, 1880. D. S. Jordan.
   Hotham Inlet, Kotzebue Sound, 1880. Capt. C. L. Hooper.

It may be not out of place to name the following common species which properly belong to the fauna:
   STICHÆUS PUNCTATUS (Fabr.) Reinhardt.
   LIPARIS Sp.
   EUMICROTREMUS SPINOSUS (Fabr.) Gill.
   TRIGLOPS PINGELU Reinhardt.
   ICELUS NAMATUS Kroyer.
   COREGONUS QUADRILATERALIS Rich.
   THYMALLUS SIGNIFER (Rich.) C. & V. Var.
   CLUPEA MIRIBALIS Girard. Signifer.
   SOMMOSUS MICROCEPTALUS (Block) Gill.

UNITED STATES NATIONAL MUSEUM, *Washington, June 28, 1882.*

www.ingramcontent.com/pod-product-compliance
Lightning Source LLC
Chambersburg PA
CBHW030349170426
43202CB00010B/1310